Literary Disinheritance

Literary Disinheritance

The Writing of Home in the Work of Mahmoud Darwish and Assia Djebar

Najat Rahman

LEXINGTON BOOKS

A division of
ROWMAN & LITTLEFIELD PUBLISHERS, INC.
Lanham • Boulder • New York • Toronto • Plymouth, UK

LEXINGTON BOOKS

A division of Rowman & Littlefield Publishers, Inc.
A wholly owned subsidiary of The Rowman & Littlefield Publishing Group, Inc.
4501 Forbes Boulevard, Suite 200
Lanham, MD 20706

Estover Road
Plymouth PL6 7PY
United Kingdom

British Library Cataloguing in Publication Information Available

Library of Congress Cataloging-in-Publication Data

Rahman, Najat.
Literary disinheritance : the writing of home in the work of Mahmoud Darwish and Assia Djebar / Najat Rahman.
p. cm.
Includes bibliographical references and index.
ISBN-13: 978-0-7391-2007-1 (cloth : alk. paper)
ISBN-10: 0-7391-2007-7 (cloth : alk. paper)
1. Darwish, Mahmud—Criticism and interpretation. 2. Djebar, Assia, 1936——Criticism and interpretation. I. Title.
PJ7820.A7Z872 2008
843'.914—dc22 2007038511

Printed in the United States of America

™ The paper used in this publication meets the minimum requirements of American National Standard for Information Sciences—Permanence of Paper for Printed Library Materials, ANSI/NISO Z39.48–1992.

To Adeeb, Fardouse, and Nadia,

my teachers always, my home.

Contents

Acknowledgements

I would like to begin my acknowledgments by warmly thanking Mahmoud Darwish who generously offered his time for interviews and who has directed me to other readers and critics, such as Subhi Hadidi. I am grateful to Joseph Parry and the editors of Lexington Books who have supported the publication of this book. Several mentors, colleagues, and friends have read earlier versions, have carried a dialogue with me over the years over my work, or have contributed in other ways to making this project possible: Mary Layoun, Prospero Saiz, Luis Madureira, Livia Monnet, Sam Slote, Jeffrey Michels, Mazin al-Nahawi, Mazin Rabie, Nezar Andary, Kristin Bergen, Manal Jamal, Elias Mikhail. I am deeply grateful to each of them for their meaningful engagement and insights. I have also presented my work in such venues as the Middle East Studies Association and the Inter-University Association of Middle East Studies at Montreal. Thanks especially to Jeffrey Sacks and Michelle Hartman for the fruitful exchanges. I would like to thank my research assistants, Rim Bejaoui and Tassia Trifiatis who supported my work during this period. The index is mostly the work of Rim Bejaoui. For material support, I am indebted to the Fulbright grants that made possible my earlier research on Mahmoud Darwish in Damascus and later in Beirut. The grant from Fonds de Québec de Recherche sur la société et la culture (FQRSC) has partially contributed to this project. I thank Gary Garrison at the Council for the International Exchange of Scholars and Michel Ledoux at the University of Montreal for facilitating the process. Earlier versions of Chapters 2 and 4 have appeared in other books. Chapter 2 was published in *A Literary History of African Women's Writings*, Pikesville, MD: Black Academy Press, 2005, under the title "Reclaiming Heritage of Disinheritance Through 'Women of the Verb' in Assia Djebar's *Loin de Médine*." Chapter 4 appeared in *Gender and Sexuality in African Literature and Film*, Trenton, NJ: Africa World Press, 2007, as "The Fragmented Heritage in the Reconstitution of Home: Assia Djebar's *L'amour, la fantasia*." "The Trial of Heritage and the Legacy of Abraham" has appeared in *Men and Masculinities* and in *Islamic Masculinities*, London and New York, Zed Press, 2006.

Introduction:

The Writing of Home through Literary Heritage

"Home, for we have no home."

—Al-Mutannabi, cited in Adonis, *Al-Kitāb*, 7.

"Home has become such a scattered, damaged, various concept in our present travails. There is so much to yearn for. There are so few rainbows anymore."

—Salman Rushdie, *East, West*, 93.

The twentieth century in particular, with its scale of wars, has launched an age of unprecedented mass displacements, as Edward W. Said has noted in *Reflections on Exile*. Exile, previously associated with an individual artist's predicament, has become too often an abject situation of the many refugees, migrants, illegal immigrants, and perpetual foreigners, each experiencing an intimate dislocation. If exile is a "discontinuous state of being," an "unbearable rift" forced between "a human being and a native place, between the self and its true home," as Said contends, it is a condition of irrecuperable loss that is fundamentally historical. (173) It is irrecoverable since no return is ever possible, even when a physical one takes place. The exile and the native place are invariably transformed. It also cannot be merely recuperated into a productive social or cultural function, although Said calls for a vigilant critical stance to emerge from such an experience. It is historical as a condition, since it results from historical events. With exile, a yearning for and thinking of home inevitably ensues. Even when the historical seems to encroach less visibly, the relation to home has changed seemingly everywhere. John Berger also points to the singularity of this past century: "Never before our time have so many people been uprooted. Emigration, forced or chosen . . . is the quintessential experience of our time." (Berger 1984: 55) And this even when it concerns a relation to the private home: "Today, as soon as very early childhood is over, the house can never be home, as it was in other epochs. This century, for all its wealth and with all its communication systems, is the century of banishment." (Berger 1984: 67) Similarly, Barbara Bonner links the preoccupation with "home" to modern transformations of societies that bear the imprint of displacements. She asks, "Have modern societies abandoned the ties with extended family and community, the natural world, ancestors, and the gods that provided meaningful connections of home in traditional times?" (Bonner 1996: ix)

Indeed our object of study here challenges efforts to chart an experience of "homelessness" across cultures and languages without particular attention to history. Even semantically, the English word "home" is widely indeterminate as to signal the danger of such imprecision.

> 'home' ... can mean, almost simultaneously, both the place I have left and the place I am going to, the place I have lost and the new place I have taken up, even if temporarily. 'Home' can refer to the place where you grew up ... the mythic homeland of your parents and ancestors that you yourself may never have actually seen, or the hostel where you are spending the night in transit. In other words, 'home' may refer to a deeply familiar or a foreign place, or it may be no more than a passing point of reference. (Bammer 1992: vii, cited in Saunders 2003: 20)

The word "home" opens various problems and possibilities that the Arabic or French equivalents may not necessarily share: How to speak of it beyond designators that specify a national homeland or a private physical space—*waṭan* as homeland, *bayt* or *manzil* as house, *malja'* as refuge, *balad* as country; or in the French *patrie*, *foyer, maison, chez soi.* "Home" in English, ironically, does not translate the Arabic or French without risking to lose the specificity of the original designators: and yet "home" is what permeates the work of the two writers, the Palestinian Mahmoud Darwish and the Algerian Assia Djebar, precisely without being named, in its complex rhetorical configurations, as I will argue further. Home for the exile is in constant reconfiguration.

In its origins, the English word "home," from the High German *heim*, Greek *kōmi* or "village" has been, according to Berger, co-opted by "moralists" and those who "wield power":

> The notion of home became the keystone for a code of domestic morality, safeguarding the property (which included women) of the family. Simultaneously the notion of homeland supplied a first article of faith for patriotism. . . Both usages have hidden the original meaning. Originally home meant the center of the world . . . Without a home at the center of the real, one was not only shelterless, but also lost in non-being, in unreality. Without a home everything was fragmentation. (Berger 1984: 55)

If home in the context of the Arab world has meant most poignantly *homeland*, the loss thereof in Palestine and its difficult reconstitution in the wake of colonialism and failed nationalisms, it necessitates a reflection beyond exclusionary nationalist imaginings, with a consciousness for the experience of the collective, hence the important contributions of Darwish and Djebar. Home has also meant in this context domestic confinement of women. Home itself is an inherited trope in their work and an historical disinheritance; home is revealed as absence and a past contested. The idea of home in both works emerges as *foreign*, as estrangement, besieged by patriarchy and mythic narrative.

Darwish has personally experienced an array of displacements: the initial flight as a child of six in 1948 with his family from his home village al-Berweh in the upper Galilee to Lebanon; the subsequent internal displacement when his family "infiltrated" his home months later to find his village no longer existing under the newly declared state of Israel; the many imprisonments and house arrests that followed throughout his youth; the self-imposed exile in 1970 to Egypt and later to Beirut; expulsion from Beirut in the aftermath of the Israeli invasion of 1982; the return to Ramallah in 1996 to live for the first time in the occupied Palestinian territories; the siege in Ramallah with the onset of the second intifada. While the siege is a "locking" in rather than a "locking out", it is a displacement of sorts, adhering as it does to unsettling one's relation to place and to freedom of movement.

Not surprisingly, given this personal history, the poetry of Darwish is preoccupied with displacement—a literal displacement, with the 1948 *Nakbah*'s rupture of history, when Palestinians were dispossessed of their homeland, and with the other losses that followed, and also a displacement of the self from itself. For Darwish, the testing of poetic limits is inextricably linked with his questioning of identity, whether in interrogating the role of poetry following the siege of Beirut in 1982 and the subsequent expulsion of Palestinians or in reflecting on the self that faces such a series of displacements. And of course the poet experiences exile (and refuge) in language. Exile, in one form or another, has always been at the heart of his literary creation.

A prolific poet, he has produced nearly thirty works and has been translated into more than twenty-five languages. While Darwish's oeuvre is seminal in modern Arabic poetry and is often considered in that context, he is also without question one of the *world*'s most important living poets. Darwish has been recognized internationally and is the recipient of many prestigious international literary awards, including the Lotus Prize (Union of Afro-Asian Writers 1969), the Lenin Prize (USSR 1983), Knight of Arts and Belles Lettres (France 1997), the Lannan Foundation Prize for Cultural Freedom (United States 2001), and most recently The Golden Wreath (Macedonia 2007). Despite having been influential in transforming the poetic landscape of Arabic poetry in the twentieth century, Darwish's poetry is only gradually becoming widely known in North America.

Almost no substantial critical study currently exists in English (or any language other than Arabic and French) that addresses the relevance and complexity of his later poetry in the articulation of exile and rewriting of the homeland.

Indeed, for a long time, anyone interested in modern Arabic poetry would have had difficulty finding substantial critical studies in English on the general subject, let alone focusing on Darwish specifically. Some exceptions to this are Terri DeYoung's study of al-Sayyab's poetry, *Placing the Poet: Badr Shakir al-Sayyab and Postcolonial Iraq* (1998), and before that Terri De Young and Issa Boullata's *Tradition and Modernity in Arabic Literature* (1997); Salma Khadra Jayyusi's *Trends and Movements in Modern Arabic Poetry* (1977); and Mounah Khouri's *Poetry and the Making of Modern Egypt* (1971). On the work of Mahmoud Darwish, critical studies include: Najat Rahman and Hala Kh. Nassar, *Exile's Poet, Mahmoud Darwish: Critical Essays* (Interlink, forthcoming in 2007); Randa Abou-Bakr's *The Conflict of Voices in the Poetry of Dennis Butrus [Sic] and Mahmoud Darwish: A Comparative Study* (Reichert, 2004); Anette Månsson's *Passage to a New Wor(L)D: Exile and Restoration in Mahmoud Darwish's Writings, 1960-1995* (Uppsala Universitet, 2003).

Critical writing in Arabic on Darwish, who has long been designated "poet of the homeland" and "poet of resistance," tends to focus on his earlier writing and on themes that reinforce nationalist readings of his work. Studies that have addressed his work since the early 1980s are few, even though the poems of this period constitute a significant portion of his oeuvre.[1] Even as his later poetry consciously marks a move away from his earlier constructions of identity, of home, and of poetry, many of his critics have not taken sufficient notice of this shift, perhaps due to the force of the poet's identification as a "national poet." A critical acknowledgement of a shift in Darwish's work has not always translated to a willingness to engage it.

While the literary preoccupation with home is not new, critical studies have yet to address its rewriting in contemporary Arabic literature. Arabic criticism tends to focus on nationalist themes. Scholarship on Francophone literature, however, has been questioning nationalist paradigms of reading and engaging the complexity of the writing. Criticism of the work of Assia Djebar exemplifies this, but the critical studies tend perhaps to place more emphasis on the question of gender in her work than on the inextricable link between Djebar's focus on women and the importance she places on questions of heritage and of home.[2] Djebar's focus on women stems from a questioning of home and is very much a project of re-examining her heritage.

Born in Cherchell, Algeria in 1936, Djebar, in many of her interviews and writing, identifies herself first and foremost as a woman writer from Algeria, as she does in 2000 in her acceptance speech of the Peace Prize by the German Book Traders Association: "J'ai été élevée dans une foi musulmane, celle de mes aïeux depuis des générations, qui m'a façonnée effectivement et spirituellement, mais à laquelle, je l'avoue, je me confronte, à cause des interdits dont je me délie pas encore tout à fait."[3] [I was raised in the Muslim faith, that of my ancestors for generations, which has shaped me effectively and spiritually, but I confess I have confronted it due to its prohibitions from which I cannot completely dissociate myself.] (Djebar 2000) If gender is at the heart of her vision of self and of heritage, then language is equally significant. Perhaps these are the two most important dimensions of her identity that present Djebar's work as a fruitful comparison with that of Darwish.

If Darwish's poetic voice often identifies with Joseph, Ishmael, and other monotheistic sons, Djebar's is that of the contestory daughter of Fatima, "*le garçon manqué*," precisely in her freedom of movement outside the home. Her work calls attention to how gender cannot be simply one more category to consider in discourses on home but informs the very visions and inheritance of it. Home has also meant literal incarceration and something of a siege for Djebar, in the traditional seclusion of women, but also for Darwish in the many house arrests of the poet and the limitations on his movement when he was still living in Palestine of 1948. For her, and for Darwish, writing is a certain exile from home, as it were, at the very least a withdrawal in order to write but also a severing from all continuity; it is also a "rapprochement, de l'écoute, le besoin d'être auprès de . . ., de cerner une chaleur humaine, une solidarité." [Coming together, of hearing, the need to be near . . . to discern human warmth, a solidarity.] (Djebar 2000) Writing signals this aporetic and conscious posture toward home.

The language that addresses her desire for rootedness or "*enracinement*" is first and foremost one of contestation: "c'est cette permanence du 'non' intérieur que j'entends en moi, dans une forme et un son berbères, et qui m'apparaît comme le socle même de ma personnalité ou de ma durée littéraire." [It is this permanent and internal 'no' that I hear in myself in a form and sonority that are Berber, and which appears to me to be even the base of my personality or literary duration.] (Djebar 2000) And if Darwish insists jealously on Arabic, writing as he does only twenty years in the wake of the *Nakbah* of 1948, Djebar's use of French highlights all the more the other languages of women in Algeria: spoken and unspoken, Arabic the mother tongue, Berber, "que pourtant je ne parle pas, est la forme même où, malgré moi et en moi, je dis 'non': comme femme, et surtout, me semble-t-il, dans mon effort durable d'écrivain." [That I do not speak and which is the form itself in which, despite myself, I say 'no' as a woman, but above all in my efforts as an enduring writer.] (Djebar 2000)

Djebar also offers a critique of religious fundamentalism that is not present in Darwish's work, although as I write this introduction, Darwish has just published a poem in *Al-Ayyām,* which responds to the violent internal conflict between Hamas and the Abbas governement.[4] The post-independence stage of Algeria allows for a different context of nationalism and religious fundamentalism than that of Palestine.

Like Darwish, she is a prolific writer, having authored more than twenty novels, but also having directed films and experimented with other forms such as the operetta. She is also the recipient of many international prizes, having capped her impressive career with her election into the exclusive Académie Française in 2006. Most notable of her prizes is the Biennale di Venezia (1979), International Literary Neustadt Prize (1996), Premio internazionale di Palmi (1998), Médaille Vérmeille de la Francophonie (1999), among many others.

This book concerns itself with the shift in the articulation of home in the works of Darwish and Djebar, one that takes account of its connection to writing through an imbricated and plural literary heritage. It considers their writing as an instance of a larger cultural expression in the Arab world. As foremost writers who have received spectacular international recognition, whose work engages the complex relation between history and literature, their work allows for an examination of a certain cultural production of the *Mashreq* or the Middle East in comparison to that of the *Maghreb* or North Africa, of Francophone literature in connection to Arabic writing. The relation to the collective has to be charted differently in each case: siege, solidarity, and separation.

An examination of their work also allows for a consideration of narrative in relation to poetry. Both writers point to the limits and possibility of the forms they use, foregrounding an inextricable link between the quest for identity and for form. Djebar's central metaphor is *aporia*: how to narrate what is not narratable, the silenced voices. How does one write the self in the language of the other? How does one testify without witnessing? How can one render a narrative in palimpsestic fragments? The aporia is the necessary but impossible task. The aporia is precisely, as its ancient Greek root suggests, the impasse and the perplexity. Darwish's poetry also interrogates the possibility of presencing that which can no longer be presenced and in a lyric that absents through excess desire. Toward an understanding of these challenges, this book is a reading of the figuring of "home" in the works of Darwish and of Djebar.

Their notions of home respond to textual delineations of heritage that have become historical. While tradition is a project for the past, heritage, as transmission, is a co-existence of past and present. They identify a long literary heritage that not only speaks of dispossession and effacement but also suggests that those very predicaments are historically enacted through nationalist and religious readings of inherited stories. They address themselves to a paternal heritage that emerges from the myths of monotheism, a heritage that forged collective identity through these stories. The patriarchal narratives that forge identity by way of submission to the authority of the father and to the exclusion of the others is revisited and reopened, since the Abraham myth brings together monotheistic narratives of submission and nationalist delineations of identity. As a result, a dialogue with the father ensues. Already, the Abraham myth grounds identity in displacement, since Abraham only becomes Abraham when he leaves home. Before that, he is Abram.

Both writers confront a paternal heritage: most immediately within the family, the absent father or the father who marks a rupture from tradition. This address distinguishes these two writers from others in the poignancy and insistence of this dialogue. And it is this dimension of their writing that marks my reading of their work. Theirs is an aesthetic quest at different stages of collective struggles, post-nationalist for Djebar, occupied and besieged in Darwish's work.

If in returning to the story of Joseph, Darwish's poetic voice claims Joseph's voice, who is betrayed by his brothers, in Djebar's vision she calls attention to the women key to the deliverance of Joseph and the hope also for the freedom of Algeria: "les femmes en Algérie, par leurs souffrances et leur parole de verité, nous libèreront de l'étau de ces années terribles." [The women in Algeria, by their suffering and word of truth, will liberate us from the vice of these terrible years.]

Darwish invokes the father who exiles, who sacrifices the future for the past, and who departs in defeat, while Djebar invokes the memory of Abraham to recall Hager's repudiation and Fatima's disinheritance. Their work exploits these ruptures and is in turn characterized by an aporetic discourse.

The monotheistic writing that constitutes heritage also marks a desire for home, a desire rendered sacred through its ties to land and lineage. For both Darwish and Djebar, that heritage has been paternal due to the absenting of a maternal heritage, figured primarily as land and language. The tradition of the transient and ephemeral father, however, provides possibility for words and for home, but only in displacement. In order to reconstitute the trope of home, they call attention to different facets of discontinuity in their heritage. My chapters attempt to locate and explore the treatment of these discontinuous moments as they emanate from a rigorous reflection on writing. The first half of the book considers the authors' engagement with their cultural heritage while the latter half examines the ways in which the writers attempt to reconstitute home.

The first chapter, "The Trial of Heritage and the Legacy of Abraham," devotes itself to the textual delineation of heritage in the work of Darwish and Djebar. It delivers Abraham as a figure of paternity and of heritage, one who is doubly bound by communal duties and divine commands. Abraham serves as exemplary of identity through discontinuity: rejecting his own home, religion, and father to follow a lonely god, he also breaks with his own children. The figure of Abraham reveals a double movement to heritage: not one that emanates from the past and looks toward the future but one that is arrested in a certain textual bind. This chiasmus forms the first discontinuity.

The second chapter, "Reclaiming an Islamic Legacy of Memory and Contestation in Assia Djebar's *Loin de Médine*," probes Djebar's effort to recall the revolutionary aspect of Islam at the time of Mohammed, one that granted inheritance rights to women, but one that was also embedded in strife from the outset with the political dominating the spiritual. She locates a rupture in this heritage of Islam that emerges with the death of the Prophet, predicated upon the dispossession and exclusion of women at a time when emergent Islam granted women inheritance rights. Djebar effectively wants to reclaim her share of that heritage of early Islam to reveal that it was always open to contestation. Her appropriation of *ijtihād* as intellectual strife, one that insists on individual interpretation rather than consensus, and the very methods of transmission of the early historical accounts of Islam, allow her to highlight the contribution of women not only to the transmission of Islam but also to its establishment. It furthermore enables her to shift the focus to women as voices of protest and transmission.

"Poetic Survival: The Post-Beirut Poetry of Mahmoud Darwish," considers Darwish's turn to pre-Islamic and Andalusian moments of Arabic literary heritage. It examines the status of poetry in his writing and the extent to which he draws from these moments conceptions of poetry and of home. His incorporation of home from these two instants chooses less prevalent motifs: it insists on desire rather than loss, and on the perpetual journey rather than the nostalgic return. Poetry itself emerges in this formulation as a figure of home. Home is no longer simply connected to land or people but to threatened longing, perpetual search, and the possibility of a poetic gathering of voices. Lyric as search and desire emerges as a discontinuity in a heritage that valorized it as return and loss.

While the previous chapters focus on a conscious interrogation of heritage by the writers, the last two name the fragment and language as discontinuities necessary to the reconstitution of home. "The Language of Home and the Fragmented Heritage: Assia Djebar's *L'amour, la fantasia*" explores the fragment as key to the reconstitution of home in Djebar's writing. It examines Djebar's foregrounding of her writing as fragmentary and her problematization of the venture of testimony. Homeland and private home are also interlinked in her work through the fractured transformation of the personal and historical home. In the case of Darwish's poetry, the son is later separated from the family, paralleling the loss of the homeland and that of the personal home as well. Through the many imbrications of the private home and the public homeland, the personal and the historical, the multiple inheritances predicated on love and imposition, Djebar also situates her writing of home among cultural figures from the past—like St. Augustine and Ibn Khaldun—that link writing and home.

The last chapter, "The Writing of Absence: Language, Rhythm, and Temporality in the Poetry of Mahmoud Darwish," establishes language as a mode of discontinuity. In his later work, *Limādhā tarakta al-Ḥiṣāna Waḥīdan?* [Why Have You Left the Horse Alone?], which expresses the desire of the poet to testify to the past and to open the "register of absence," Darwish's language emerges as rhythm not only in the incorporation of musical elements such as rhymes and meter but also in the primary emphasis on sound. Poetry then not only rearranges the referentiality of things in their possibility but further performs the movement of home as errance. A link is made with Sufism due to its enrapture with language, and because it was a rupture in writing from what preceded it and within its own cultural context. It is a writing that becomes its own home. The marginal experience of Sufism within an Arabic tradition reveals an experience that sought its being in language. Darwish's turn to language becomes akin to the Sufi one. Darwish seems moved by this Sufi notion of language where language is listening to presence and is a movement of becoming, where writing is the only possession of self.

In the latter work of Darwish and in the fiction of Djebar, home announces itself as a trope and is figured specifically as a metaphor, as in the Biblical words translated as "*Man goesth to his long home.*" (Eccles. xxi. 5) And as a temporal and spatial metaphor, home performs itself. It betrays itself as absence and at the same time as the possibility of form due to metaphor's materialization of an invisible union between apparent dissimilarities. (Arendt 1968: 13-14) The prevalent associations of home with belonging and dwelling are extended in the above Biblical formulation to death. The work of the writer specifically links home to an unbounded temporality where the passage through time and space does not begin nor end. Darwish writes: "And travel led me to travel/ and I don't see a country there." (Darwish 1994: 107)

For Darwish, the creation of homeland becomes the work of the poet: "the countries between my hands are the work of my hands." (Darwish 1994: 382) In so far as he approaches home as absence (due to literary as much as historical reasons that will be clarified in chapters 3 and 5), he sees writing as the only guard against absence: "It is absence of countries that I shape in words." (Darwish 1994: 299) Poetic language, despite its limitations, becomes a way of guarding off disappearance. Writing for both is a limit in the project of reconstitution: for possession and dispossession.

> Past is what I see
> for one a kingdom of dust and his crown. So let my language
> triumph over time the enemy, over my descendants,
> over me, over my father, and over disappearance that does not
> disappear
> this is my language and my miracle
> ...
> and the sacred of the Arab in the desert
> who worships what flows from rhymes like stars on his cloak,
> and he worships what he says
>
> it is necessary for prose, then
> it is necessary for divine prose for the prophet to triumph.
> (Darwish 1995: 118)

Language here is the only reality, the only possible triumph over inherited ways of establishing identity, and the only resistance to traditions of dispossession. However, the poetic gaze is limited, for it can only see the past and therefore is not prophetic. The self too is limited, for it fluctuates between being present and being emptied by travel, performing the temporality of the poem. The language of this poem, on the other hand, and especially in this passage, recalls the language of the Qur'an in its rhythm and in its words. Hence it recalls the Qur'anic claim of language as miracle and the particular status that Arabic language acquires after the appearance of the Qur'an. For Darwish, then, language has the paradoxical power to absent and the power to guard against absence, hence the need for poetic reconstruction.

In seeking to be part of a continuing, collective work of reconstruction, an endeavor that would allow for new figurations of home to emerge from the inherited myths, Darwish and Djebar consider these myths before they are foreclosed by history in an attempt to find an opening in how history reads them and to reveal history's encroachment upon myth. Their texts foreground the way in which history has read the Abraham myth to result in nationalist configurations of identity. The realm of myth is revealed to be that of metaphor where identification between history and myth emerges out of seeming difference. And with Darwish, poetry brings both myth and history together through the heritage selected to expose this structure of identification, a heritage that emerges not only from within the bounds of literary texts but also from the historical readings of them. Djebar proclaims: "Ce fut dans ce corps à corps avec l'Histoire que j'écrivis *L'amour, la fantasia*, puis *Ombre sultane* et la suite d'un quatuor romanesque d'Alger." [It is with this struggle with History that I wrote *L'amour, la fantasia*, then *Ombre sultane,* and the rest of the quartet on Algiers.] (Djebar 2000)

They seek alternate forms of history that would not foreclose the old myths and that would overcome readings and enactments of dominant histories. In their search for form, they pose poetry and literature as possibilities of such an alternative. Whereas myth and history rely on a narrative structure, Djebar's work resists narrative in its valorization of the fragment. And in foregrounding fiction, it challenges the impetus for mimesis and closure. Literature remains aporetic. Darwish, however, identifies poetry with history in its desire to write the beginning of things, but poetry remains even farther from myth or history. Darwish's poetry, which insists on interruptions, has the capacity to continue its tropic figuration of home endlessly. The notion of poetry that emerges in his work is that of perpetual search.

The work of Darwish and Djebar brings together poetry and history as well as the political and the poetic in the way it delves into the past. The political contests the past as tradition and authority; it seeks an opening in how history reads the past, which takes account of the collective. Whereas Djebar attempts to "resuscitate" this dead past and articulate the silenced voices of women, she is ultimately aware, as is Darwish, of the impossibility of reclaiming this past as it was. But Hannah Arendt points out (citing Walter Benjamin), "that although the living is subject to the ruin of the time, the process of decay is at the same time a process of crystallization." (Arendt 1968: 51) It is this possibility of transformed and fragmented poetic survival that guides their endeavor.

In examining Benjamin's relation to the past, Arendt writes that:

> Insofar as the past has been transmitted as tradition, it possesses authority; insofar as authority presents itself historically, it becomes tradition. Walter Benjamin knew that the break in tradition and the loss of authority which occurred in his lifetime were irreparable, and he concluded that he had to discover new ways of dealing with the past. In this he became a master when he discovered that the transmissibility of the past had been replaced by its citability and that in place of its authority there had arisen a strange power to settle down, piecemeal, in the present and to deprive it of 'piece of mind,' the mindless peace of complacency. (Arendt 1968: 38)

The loss of authority in the transmission of one's collective past is precisely what Darwish and Djebar confront, responding to the fracturing of the past in an attempt at its reconstitution from the perspective of the defeated and silenced. Benjamin's strategy had been to destroy in order to preserve. His is a writing that wrenches fragments out of their context and puts them in new ones in order to create new figuration of history and to avoid easy identification. Benjamin uses quotes, as Arendt indicates, with "the double task of interrupting the flow of the presentation with 'transcendent force' . . . and at the same time of concentrating within themselves that which is presented." (Arendt 1968: 39) If Benjamin's work is one of identifying those moments of rupture that tradition does not deliver, Darwish and Djebar also follow him in their emphasis on the discontinuous. For tradition is able to impose its order and authority onto the past only by denying discontinuities. (Arendt 1968: 44) Those discontinuous moments are important, then, because it is only through them that "the past [speaks] directly." (Arendt 1968: 40) Reading, being attentive to the rhetorical complexities and plays of the text, becomes a crucial preliminary aspect. Such a reading would not recreate another continuist, master narrative along the axis of oppressive tradition but would reveal how tradition is revived and simultaneously challenged at each moment. Hence the necessity of the threatening task in a critical present that faces the effacement of the past and the tyranny of tradition.

Many Arab Writers are preoccupied with "home." As Muhamed Shukri has indicated in an interview with *Banipal*, novels are often linked to personal lives in the Arab world, because there is a search for a history lost stolen by colonialism. Autobiography evokes a sense of history in its readers because it is inspired by the events that the country has undergone. (Shimon 1999) While each treatment of home is unique—where the emphasis may be the work of memory, the nostalgia for the beloved city, the tearing violence of war, or the rejection of all belonging within the family, or the freedom of exile—there are two tendencies: the secularized re-enactment of religious myth as well as the spatialization of home as siege of internal confinement and external errance.

> Phénomène courant dans la production romanesque contemporaine, cette figuration de l'espace patrimonial lié à la figure prophétique de Muhammad est, cependant, investie dans une vision qui n'a rien de religieux, qui est même résolument laïque. La figure et le parcours de Mustapha dans *La Saison de la migration vers le nord*, le célèbre roman de Tayyib Salih, en témoigne de façon éclatante. [In the contemporary production of novels, a wide phenomenon is the figuration of the patrimonial space tied to the figure of the prophet Mohammad, a vision that has nothing to do with the religious and which is resolutely secular. The figure and the journey of Mustapha Said in *Season of Migration to the North*, the famous novel of Tayeb Salih testifies to this in a striking fashion] (Hallaq 2002: 15)

Such examples that call attention to symbolic spaces of heritage are literary works by Muḥammad Shukri where the journey from the Rif to the city of Tangier is emblematic of Mohammad's journey; Ibrahim Kawni where the desert journey is from the everyday to absolute emptiness; Jurj Salim where the ability to find home is no longer to be taken for granted; Jabra Ibrahim Jabra, Walid Ikhlasi, Ghassan Kanafani, Ḥanan al-Shaykh, Gamal Ghitani, Huda Barakat who also write about home as siege, whether as confinement to the interior or exile to the exterior. (Camera d'Afflito 2002: 121).

> L'espace est la projection de l'angoisse, celle de l'emprisonnement dans l'exigu ou celle de l'errance dans un monde sans repères. Exprimant en

> premier lieu le sort du Palestinien confiné dans son camp ou jeté dans le désert du monde qui, à peine, entend ses cris, il reflète aussi la situation d'une humanité aux abois . . . la dysphorie caractérise également l'espace de la libanaise Hanan al-Shaykh . . . le sort réservé à la femme (arabe) y est figuré à travers la double opposition intérieure, extérieur et inclusion/réclusion, lesquelles renvoient de toute manière à l'exclusion. Il en est de même des œuvres de l'Égyptien Gamal Ghitani et de la Libanaise Huda Barakat . . . où l'espace compartimenté, cloisonné et rétréci, structure un univers livré à l'exercice d'un pouvoir arbitraire sans limites. [Space is the projection of anguish, that of imprisonment in scarcity or that of wandering in a world without landmarks. Expressing first of all the fate of the Palestinian confined in a refugee camp or thrown into the desert of the world which hardly hears his cries, it reflects also the situation of humanity at bay . . . anguish also characterizes the space of the Lebanese Hanan al-Shaykh . . . a fate reserved to the (Arab) woman is figured through the double opposition interior/exterior and inclusion/reclusion, which means essentially seclusion. It is the same with the works of the Egyptian Gamal Ghitani and of the Lebanese Huda Barakat where space which is compartmentalized, cloistered, and narrow structures a universe delivered to the exercise of arbitrary power without limits.] (Hallaq 2002: 14)

The search for the articulation of home that surpasses its violent enactments, the effort to do so consciously through an engagement with myths of the past and a revisiting of heritage, in a privileging of the aporetic and the rhetorical, is what is of particular interest in the work of Darwish and Djebar. Their work, which spans four decades and is in continual transformation and becoming, is one of reconstitution, an opening to the political.

Notes

1. Darwish has produced nearly fifteen collections of poetry since the Beirut 1982 period. Studies of Darwish's work in Arabic tend to focus on the question of land and resistance in his poetry. See for instance Shakir al-Nabulsi, *Majnūn al-Turāb: Dirāsah fī shi'r wa Fikr Maḥmūd Darwīsh* [The Mad Poet of the Land: A Study of the Poetry and Thought of Darwish] (Beirut: al-Mu'assassah al-'Arabiyah lil-Dirāsāt wal-Nashr, 1987); 'Abd al-'Aziz Muwafī, "Thunā'iyāt al-Arḍ/al-Mar'ah wa intihāk al-Muqadas: Qirā'ah fī Dīwān *A'rāss*," [The Coupling of Land/Woman: A Reading of Darwish's Weddings] *Mahmoud Darwish: An Arabic Perspective by Fourteen Critics. Al-Qahirah* 151 (1995): 62-69; or Raja al-Naqash, *Maḥmūd Darwīsh, Shā'ir al- Arḍ al-Muḥtallah* [Darwish, Poet of the Occupied land] (Beirut: al-Mu'assassah al-'Arabiyah lil-Nashr, 1972). There have been very few studies on Darwish in English. A notable exception has been Barbara McKean Parmenter's *Giving Voice to Stones,* which considers his work as part of its study on Palestinian literature. Barbara McKean Parmenter, *Giving Voice to Stones: Place and Identity in Palestinian Literature* (Austin: University of Texas Press, 1994).

2. On the major criticism on Djebar's work, see for instance Mireille Calle-Gruber, *Assia Djebar, ou la résistance de l'écriture. Regards d'un écrivain d'Algérie* (Paris :

Maisonneuve & Larose, 2001) and *Mises en scènes d'écrivains: Assia Djebar, Nicole Brossard, Madeleine Gagnon, France Théoret.* (Quebec and Grenoble : Le Griffon d'argile, 1993); Jeanne-Marie Clerc, Assia Djebar: *écrire, transgresser, résister* (Paris: L'Harmattan, 1997) ; *Assia Djebar et Sembène Ousmane: littérature et cinéma en Afrique francophone*, edited by Sada Niang (Paris: L'Harmattan, 1996) ; Mildred Mortimer, *Assia Djebar* (Philadelphia: CELFAN, 1988); Jean Déjeux, *Assia Djebar. Romancière algérienne, cinéaste arabe* (Sherbrooke: Sherbrooke Univ. Press, 1980); Winifred Woodhull, *Transfigurations of the Maghreb* (Univ. of Minnesota Press, 1993); Harrow, Kenneth, *The Muse and the Marabout* (Ed. Heinemann, 1993); Lise Gauvin, *L'écrivain francophone à la croisée des langues* (Paris : Karthala, 1997).

3. All translations are my own, unless otherwise indicated.

4. Mahmoud Darwish, "Anta munthu al-āna ghayrak," [You Are No Longer Yourself] *Al-Ayyām*, 16 June 2007.

Part I

Revisiting a Heritage of Dispossession

Chapter One

The Trial of Heritage and the Legacy of Abraham

> *I could conceive of another Abraham—to be sure, he would never get to be a patriarch or even an old-clothes dealer—an Abraham who would be prepared to satisfy the demand for a sacrifice immediately, with the promptness of a waiter, but would be unable to bring it off because he cannot get away, being indispensable; the household needs him, there is always something or other to take care of, the house is never ready; but without having his house ready, without having something to fall back on, he cannot leave—this the Bible also realized, for it says: "He set his house in order."*
>
> —Franz Kafka, cited in Walter Benjamin's *Illuminations*, 129.

When Kafka expresses the possibility, and the desire, to textually re-envision the inherited figure of Abraham, he is echoed by contemporary Arab writers contending with Abraham's presumed legacies: nationalism and religious fundamentalism. Kafka envisions an Abraham who would not be easily bound by the various monotheistic traditions and nationalist readings. He would fail to meet the demands of his household and to become patriarch, but he would nonetheless be diligent in his quest. He would also fail to meet the sacred commands, though he may be always ready, being "indispensable" to his family. Kafka's Abraham represents a fragile but arresting possibility before it is textually foreclosed. He is a figure, more specifically, of the double bind, one that demarcates the conflict and suspended difference of the divine commands and the communal duties. Kafka wants to insist on this difficult impasse, since Abraham never manages to establish order in his house. His paternity is already in question in the biblical story, even as it is being consolidated.

Abraham is fundamental for monotheistic, patriarchal demarcations of identity. Hence, a specific examination of Islamic articulations of his identity intimately linked to conceptions of patriarchy, nationalism, and fundamentalism, requires one to turn to the Old Testament to explore how Abraham is later incorporated and reworked in the Qur'an as Islam attempts to inaugurate its difference from older monotheistic traditions. While identity in all monotheistic traditions seems construed along a father-son nexus, the Qur'an reveals a different emphasis on the relationship between father and son. In introducing Abraham as a rebelling son, Islam reworks the bonds of filiations so that the son is valorized in his faith to his God and not in his submission to his father. The son's questioning of his father's traditional beliefs is encouraged as *ijtihād* or intellectual labor necessary for faith. Abraham nonetheless emerges as a figure of ambivalence—as father and rebelling son—who will become in Islamic readings the father of submission.

In the latter part of this essay, the writings of Djebar and of Darwish present two contemporary literary responses to Islamic and biblical constructions of identity. Both writers are engaged in re-examining their heritage, which they identify as paternal. The Abraham story is revisited, since it combines nationalist and religious constructions of identity and forges collective identity by way of submission to the authority of the father and exclusion of the other. They suggest that this long literary heritage speaks of dispossession, exclusion, and that those predicaments are historically enacted through nationalist and religious readings of inherited myths. They expose nationalist demarcations of identity that have failed and brought on a crisis of collective identity in Algeria and elsewhere where a pluralist past is denied, women are secluded from public life, and any voice of difference is silenced.[1] They reconsider these monotheistic myths before they are foreclosed into monolithic meaning by history to explore new ways of thinking about identity. Djebar invokes the memory of Abraham to recall Hagar's repudiation and the overall exclusion of women. Darwish invokes the father who exiles, who sacrifices the future for the past.

Walter Benjamin introduces the citation of Kafka above when speaking of narrative (Kafka's in particular) as the possibility for the postponement of the future. Benjamin reads the desire for the deferral of closure as a desire for hope. (1969: 129) To postpone the future is to defer closure, to foreclose violent formations of identity, and to entertain the possibility of new readings. Perhaps Abraham is the figure that refuses closure as Kafka envisions him and as Darwish and Djebar read him. While he is invoked by Darwish and Djebar as an emblem of paternal heritage predicated on submission, exile, and the sacrifice of the son, he is interrogated again to allow for hope, home, and future. It is a collective effort of rereading that would allow for new stories to emerge from old myths.

For what would it mean for Abraham to "set his house in order?"[2] Why is it necessary to do so before the sacred tasks can be carried out? God proclaims in

Genesis 18:20 that he has chosen Abraham precisely because he can keep order in his household and by extension maintain the covenant with God, so "that he may charge his children and his household after him to keep the way of the lord by doing righteousness and justice; so that the Lord may bring to Abraham what he has promised him." (New Revised Standard Version 1962)[3] But more importantly, how did Abraham presumably "set his house in order?" Is it by division? One woman kept, one exiled? One son claimed one disinherited? These questions can hardly be excluded as outside the parameters of the binding of Isaac. (Or is it Ishmael?) Is the sacrifice of the son to God or to the other woman? Is not the house already in disorder because of the birth of Isaac and the conflict of inheritance that will lead Sarah to demand the exile of Hagar and Ishmael? The division among the women and their sons carries with it double promises from God on behalf of Isaac and Ishmael. To Hagar, too, God promises that Ishmael will be "a great nation." (Genesis 21: 18) From these familial segmentations will be a separation of nations.

Perhaps one way for Abraham's house to be in order is to guarantee sole inheritance for Isaac. But, then, having put his house in order, Abraham would blindly climb the mountain to disorder again, where, without God's change of heart, his heir seems fated to perish. In fact, the event of the binding of Isaac is marked by disorder. Genesis 22 begins with Sarah's exclusion from this event and from the family of father and son. Sarah, Isaac, Hagar, and Ishmael all end up in different places. The Old Testament relates that when Sarah died in Hebron, "Abraham went in to mourn for her." (Genesis 23: 2) As Jon D. Levenson notes, Abraham "dwells in Beer Sheva, far from Isaac, far from Sarah who is in Hebron, far from Ishmael and Hagar in Egypt. In the end, Abraham is close only to God." (1998: 259) In the Qur'an too, Abraham will have divided houses as he journeys to see his son Ishmael and return to his wife Sarah, although the reason for this "exile" is less directly attributed to Sarah's rivalry: "Abraham said: 'Lord make this a secure land . . . I have settled some of my offspring in a barren valley near Your Sacred House, so that they may observe true worship, Lord.'" (*The Koran* 14: 36)[4]

Abraham's house has never been in order, for disorder is written into paternity as the Qur'an also relates. Beyond the general impossibility of ascertaining the certainty of paternity, Abraham himself needed divine intervention to father Isaac; he is already an old man and Sarah has passed her childbearing years. The foundation upon which the claim to paternity is made is never secure. One asks with Carol Delaney: "*Is Isaac his to sacrifice?*" (1998: 22) Implied also in the rendition of Abraham's attempted act of sacrifice is the valorization of paternity over and above any parental claims that the mother, who neither knows nor is asked, can make. His is a paternity predicated not simply on an acknowledged biological relationship, nor a social role based on that relationship, but one, as Delaney states, that "has meant *the primary, creative, engendering* role . . . The notion of paternity, therefore, already embodies *authority* and power and provides the rationale for a particular constellation of the family and the structure of relations within it." (1998: 7-8) The valorization of paternity creates a certain family order out of unstable elements where the father's claim to paternity has to be shared with another, where the mother is made absent, and where the future of the son is offered to the past-God. This is the heritage of paternity received as social (and political order) from the myth of Abraham filtered through the various traditional accounts. In such a rendition as the Old Testament's, which launches the "patriarchal narratives," the divine and paternal powers of creation and annihilation are henceforth interwoven, and the only story that remains, as Delaney points out, "could only be a story of recognition, that is of acknowledging and submitting to the one true God." (1998: 21)

Why is paternity so important? What order does it uphold? In the Old Testament, paternity guarantees inheritance of home and identity, but through the dispossession of others. The promise of paternity is made in the same breath as the promise of land. God commands Abraham: "'Leave your country, your family and your father's house, for the land I will show you.' . . . Abram passed through the land as far as Shechem's holy place . . . the Canaanites were in the land . . . 'It is to your descendants that I will give this land.'" (Genesis 12: 1-7) This is a covenant not revealed as such in the Qur'an. Rather, the emphasis throughout is on Abraham's leaving his father the idolater. Even his descendants will be subject to their faith. "'And what of my descendants?' asked Abraham. 'My covenant,' said He, 'does not apply to the evil-doers.'" (*The Koran* 2: 125) It is significant that the possession of land does not happen in Abraham's lifetime in the Old Testament. Even his immediate descendants will be without a home, "sojourners in a land not theirs." (Genesis 12: 13) Although they eventually create a new home, this promise is deferred and mediated through divine threats that Israel's inheritance will be broken. (Schwartz 1997: 129) The land remains a promise, though a strict, literal nationalist reading has attempted its actualization. "Almost every promise made to Abraham," Silvano Arietti points out, "concerns not the present but the future." (1981: 108) And though Abraham begets Ishmael and Isaac, the question remains: is paternity ever fulfilled? (Delaney 1998: 124) Genesis 22:19 relates that Abraham, after his attempted sacrifice, returned to his men whereupon they set off to Beersheba and lived there. It does not mention Isaac. Although Isaac ultimately resurfaces to hear Jacob, this still leads Delaney to ask, 'Where is Isaac?' The ending of Genesis 22 establishes the patriarchal lineage through Abraham's brother Nahor, "as if Isaac had ceased to exist." (Delaney 1998: 124)

Abraham's biblical story centers on paternity, on Abraham's desire to have a son who will be the fulfillment of God's promise so that he can be a "father of nations." His identity is inscribed in his paternity and is divinely ordained. Even the name of Abraham etymologically denotes fatherhood. The deity of the Old Testament changes Abraham's name from Abram (or "exalted father") to Abraham (or "father of a multitude"). (Genesis 17: 5) Not only is he favored for his paternity; he is also a father to a heterogeneous (and conflicting) collectivity after God's image in the Torah.

But Abraham himself occupies an ambivalent position in relation to paternity. Both a father and rebelling son in Islam, he is obligated to God at the expense of his own father, his own fatherhood, and his own son. He replaces his father and the visible idols for the invisible One. (Arietti 1981: 57) The Islamic rendition of the story of Abraham greatly emphasizes the encounter between Abraham and his own father, going back further into his life than does Genesis. It follows the post-biblical *Midrashim* story, and we encounter a defiant son destroying the idols worshipped by his people. While they decide to burn Abraham, his own father waits among the crowd. (*The Koran* 37: 109) Just as he displaces his father for his faith, so is his own father willing to sacrifice him for his own faith: "Do you dare renounce my gods, Abraham?" (*The Koran* 19: 46)

Abraham is pivotal to Islam, which traces itself back to him as an originary monotheistic religion, and which considers both Judaism and Christianity to have shared this message of monotheism only to distort it. So Islam claims to be both the new and the old faith. It is precisely to restore people to the faith of Abraham that Muhammad was sent. The Qur'an asserts that "Abraham was not a Jew, neither a Christian, but he was a pure monotheist (*ḥanīf*) and one who submitted (*Muslim*) to God; certainly he was never of the idolaters." (Cited in Delaney 1998: 162) In considering Abraham as a pure monotheist, Islam continues from previous traditions and succeeds in having that status acknowledged still today, as evidenced by the link it makes between Abraham and Muhammad. The parallels between the two prophets in the Qur'an include repeated references to them as breakers of idols.

When Islam delivers Abraham as a youth in search of a God among the gods, it is essentially defying the fatherly conception of the Old Testament where biological fathers are conveniently monotheistic believers. (*The Koran* 6: 75) It reconfigures affiliation and replaces the allegiance to the pagan and biological father with that of God: "show kindness to [your] parents. But if they bid you serve besides Me deities you know nothing of, do not obey them." (*The Koran* 29:7) So in having the story of the father, and Abraham as a rebellious son, it accentuates the faith of Abraham. In a sense, Abraham becomes another Adam, but one whose genealogy is of prophesy. And among the prophets, he holds a special status, being linked with a new conception of divinity and due to his line of descendants being one. He made his heritage one of prophecy, so that all the prophets that succeeded him were of his line of descent. And God, the Qur'an relates, took him as a friend.

It is a fragile paternity in a process of consolidation. A father and a son, Abraham is the figure of the patriarch and of heritage. Abraham upholds paternity to such an extent that he is willing to sacrifice his desire for fatherhood to the divine vision. He submits and in his submission he reigns over his desire. The faith of Abraham knows no bounds, and his possession of his paternity is predicated on the selfless abdication of all for the One God. The attempted sacrifice is the act that binds Abraham's identity as patriarch to his excessive faith and binds the heritage given to the son.[5] It furthermore has historically "bound" our reading of Abraham.[6] Through religious and nationalist readings, he has been received as patriarch and emblem of faith. The binding of Isaac has been the inherited story that demarcates heritage as paternal, faith as submission, where inheritance is possible only through submission to the patriarchal authority and at the same time threatened by that very faith. The Qur'an avoids the pitfalls in the Old Testament, however. For Abraham speaks to his son about his dream and asks him for his judgment: "He said: I see in a dream, my son, that I sacrifice you, so consider what you see fit. He [the son] answers: Do as you are commanded, you'll find me, God willing, forbearing." (*The Koran* 37: 102-111)[7]

Abraham becomes the closest image to God, not only fathering the Jews and Arabs but being claimed by all three monotheistic religions, being willing to sacrifice his own son as perhaps the Christian God was willing to do. He is not only the beginning of monotheistic religions, he is also their essence: "Who but a foolish man would renounce the faith of Abraham? We chose him in this world, and in the world to come he shall abide among the righteous. When his Lord said to him: 'Submit,' he answered: 'I have submitted to the Lord of the Universe.'" (*The Koran* 2: 31)

Abraham ultimately promotes dissension rather than community, as Regina Schwartz notes: "It could have been one community. Sadly enough these revisions succumbed to competition for the status of the true children of Abraham, to the scarcity principle." (1997: 159) Not unlike the monotheistic Old Testament God who cannot recognize all peoples as his own and who cannot give blessings to all, so Abraham can inherit only one son and dispossess the other, and can keep only one woman and exile another. While Abraham stands behind all three monotheistic religions as the past, he may also be the figure of future and promise as Kafka and the work of Darwish and Djebar implicitly suggest. It is only through opening these myths again to new readings that the possibility of new stories emerges.

The story of Abraham in its many forms remains contemporaneous. It is a heritage of sacred writing that has translated to profane nationalist and fundamentalist configurations of identity. If one is to acknowledge with Schwartz and Delaney that secular ideology has its roots in religious texts, one can further specify that nationalism may have its foundation in the Abraham story. The divine promises to Abraham of land and of paternity over many nations are the key moments in Genesis, a link that nationalism also makes. While the Bible is too heterogeneous to provide unambiguous demarcations of a "nation" or a "people," nonetheless it has been too often authorized as "a manual for politics." (Schwartz 1997: 123)

There is an intimate connection between the development of European nationalism and the wide-spread reading of biblical narratives as Schwartz indicates: "this Europe—filled with Bible stories about peoples—was also a Europe on the road to carving itself into new peoples, into nationalisms." (1997: 7) The biblical preoccupation with collective identity is filtered through German nationalism, so that modern nationalism is conceived through the interpretive work and reading of the German versions of biblical narratives: "In a disturbing inversion, soon nationalism was authorized by the once-holy writ. A text that had once posited collective identity as the fiat of God ('I will be your God if you will be my people') came to posit collective identity as the fiat of the nation authorized by God ('one nation under God'). Where nationalism is not explicitly authorized by God, it replaces God." (Schwartz 1997: 11-12)

The Hebrew Bible has had a tremendous impact on formulations of identity. In its biblical delineation, identity is linked with a unilateral notion of heritage. It is through inheritance, whether of faith or kinship, that collective identity is consolidated to the exclusion of all others. Even the promise of land is one that is inherited through the sacred words; land, like identity, is not to be gained through exchange with others but against them and at their expense. Schwartz attributes the violence in collective identity formation to monotheism where a "principle of scarcity" permeates. The monotheistic God not only demands exclusive adherence but also confers exclusive blessings not to be shared by all.

A questioning of nationalist paradigms leads necessarily then to a re-examination of the cultural paradigms that father modern ideologies. What has strongly carried into the Qur'anic rendition is the obligation of the submissive and obedient son. The binding of the son has led to the binding of a one and "true" reading. The need remains henceforth for rereading to make space for hopes that ideologically ritualized readings exclude.

Both Darwish and Djebar are engaged in such an endeavor of reading. In invoking Islamic stories informed by biblical ones, the two writers locate their heritage with Abraham and his ensuing legacy.[8] The paternal figure in their work as emblem of faith and submission predicated on the exile and sacrifice of the son is re-examined to allow for home, hope, and future without exclusion, submission, or disappearance. Both of their literary ventures involve an attempt at reconstruction, a work that implies a collective effort. The work of reconstruction through narrative and poetry would allow for new stories to emerge from the old myths.

The patriarchal narratives that forge collective identity by way of submission to the authority of the father and at the exclusion of the other are revisited, since the mythical has always encroached upon the historical and history has always attempted to speak for myth. Already the Qur'an foregrounds the mythic status of Abraham: "People of the Book, why do you argue about Abraham when both the Torah and the Gospel were not revealed till after him? . . . Indeed you have argued about things of which you have some knowledge. Must you now argue about that of which you know nothing at all?" (*The Koran* 3: 65) Unlike other prophets who are invoked directly and whose stories are told after they have been named, Abraham is often introduced in relation to his story: "Tell of Abraham." or "recount . . . the story of Abraham." (*The Koran* 6:75, 19:40) And yet the Qur'an has been received as another closed patriarchal narrative.

The family drama of one father, two women, and two sons continues to be played out not only in the literary world but in the critical, historical present as well. A father to two peoples, Abraham is the figure who brings together, if not violently binds, myth and history. What is more symbolic of this binding than the violence in Hebron perpetuated by the Jewish settler upon the praying Moslems, a violence that takes place at the presumed tomb of Abraham.[9] These simultaneous claims to the historical paternity of Abraham are predicated on the inherited accounts and myths of monotheism. With the patrimony of Abraham that continues to be claimed and proclaimed historically, is not one ultimately still within the mythic? The myth of Abraham continues to be read as a story of origins that forges collective identities and identifications of home. But these origins are mythic, for Abraham's beginnings as the accounts relate and as history bears out are always elsewhere. And yet his tombstone remains a politically contested site in history. And Hebron remains a volatile place.

In seeking to be part of a continuing work of reconstruction that would allow for new figurations of home and identity to emerge from the inherited myths, Darwish and Djebar attempt to find an opening in how history reads myth to reveal its encroachment on myth. Djebar writes:

> For . . . years I had been an uncomfortable witness of the fundamentalist rise in public life . . . I told myself that the only kind of response of which I was capable, as a writer, was to go back to the written sources of our history. I wanted to study . . . this specific period that the fundamentalists were in the process of claiming for themselves, deforming . . . from the standpoint of facts as well as the standpoint of intent. (Cited in Zimra 1993: 122-23)

Darwish and Djebar foreground the way in which history has read the Abraham myth to result in nationalist and fundamentalist configurations of identity. Myth, which suggests comparisons and connections out of disparities, provides writers with a world in which everything can be identified with everything else. The realm of myth is revealed to be that of metaphor where identification between history and myth emerges out of seeming difference. History haunts myth and tries to identify with it, for myths also impose a narrative structure on events and desires. And with Darwish and Djebar, poetry and literature bring myth and history together through the heritage selected to expose this structure of identification, a heritage that emerges not only from within the bounds of literary texts but also from the historical readings of them. They seek alternate forms of history that would not settle too quickly the meaning of the old myths and that would overcome readings and enactments of dominant histories.

In Darwish's and Djebar's invocations of Abraham as a figure of heritage, there is an implied suspicion that Abraham, who is doubly bound, reveals a double movement to heritage: not a heritage that emanates from the past and looks toward the future, but one that is arrested in a certain textual bind, in a perfect Benjaminian historical gesture, that turns back to the past while being propelled toward the future. Such a heritage looks upon piling heaps of ruin, as Benjamin envisioned that turning back, and inevitably produces that textual lineage in a narrative binding. And the two writers are well aware that textual production also creates its own progeny.

A dialogue with the father ensues for both writers. For both Darwish and Djebar, that heritage has been paternal because of the textual silencing and historical loss of the mother, figured previously and respectively as land and language, that surer but irrecoverable remainder. The heritage of the transient and ephemeral father, if absent, provides possibility for words and for home but only in displacement. Darwish writes: "I learned all the words and how to take them apart so I can form one word, homeland." (1994: 327) And as Abraham's chosen deity is intangible, so have Darwish's and Djebar's notions of home been inaugurated in words that respond to textual delineations of heritage that have become historical: "the countries between my hands are the work of my hands." (1994: 382) Djebar invokes the memory of Abraham to recall Hagar as the one left behind, as that inheritance that has not become part of any tradition and yet continues to be inherited. "Abraham accompanies Hagar and the child . . . until the site of Mecca, between the two hills of Safa and Merwa. /Then Abraham leaves. There, they are alone/ Ishmael is thirsty/ Ishmael is going to die." (Djebar 1991: 302) Darwish invokes Abraham as the father who always leaves, the father who could not defend his sons, neither to celestial sacrifice nor to the fears of Sarah: "And every absence is my father." (1994: 102) Perhaps for both Darwish and Djebar, Abraham is ultimately the site of contestation that remains, a remainder not only through the historical conflicts that are contemporaneous but also through the textual production.

Darwish's poetry often addresses the father or the forefathers; and, often, it has the form of a question, an accounting, or trial as evidenced by his titular question about the departure, "Why have you left the horse alone?" He does not invoke Abraham directly but addresses him through Ishmael and all the other sons. His poetic voice gathers the sons with whom it identifies: Ishmael, Joseph, Cain, and other exiles. The poetic voice also addresses his own father and literary forefathers, such as al-Mutanabbi and Imru'u al-Qais. When there is no faith, there can be no submission and no silence for the son. Ishmael dialogues with and interrogates the father through the poetic voice: "Where are you taking me, father? /In the direction of the wind, my son . . . / – Who will live in our home after us, my father? / – It shall remain as it was, my son." (Darwish 1995: 32-33) The saddened and sympathetic voice of the son holds the father accountable not to condemn him but to reopen the register of events to reinvent the outcome.

Poetry for Darwish is not only a staging of voices but also a space of survival. It seeks an inheritance that will not dispossess and that will open toward a future. "I look upon a procession of ancient prophets/as they climb barefoot toward *Orshalim*/And I ask: Is there a new prophet/for this new age?" (1995: 13) The search for new prophets is an acknowledgement that the old prophets, including Abraham, still loom as ghosts over the place and its absence. The father becomes ghost, ghost of self that haunts the memory of place. The father's departure from his house occupies the question of Darwish's poetic voice: "Why have you left the horse alone?" Through the paternal response, "for homes die without their inhabitants," he inherits a notion of home in its absence from the one who left. The voice of the son, which recognized only the departure, learns through dialogue with the father how home cannot be dissociated from a paternal heritage, and a paternal failing, and from the question and the words. The haunting is not only of the past and its failings, but also of the future and the limits of the poetic endeavor.

Like Darwish, Djebar frames her narratives with the figure of the father, whether it is her Algerian father, the literary fathers of St. Augustine and Ibn Khaldun, the French chroniclers, or Abraham. Hers is an inheritance usually bestowed on males. Aware of being privileged to receive this heritage of writing, she uses it to interrogate the father figure and to "resurrect" the silenced voices of women:

> My fiction is this attempt at autobiography, weighed down under the oppressive burden of my heritage . . . But the tribal legends criss-cross the empty spaces, and the imagination crouches in the silence when loving words of the unwritten mother-tongue remain unspoken – language conveyed like the inaudible babbling of a nameless, haggard murmur . . . How shall I find the strength to tear off my veil, unless I have to use it to bandage the running sore nearby which words exude? (1993: 218)

Djebar is haunted by the necessity and the impossibility of such a project. She names Abraham explicitly to recall these female suppressed voices, which are marked as discontinuous moments in heritage.

The heritage of Abraham for Djebar is the heritage of Ishmael and his mother: exile and repudiation: "Hagar the repudiated, because she is the first." (1991: 302) And this heritage is replayed in Islam for her. Political strife embedded in the Islamic community will have its familial roots where patriarchy is impotent, just like Abraham's predicament. The multiple marriages of Muhammad never guarantee any unity or order in the household. She recalls specifically Fatima and her inability to inherit either spiritually or materially from her father: "There is also her right as a daughter, her share of the inheritance. In this second controversy, she will fight alone." (1991: 78) She conjures Hagar as if to announce a beginning to a tradition of disinheritance. Djebar seeks the source for the legacy of Ishmael who ultimately repeats the repudiation of his father Abraham, upon the injunction of the father. And Ishmael submits.

While Djebar increasingly links the legacy of Muhammad to that of Abraham, locating Islam within this fixed paternal heritage of sacrifice and dispossession, she at the same time recalls Hagar as the body of struggle. It is precisely the dance of Hagar, as she searches for water for the thirsty Ishmael in the desert, frantically traversing the two hills of Safa and Merwa, that is the added story of Islam and that provides the possibility for inclusion, struggle, and survival. It is this dance that stages the fiction and this fiction that allows a voice to emerge through the body. "The child, in disarray . . . scrapes . . . the sand . . . when finally the water surges forth/ finally a source/ finally a music/ of beginning/ Hagar, dances in an abandoned folly, Hagar listens/ Hagar stops." (1991: 303) This is not only the supposed beginning of the sacred spring of *Zamzam* that runs in Mecca to this day, but it is also the commencement of possibility.

Djebar also points to the convergences and separations of traditions inherited. This heritage, encompassing an Islamic tradition predicated upon submission, offers her the opportunity for dialogue through the song of Abraham. In music, one can locate the promise: "Tradition would seem to decree that entry through its gate is by submission, not by love. Love which is the most simple of settings might inflame, appears dangerous. There remains music." (1993: 169) In her reading of the ballad of Abraham, she sees love valorized in the story of Abraham toward his son (and Muhammad toward his wife Khadija as well as toward his daughter Fatima in *Loin de Médine*), a love rendered secondary to submission if not altogether ruinous in traditional Islam. It is this inherited cultural moment that will lead both Darwish and Djebar to point to the ruptures of their heritage. In focusing on the father-daughter relationship, Djebar recalls Muhammad's own intervention on behalf of his daughter. "Fourteen centuries have elapsed: it seems that no father has since, at least within the community of Islam . . . developed such a compelling defense for the tranquility of his daughter!" (1991: 68-69) Djebar's focus on the daughter allows for healing and for inclusion.

Djebar imbricates Abraham's cultural patrimony with a menacing present in an indictment against contemporary Arabia and Algeria: "Abraham has returned, retracing his steps." (1991: 305) The violent legacy of Abraham, authorized by a blind paternal faith turned law, is in the continual displacement and dispossession of Hagar. Danielle Shepherd's comment on *L'amour, la fantasie* is appropriate as well for Hagar: "Woman sees herself called upon incessantly to conquer the laws of necessity and to advance regardless of destiny." (1996: 188) The struggle of Hagar, embodied in her frenzied dance, is to survive; and the need for survival still remains. Djebar's endeavor of writing is likewise one of struggle and survival, simultaneously a displacement of the father and a transgression against him. For her, writing is associated with the father, for she learns it from him and against his prohibition (on love letters, for instance).

We return to Kafka who wants to consider Abraham not as an inaugurating figure of paternal authority and submission, nor even as the everyday man who meets his communal duties, but as a figure of the double bind where the demands of the everyday never cease and his devotion to the divine is neither compromised nor fulfilled. This bind inhabits the center of this figure of heritage as a discontinuity. So, ultimately, whether one shares Kafka's vision of Abraham or not, one certainly needs his interrogation of this figure of heritage. Not unlike Kafka, both Darwish and Djebar invoke, through Abraham, this arrested vision of myth to point to its possibilities before its narrative closure. This mythic moment endows the writers with the ability to abide before the damage of old myths. This arrested moment further grants an opening for new conceptions of identity and of home to emerge from the old. It allows at the very least for a marking of that desire.

Notes

1. In Algeria, violent conflict has ensured since the nationalist government canceled the 1992 elections because Islamic fundamentalists won by a landslide. Supporters of the Front Islamique du Salut, or Islamic Salvation Front, which presented the only alternative to a corrupt nationalist dictatorship, and those concerned about their rights under fundamentalists immediately protested. Civil strife continues in Algeria. In Israel, the mere suggestion of including Darwish's poetry in the country's high school curriculum threatened to dismantle the government and the second uprising unfolds violently as a result of one group imposing its nationalist claims at the expense of the other.

2. While Kafka, as cited by Benjamin, attributes the expression "He set his house in order" to the Old Testament, the origin of this phrase is uncertain. The expression cannot be strictly traced to the German versions of the Hebrew Bible. It seems to be put into play by the two writers based on a verse in Genesis 22:9, which is the closest biblical phrase to Kafka's and is said in the context of binding: "Abraham laid the wood in order, and bound Isaac." See Robert Young, *Analytical Concordance to the Bible: Authorized Edition Revised* (NY: Funk & Wagnall's Company, 1936). Moreover, Benjamin does not cite the source of Kafka's words.

3. Subsequent references are to the *New Revised Standard Version* (New York: New American Library, 1962).

4. *The Koran*, translated by N. J. Dawood (New York: Penguin Classics, 1999), 14:36. I have modified the translation of this particular verse. I use the spelling "Qur'an" rather than "Koran," although I rely on Dawood's translated version.

5. One cannot account for all the readings that this episode has generated. Noteworthy are the readings of Immanuel Kant and Søren Kierkegaard. While monotheistic religions have read this binding as testimony to Abraham's faith, it was Immanuel Kant who began in the philosophical tradition a reopening of this reading based on a notion of universal ethics. Kant argues that an action that is considered wrong in itself cannot be deemed right as a result of divine directive. He wants to ground a moral actor not on "laws proceeding from another person's act of choice" but on "inner laws that can be developed from every man's own reason" and that would constitute "universal ethics" (Cited in Jon D. Levenson, "Abusing Abraham: Traditions, Religious Histories, and Modern Misinterpretations," *Judaism* 47 (Summer 1998): 260. Søren Kierkegaard's defense of Abraham in *Fear and Trembling* is a response that underscores the conflict within Abraham. Kierkegaard insists on the "dread" that Abraham presumably experiences, a tension that results both from his faith in God's promise and from his love for his son. If the ethical for Kant is universal and directed from within itself, faith for Kierkegaard is so radically individual that it is incommunicable; it isolates and places the individual above the universal because of his/her unmediated relation to the absolute. Søren Kierkegaard, *Fear and Trembling*, translated with introduction and notes by Walter Lowrie (Princeton: Princeton University Press, 1968).

6. I am referring to the work of Mahmoud Darwish and Assia Djebar since the early eighties.

7. The massacre in Hebron took place on 25 February 1994 at the Cave of the Patriarchs, known as Abraham's tomb. A Jewish settler from Hebron, Dr. Baruch Goldstein, entered the Mosque where Moslems were praying and opened fire, killing twenty-nine of them before he was killed. Nothing immediate is known to have triggered this event, although Hebron is often tense because of the competing religious claims on its sites and because the Israeli settlements are inside the city.

8. Translations of Darwish's poetry from the Arabic are mine.
9. Translations from the French are mine.

Chapter Two

Reclaiming an Islamic Legacy of Memory and Contestation in Assia Djebar's *Loin de Médine*

"*Satan, being thus confined to a vagabond, wandering, unsettled condition, is without any certain abode; for though he has, in consequence of his angelic nature, a kind of empire in the liquid waste or air, yet this is certainly part of his punishment, that he is . . . without any fixed place, or space, allowed him to rest the sole of his foot upon.*"
—Daniel Defoe, *The History of the Devil: Ancient and Modern*, n.p.

"*Woman is the mountain who must go to Mohammed.*"
—Luisa Valenzuela, *Women's Voices from Latin America*, 165.

When Assia Djebar symbolically locates the women of early Islam, "women in movement," far from Medina—already a locus of exile for Muhammad and his followers—she is working against an inherited monotheistic notion of exile that dictates that any deviation or displacement of an established order is morally charged.[1] No longer are the paradigmatic figures of exile the revolting Satan, the easily tempted Eve, or the murderous Cain. Instead she calls forth the rhythmic wandering of the ancient Hagar and the legacy of struggle she leaves for the daughters of Ishmael. While the condition of wandering has been associated with a spirit of revolt manifesting nothing short of a dubious moral standing, Djebar wants to connect the duplicitous notion of wandering to a spirit of revolt imprecated in a quest for knowledge borne by strife (or as she names it *ijtihād*, a quest that Islam favors. The pursuit of knowledge and the condition of wandering are henceforth inextricably linked.

The Qur'anic revelation has few interdictions on learning.[2] It encourages the believers to leave home and seek knowledge, necessarily tying this search with displacement. The revelation itself bequeaths knowledge—and submission—as it is delivered to the illiterate Muhammad away from home: "'*Lis!' ordonne l'ange Gabriel dans la caverne. 'Mais je ne sais pas lire', doit murmurer l'ancien berger. 'Lis!' répète Gabriel qui n'a pas 'écouté' . . . L'écriture ainsi se présente divine, liberté première, essence: elle devient chair et chant tracés ensemble.*" ["Read!" The angel Gabriel commands in the cave. "But I don't know how to read," the former shepherd must have murmured. "Read!" Repeated Gabriel who did not "hear"...Writing henceforth presents itself as divine, first freedom, essence: it becomes flesh and song traced together] (Djebar 1993: 9) Mohammed's knowledge of the divine writing will bring forth a rebellious voice against the idol worship of the powerful tribes of Mecca. This call to seek knowledge, even as it implies movement, exile, and rebellion, Djebar takes up as her desire for *ijtihād* and her duty to faithfully submit to the divine.

In *Loin de Médine*, she attempts, through writing, to reclaim early Islam as her heritage in order to locate a rupture within it in the active silencing of women and absenting of their voices, their bodies, and their rebellions. Djebar effectively wants to reclaim her share of that heritage to reveal that it was always open to contestation. In her effort to "revive" the forgotten voices, Djebar increasingly links the legacy of Mohammed to that of Abraham, locating Islam within this fixed paternal heritage of sacrifice and dispossession. At the same time, she recalls Hagar as the body of struggle and possibility of survival. Through her writing and her intellectual attempt at *ijtihād*—not the traditional meaning that insists on consensus or *ijmā'* but proffering her own individual interpretation—she turns to an Arabic and Islamic heritage in appropriating the very methods of transmission to question the present of Islamic fundamentalism and ineffective nationalism. Djebar relates the past to the present as will be evident in order to show that the move is predicated upon the dispossession and exclusion of women.

In this, she follows a trajectory of Middle Eastern and North African women writers engaged in a reflection on the place ascribed to women within their tradition. These women include such early figures of the twentieth century as the Algerians Fatima Amrouche and Marie Louise Amrouche as well as the Egyptians Huda Sha'arawi, and Aïcha 'Abd al-Rahman. More contemporary women include Fatima Mernissi and Nawal al-Sa'adawi. Djebar herself traces this tradition of women writers to ancient times, to the people of the Touareg and to Zoraida, the first Algerian woman to write. For Djebar, a tradition of women writers has always existed in the Maghreb.

Like much of Darwish's work, this is an intervention in the present and an engagement with the past. Whereas Djebar responds to a specific event, the rise of Islamic fundamentalism in Algeria, Darwish's later work tends to distance itself from poetry as response, although it cannot altogether disengage from the historical even in such works as *Sarīr al-Gharībah* which presents itself as a collection of love poems. Both writers, however, foreground the aesthetic dimensions of their projects. Gender rarely is brought to bear in his work except in its symbolic and mythic dimensions. The struggle is envisioned in more abstract human dimensions. Like Djebar, however, Darwish is interested in the religious myths and stories and how they create political realities.

Through writing, Djebar in turn seeks to recall the revolutionary aspect of Islam at the time of Muhammad, one that promised, among other things, more rights and participation to women. And yet, as Djebar reminds us, while Islam undoubtedly created a "social revolution," its spiritual and political aspects have been from the beginning in conflict. Djebar and others such as Fatima Mernissi suggest that while this social revolution was nothing less than a feminist revolution in sixth-century Arabia, it was ultimately an aborted one. (Lee 1996: 60) It is the political that has overshadowed the spiritual. This failure is evident in the manifest split between spiritual Islam and its political practices ensuing especially after the death of Muhammad. Djebar indicates that this split survives today: "*Et tandis que l'Islam recommande 'd'aller jusqu'en Chine pour quêter le savoir,' chacun crie haro sur la fillette qui, à douze ans, fait un pas hors du seuil, vers la première placette publique.*" [And while Islam recommends "going all the way to China in search of knowledge," each denounces the young daughter, who at age twelve, steps outside the threshold toward public space.] (Djebar 1993: 8) Djebar's novel, *Loin de Médine*, traces the wanderings of political Islam from its spiritual inception, rewriting the history of Islam by centering on the process of dispossessing women, and binding the oblivious present to the living past. (Zimra 1993: 121) Medina emerges as a center of political power, a "trope for Islam," predicated on the marginalization of women. (Zimra 1996: 831) Djebar, in turn, sets out to "recall" these rebellious and rare women who were relegated to forgetfulness: "Des Musulmanes de la plus rare espèce: soumises à Dieu et farouchement rebelles au pouvoir, à tout pouvoir—ainsi se perpétuera le sillage de Fatima, en Syrie, en Irak, plus tard en Occident musulman." [Moslem women of the rarest kind: submitted to God and ferocious rebels against power, against any power—and so the trail of Fatima will be perpetuated in Syria, in Iraq, and later in the Moslem West.] (Djebar 1991: 99-300)

In this work, as in *L'Amour, la fantasia*, Djebar relies on traces and fragments in order to call attention to the voices of women narrators and women rebels that surrounded the life of the Prophet Mohammed. She reads the historical accounts of the early Islamic century, a period that begins with the death of the Prophet. Relying on the chronicles of the first two to three centuries of Islam of the historians Ibn Hashem, Ibn Saad, and Tabari, she highlights the contribution of the early women not only to the transmission of Islam but also to its establishment. (Crosta 1996: 55) She focuses on the time of the initial dissensions in Islam with the first Caliphate, conflicts centered around questions of material and spiritual inheritance, "the thirty or so years that Moslems call 'the Great Discord'": "Entering into Tabari's world, I was finally able to evoke all that he had, but purely from a woman's standpoint." (Zimra 1993: 125) While women traverse the texts of these historians, they only appear fleetingly:

> Musulmanes ou non musulmanes . . . elles trouent, par brefs instants, mais dans des circonstances ineffaçables, le texte des chroniqueurs qui écrivent, un siècle et demi, deux siècles après les faits. Transmetteurs certes scrupuleux, mais naturellement portés, par habitude déjà, à occulter toute présence féminine . . . Dès lors la fiction, comblant les béances de la mémoire collective, s'est révélée nécessaire pour la mise en espace que j'ai tentée là, pour rétablir la durée de ces jours que j'ai désiré habiter. (Djebar 1991: 5)
> [Whether Moslem women or non Moslems . . . they traverse briefly but in unforgettable circumstances the texts of the chroniclers who write, a century and a half, two centuries, after the facts, transmitters who are certainly scrupulous but naturally carried by habit to eclipse all feminine presence. Henceforth, fiction, overwhelming the benefits of collective memory, reveals itself necessary for the staging I attempted there, for the re-construction of these days that I desired to have lived.]

In a familiar move, as in her other works, Djebar foregrounds the fictionality and necessity of such a literary endeavor of reconstruction, one that foremost bears her own desire. She especially endeavors to "recreate" the narrations of these female transmitters that pass briefly through the early (and later accounts of Islam) and to "resurrect" the voices of the forgotten women: "de multiples destinées de femmes se sont imposées à moi: j'ai cherché à les ressusciter . . . Femmes en mouvement 'loin de Médine,' c'est-à-dire en dehors, géographiquement ou symboliquement, d'un lieu de pouvoir temporel qui s'écarte irréversiblement de sa lumière originelle." [Multiply destined women are imposed on me: I wanted to resuscitate them . . . women in movement "far from Medina," that is to say outside, geographically and symbolically, a place of temporal power that irreversibly breaks away from the original light] (Djebar 1991: 7) In such a paradoxical if not impossible project that seeks to raise the dead bodies as living voices, she ultimately grants power not so much to the mirage of voices but to the creative voice. She relies on these writings of the chronicles as a basis from which she can construct her own notion of heritage and to situate herself with these women of the past, "far from Medina."

Djebar's use of authenticated sources is strategic, as Sonia Lee claims, since it allows her to only focus on recreating the past and to avoid engagement in debates around the historical truth of the narrator's claims. (Lee 1996: 57) "For Djebar to use Tabari [the most famous of the other two that she uses] is immediately to stand behind an authority no one, whether devout believer or lay historian, will dare contest." (Zimra 1993: 120) The importance of the historical commentators cannot be over-emphasized since they provide, through their exegesis, a historical understanding to the Qur'an: "For a true believer, the Qur'anic verses . . . must be read in concert with the Prophet's sayings . . . comments intended to clarify the revelation. In this process of Qur'anic exegesis, socio-cultural factors intervene, especially where the original *ḥadīth* is quite pithy . . . as . . . in the conflict between Fatima and the Khalifs." (Zimra 1993: 120)

Her use of epigraphs also has the strategic purpose of situating her work in relation to specific cultural heritages, both "legitimizing" it and, at the same time, undermining the presumed continuity of her texts and those preceding it. The Ferdousi epigraph, for instance, situates her work within an established historical tradition: "Tout ce que je dirai, tous l'ont déjà conté; tous ont déjà parcouru le jardin du savoir." [All that I will say will have already been said; all has passed through the garden of knowledge.] (Djebar 1991: 7) Patricia Geesey suggests that Djebar, by choosing this particular citation, is locating her text specifically within a tradition of epic that narrates the familiar. (Geesey 1996: 42) Djebar's desire for epic as a source of memory is already marking her stance of *ijtihād* or contestation not on the grounds of proclaiming false that which has been written but to mark an entrance into a dialogue both on religious and political grounds, however unusual it may be through this work of fiction that insists on aporia: "Et il y eut alors un étrange dialogue entre lui et moi, entre moi, son ressuciteur, et le vieux temps remis debout." [And there was a strange dialogue between him and me, between myself, his resuscitator, and old time] (Djebar 1991: 7) Unlike Darwish who sees his poetic project as one of lyric-epic in the post Beirut period which involves writing a genesis of a collectivity without narrative, as I will elaborate in the next chapter, Djebar does not foreground epic as the primary endeavor here. The Jules Michelet epigraph points to the importance of dialogue for Djebar, especially in her work to reclaim a time past. It is a contestation that forms part of the intellectual heritage proclaimed by Islam. "Plus loin . . . les groupes s'affrontent: entre les *Mohadjirs*, les Migrants mecquois, d'une part et les *'Ançars* médinois, d'autre part; entre les clans mêmes divisants . . . le problème de la succession donne lieu à des querelles." [Further on . . . the groups confront one another: the *Mohājirūn* or the Emigrant Meccans on the one hand and the *Anṣār* of Medina on the other hand . . . even within the divided clans . . . the problem of succession leads to fights.] (Djebar 1991: 11) This first and violent contestation already involves conflicts over inheritance.

The Opening of Heritage through the Work of *Ijtihād*

For Djebar, *Loin de Médine* stems from a desire for *ijtihād*, a "desire to interpret" (Djebar 1991: 6), to partake in the shaping of tradition, perhaps to allow for other possible future outcomes. She means *ijtihād* not in the sense of holy war against others, a sense associated with *jihād* that is all too familiar today. Rather she chooses to locate its meaning in the intellectual effort that creates an internal strife, that would offer an opening for questioning and dialogue in her "quest for truth," "effort intellectuel pour la recherche de la vérité—venant de *djihad*, lutte intérieure, recommandée à tout croyant." [intellectual effort for the search of truth—coming from *jihād*, interior struggle that is recommended to each believer] (Djebar 1991: 6n) As George Lang shows, Djebar undermines this constructed opposition between jihād as active yet static struggle or holy war and *ijtihād* as dynamic, free interpretation. In Djebar's work, they emerge embedded in one another:

> jihad and *ijtihād* each anchor one end of a dialogical continuum running from holy war through conversion, maieutic, and on to the hermeneutics of *ijtihād*. War is, after all, innately dialogical, but interpretation has an intrinsically agonistic side, and the continuum jihad/*ijtihād* has as well a particular configuration in the Maghreb, where texts are intensely transtextual—an expression preferable to 'intertextual' to emphasize their invasive nature, a characteristic rooted in the history of the region and in the imperative practice of Islam, which began, after all, with God's edict to Muhammed at the first moment of revelation: *iqrā'!* (read/recite). (Lang 1996: 2)

Before the meaning of *jihād* solidified into a meaning of struggle as war in a juridical tradition, it had multifarious meanings. The root of the word "jihād" consisting in the Arabic root *j-h-d* "had the pre-Qur'anic meaning of striving, laboring, or toiling, and in the thirty-six instances where the word occurs in the Qur'an was used 'classically and literally in [that] natural sense.'" (Ali cited in Lang 1996: 3)

Her notion of *ijtihād* as intellectual strife allows her to shift the focus to women—not only the struggles of the early women of Islam but contemporary Muslim women struggling against nationalist and fundamentalist configurations of identity. Winifred Woodhull differentiates between Djebar's tentative demarcations of identity, that emerge in response to rigid and exclusionary formulations, from fundamentalist ones: "Because Djebar's insistence on the search for form allows only for provisional, strategic identities, the latter are quite distinct from the essentialist Muslim identity that religious and other conservatives want to assign to Muslims in every historical period and every culture." (Woodhull 1993: 33) Djebar's text does not allow for closure; it remains aporetic, as seen in the filial figures of Fatima and Aïcha who represent irreconcilable meanings at the heart of their struggle, that of the daughter and the wife respectively.

Through her work of *ijtihād,* Djebar shows how women of early Islam were fundamental to the emergence of Islam. (Zimra 1996: 827) Her concept of *ijtihād* is one where heterogeneous narratives contest each other, brought together and juxtaposed, where fictional accounts are allowed to propagate from traditional *isnād* (or chain of transmission) narratives. Henceforth women's writing takes its place in the traditionally masculine domain of *jihād* not to reinforce the communal thrust for consensus but to undermine the very basis of that consensus. (Lang 1996: 7)

> Classical Sunni *ijtihād* was a ratiocinative procedure whose aim was to establish consensus among scholars alone 'competent to exercise [it]' (Hourani 1991, 68) . . . For her part, Assia Djebar so closely ties the question of *isnād* to alternative lines of narrative development that her *ijtihād* falls beyond rati-

ocination. In the first place, by speaking of her personal will, she connects renewal of interpretation with inner struggle, a notion by no means alien to Islamic thought but suspect from the point of view of the *'ulumā'* (the learned), whose goal was *ijmā'* (consensus), and who holds the monopoly on *ijtihād* as usually construed. Furthermore, by constructing a montage of substitute fictional episodes that various *isnād* generate, Djebar undermines the procedural rationality that was the premise of both classical *ijtihād* and modernist revisionism dating from the colonial period. (Lang 1996: 8)

Djebar's strategic attack on historical Islam is one launched while she follows the percepts of the Qur'an and the *Ḥadīth* that call on the believers to engage in an interrogation of their faith.

Relying on the *Ḥadīth* for her own attempts at *ijtihād* and reconstructions, she follows its tentative trajectory: "Un *ḥadīth* n'est jamais tout à fait sûr. Mais il trace, dans l'espace de notre foi interrogative, la courbe parfaite d'un météore entrevu dans le noir."[3] [A *ḥadīth* is never completely certain. However, it traces in the space of our interrogative faith the perfect curve of a fallen star as seen in the dark] (Djebar 1991: 63) Djebar not only relies on the material of the *Ḥadīth* but more importantly appropriates the structure of *isnād* and *Ḥadīth* transmission into her own discursive methods. She reenacts the chain of transmission in order to reconstruct the voices of women and to center them, an act of reconstitution that is inextricably an act of reading. This way, she allows the narrative voices of women to permeate the male-dominated *isnād*. Traditionally, the process of verifying authentic *Ḥadīths* from false ones was very important in the first centuries of Islam, for the corpus of *Ḥadīth* can be easily manipulated for political ends.[4] Djebar, in turn, establishes a dialogue in her narrative between "fact" and "fiction." (Geesey 1996: 45) There is already a certain affinity between the way the *Ḥadīth* proliferates different narrations around the same event and Djebar's polyphonic style of writing to which we have become accustomed. (Geesey 1996: 44) Djebar in effect demonstrates in her text that heterogeneity has always been inherent to Islam: "'*Islam*,' *dit-on, se traduit par soumission. Se trahit?*" ["Islam," one says, translates to submission. A betrayal?] (Djebar 1993: 7)

Already in the way it translates its mission as submission, it betrays itself. Those who make the claim for its essential submission forget the intellectual rigor that it commands. Lang points to the "inherently agonistic" nature of the *Ḥadīth* accounts. (Lang 1996: 7) Furthermore, Fischer and Abedi call attention to the process of producing meaning in the foundational texts of Islam, one that involves "dissimulation": "The . . . structure of Qur'an and Ḥadīth . . . [plays] upon appearances and resemblances . . . that may or may not be grounded . . . depending upon the perspective and knowledge of the interpreter. It is a structure necessitating a critical sense, but one ambivalently also permissive of uncritical belief and false leads." (Cited in Lang 1996: 7) Lang likewise reminds us that the conflict emerging from diverse interpretations had from the beginning real political ramifications, but that the shutdown of *ijtihād* was also the result of certain Islamic epistemological practices.

> Interpretation was open, though conflict was far from purely hermeneutic. In fact the great schism between Sunni and the Shi'ite currents anticipated in the first passages of *Loin de Médine* dates from the second Islamic generation, and the Maghreb itself was the scene of intense military and doctrinal clash, starting with the appearance of the Kharijis around 740 A.D. More than the result of political rivalry, however, the subsequent hardening of doctrines—the closing of 'the gate of *ijtihād*' (*bāb al-ijtihād*)—might also be understood as an inevitable consequence of what one might call Islamic epistemology. (Lang 1996: 6)

The structure of Djebar's narrative opens the gate of interpretation once again, offering another mode of *isnād* by presenting a plurality of voices traditionally submerged and reinforcing the thematic focus on women. Voices of the transmitters in the first-person narration or in italics are presented as direct transcription from the oral and alternate with accounts of women by the author herself as third-person reconstruction.

The Severing Poles of Opposition: Fatima and Aïcha

Long since the emergence of Eve as the first woman and an emblematic one, women prone to wandering have been perceived as a threat to the security of the home, hence the desire to hide and dispossess them, rendering them confined inhabitants of oblivion. Women clearly constitute a force of opposition in Djebar's text, however, falling mostly between the two poles of the transmitter Aïcha, whose name promises life and whose political aspirations are in tune with the temporal powers of Medina, and Fatima, the force of contention and doubt to the political leadership that misinterpreted the Prophet's words and were cause for her disinheritance. As in her other texts, women are figured primarily in relation to patriarchy as daughters (and wives); in this specific instance they are all daughters of Ishmael, inheritors of his mother's exile and repudiation.[5]

Djebar looks back to Islam's early process of consolidation of power to reveal a community that is being established at the outset beyond Mecca and Medina, one that strengthens its existence at the expense of women and by means of their exclusion. While these women rebels are invoked for various reasons, they all meet the same fate of disappearance in the early chronicles of Islam and in the collective memory of its believers.[6]

While Djebar is scrupulous in naming women who made an impact in the history of Islam, including such figures as Oum Fadl who "porte en elle tout un passé récent." [carries within her a very recent past] (Djebar 1991: 56) and who becomes an important transmitter, she places the focus on Fatima, the Prophet's daughter, and Aïcha, his wife. Indeed the opposed stances of Fatima and Aïcha textually and discursively frame the plurality of other women's voices, and will eventually lead to factional divisions within the Islamic community.

Already while Muhammad is dying, he asks for his cousin Ali in order to relay his last words, fearing that this tentative community will fall into error. Two of his wives, Djebar relates, warn their fathers as well. Aïcha brings her father Abou Bakr, Hafça brings her father Omar ibn al-Khattab, and the others look for the Prophet's cousin. At the brink of death, the community is already ripe for political strife. The ensuing schism will have familial roots.

> Comme si le corps de l'Islam devait se diviser, enfanter par lui-même luttes civiles et querelles, tout cela en tribu payée à la polygamie du Fondateur. Comme s'il fallait épouser de multiples fois pour rassembler et transmettre un pouvoir multiple certes, mais par là même jamais unifié. En l'occurrence, les épouses, futures veuves, amènent pour la plupart leur père; de fait, ce seront les deux beaux-pères du Prophète qui, l'un après l'autre, succéderont par leur mérite personnel il est vrai, plutôt que grâce à leur alliance. (Djebar 1991: 59)
> [As if the body of Islam must divide, itself fostering civil struggles, all in a tribute paid to the polygamy of the Founder. As if it was necessary to marry many times to reassemble and transmit a multiple power certainly but one never unified. At the time, spouses, future widows, bring for the most part their fathers; in fact it is the fathers-in-law of the Prophet who, one after the other, will succeed by their personal merit, it is true, more so than due to their alliance.]

This is the stage that Djebar sets through her fiction. The conflict is precipitated through women who, divided from one another as co-wives and with different allegiances, fashion their own vision of filiations, ones that appeal to the father. The question of succession lingers open after his death as a result of his silence. "L'agonisant a donc désiré un scribe, un confident qui puisse écrire fidèlement ses recommandations. Trois au moins se sont présentés à son chevet. Il a eu un regard de désolation et il a tourné la tête vers le mur. Il n'a rien voulu dire." [The dying man had wanted a scribe, someone to confide in who would be able to write faithfully his recommendations. Three at least presented themselves at his bedside. With a look of desolation, he turned his head toward the wall. He didn't want to say anything more.] (Djebar 1991: 11) The privilege of the scribe, Djebar reminds us, does not bestow temporal succession. Had the Prophet had a son, he would have been the natural choice for the scribe but not necessarily for the guide of the *Ummah* (people, nation, and community). The successor would then have been named, and it would have avoided much of the dissension that ensued after the death of Muhammad and that continues today. The failure of the will of Muhammad to be written further links heritage to writing, where writing could circumvent and call into question repressive tradition.

Patriarchy will prove to be violently impotent in this family affair that precipitates the struggles within Islam. The strength of familial filiations always falls short. Djebar from the beginning announces the ambivalence of the personage of Ali in this Islamic tradition. He is not only the cousin of the Prophet, he is also his adoptive son as well as son-in-law (not to mention the Prophet's reference to him as his brother, since Muhammad himself was raised by his uncle, Ali's father, after the death of his parents and his grandfather. Fatima will reiterate this when she refers to her father as the "brother [of her] cousin."). It is not only his blood ties that will render him problematic; his special relation to Muhammad will as well. "Certains affirment que Ali seul ne veut pas quitter le chevet du Messager, dédaigneux de l'héritage temporel." [Some attest that Ali alone did not want to leave the bedside of the Messenger, disdaining temporal inheritance.] (Djebar 1991: 12) Djebar, however, does not locate the strife within Islam with Ali, as theologians and Shiites have, the latter siding with Ali as the one privileged to inherit the caliphate. Djebar chooses to focus, instead, on the forgotten Fatima as a locus of dissension.

Fatima only survives her father, Muhammad, by six months, dying at twenty-eight. She is remembered as the mother of Hassan and Hussein, "les futurs martyrs, dont le drame culminant à Kerbela, fissurera, plus de cinquante années plus tard, le devenir Islamique." [the future martyrs, for whom the drama will culminate at Kerbela and will fissure, more than fifty years later, the Islamic future.] (Djebar 1991: 57) She, like her mother Khadija, will be the sole spouse for her husband while alive. She is also the sole inheritor of the Prophet.[7] "Fatima, fille du Prophète, avance au premier plan du théâtre islamique également comme épouse et mère de trois martyrs—morts de main islamique: Ali, Hassan et Hossein. Son ombre revendicatrice s'étend sur le corps entier, quoique bifide, de l'Islam séculier." [Fatima, daughter of the Prophet, will advance to the first stage of the Islamic theater, equally as wife and mother of three martyrs—killed by an Islamic hand: Ali, Hassan, and Hossein. Her shadow extends over the entire body of secular Islam] (Djebar 1991: 60)

Fatima will be denied both her spiritual and material inheritance. Djebar points out that had Fatima been a son, the fate of Islam would have been different, "quelle que fût l'épouse mandée par le mourant, elle n'aurait pas manqué d'amener 'le' fils, sinon son fils." [no matter which wife would have been commanded by the dying man, she would not have failed to bring 'the' son, if not her son] (Djebar 1991: 59) Fatima is a rupture in the patrlineal line as daughter and in the continuity of the Islamic heritage as a force of protest.

> Oui, Mohammed est *abtar;*[8] du coup, Fatima assure, par ses fils, le désir trop humain de son père. Malgré sa mort prématurée, elle pressentira que, des décennies après, se préparait le sacrifice terrible que la famille du Prophète aurait à subir . . . Tentative de la fille aimée croyant parer à la déshérence et annonçant au contraire la dissension fatale! (Djebar 1991: 60)
> [Yes, Mohammed is without sons; suddenly, Fatima, through her sons, fulfills the all too human desire of her father. Despite her untimely death, she will have the presentiment that the oncoming decades will prepare the terrible sacrifice that the family of the Prophet would have to undergo . . . the attempt of a beloved girl believing herself to be warding off the disinheritance but announcing to the contrary the fatal dissension.]

The daughter is relegated to a shadowy retreat even as he is dying. At the death of the Prophet, Djebar relates, there is no description of the daughter but only of the wives: "le Prophète meurt dans les bras de Aïcha, ses autres épouses se lamentent les premières . . . Rien, ce jour-là, de rapporté explicitement sur Fatima." [The Prophet dies in the arms of Aïcha, his other wives will lament first . . . Nothing on that day, is explicitly brought back on Fatima.] (Djebar 1991: 58) Djebar suggests that Fatima's position as daughter also puts her at a disadvantage in relation to the co-wives:

> les co-épouses prennent le pas, au seuil de la mort . . . sur les filles. Mohammed, sur le point d'exprimer son dernier désir de guide des hommes, a besoin de ses femmes comme messagères . . . Les épouses soignent les hommes, les 'portent'; les filles, elles à la limite, font plus: comme Fatima, donner des garçons à leur père. (Djebar 1991: 60)
> [the co-wives will take the lead, at the threshold of death . . . over the daughters. Mohammed, about to express his last desire as guide of men, needs his wives like messengers . . . the wives look after the men, 'carry them'; the daughters, at the limit, do more; like Fatima, they give sons to their father.]

Djebar, nonetheless, valorizes the daughter over the wife as the one who allows for (an alternate) heritage. Fatima's position as daughter, however, reveals how filial relations are set in a strict hierarchy along gender lines of descent, despite the simultaneous negotiations of filiations along belief rather than blood that Muhammad's revolution was able to achieve.

Fatima is important for Djebar because she is the voice of refusal to a tradition of Islam consolidating itself to power predicated on the disinheritance of others and on the oblivion of dissident voices. She shores that initial protest against the dispossession of women that began before the death of the Prophet and continued six months afterwards until her own death, a refusal that still resounds today for many women. (Djebar 1991: 67)

Her initial refusal will be mediated by her father, the first to object in Medina on behalf of his daughter. It is a public refusal to grant Ali the permission to marry the daughter of Abou Jahl, "l'ennemi de Dieu" [the enemy of God]:[9] "Ma fille est une partie de moi-même! Ce qui lui fait mal me fait mal! Ce qui la bouleverse me bouleverse!" [My daughter is a part of me. What hurts her hurts me! What upsets her upsets me!] (Djebar 1991: 68) Djebar comments that Muhammad's impassioned refusal on behalf of his daughter has fallen on deaf ears: "Quatorze siècles se sont depuis écoulés: il semble qu'aucun père depuis, du moins dans la communauté de l'Islam, plus aucun père ne . . . développa une défense aussi ardente pour la quiétude de sa fille!"[10] [Fourteen centuries have since passed: it seems that no father has since, at least in the community of Islam, no father has . . . developed such an ardent defense for the serenity of his daughter!] (Djebar 1991: 68-69) While Muhammad acknowledges the Qur'anic command that a male be permitted to marry four times if he can be fair and can provide—a qualification that has long been read to be an admonition in itself against polygamy—in this particular case he refuses, worried, as he claims, that he would shake his daughter's faith, on the grounds that "la fille de l'Envoyé de Dieu ne se rencontrera pas dans un même lieu avec la fille de l'ennemi de Dieu, cela, non, jamais! . . . Jamais!" [The daughter of the Messenger will not meet in the same place with the daughter of the enemy of God, this, no, never! . . . never!] (Djebar 1991: 74) Djebar recognizes the father addressing the Messenger "pour oser dire tout haut son désarroi de simple mortel: 'Je crains que Fatima ne se sent troublée dans sa foi!'" [for daring to voice his derision of a simple mortal: I fear that Fatima will be troubled in her faith!] (Djebar 1991: 75)

Her disinheritance seems inevitable after her father's death, since he is the one to mediate between his daughter and the community. For Fatima the wife turns to her father with her first protest. And the father intervenes. Her refusal will find no viable force against a hegemonic face of Islam after his death. Clarisse Zimra argues that the force of the protest that only carries force with the father's words can only be momentary:

> The paradox is that, for the wife's private choice to be respected, she must accept the daughter's public voice. Her agency must be mediated by the Father's Word, in defiance of his own stated practice of polygamy, a conundrum he tries to circumvent by questioning his daughter's faith. Such is the contradiction that *Loin de Médine* explores but cannot untangle and upon which, it concludes, all successive attempts at individual freedom will founder. It is to this ambivalent moment concretizing an agency that Djebar wishes us to attend: original yet not originary, for the father's approval that should shore it up eventually yields to the political needs of the Prophet. (Zimra 1996: 831)

Djebar's narrative revolves around this arrested moment, this "contradiction" or double bind, where the father's intervention is necessary for the daughter's emancipation. She does not resolve this aporia, as if to suggest the outcome, the legacy of disempowerment could have been and could be otherwise. The importance of her father's stance is in making public their shared refusal. In this he places more importance in the filial relationship of father-daughter than in the husband-wife relationship, proclaiming his daughter as part of himself. He, furthermore, grants his daughter, and by extension women in general, more power in a social order that privileges the husband. (Zimra 1996: 831) The role of the father as protector is limited, however, since he also has to safeguard her from his own practices.

> The father's original position, taken out of love for his human child, is immediately fraught with the equivocation of the leader who understands that all private decisions will have public, hence future political consequences that may fracture a fragile consensus still in the making. (Zimra 1996: 832)

The refusal of Fatima two or three years later will be along different lines. She will protest the temporal succession of the caliphate on behalf of her family and her self. (Djebar 1991: 75) The male family members of Muhammad will initially refuse to pledge their allegiance to the new caliph. Ali will refuse as long as Fatima is alive. Their refusal meets with coercion and threats. Already dissension over the temporal succession is taking place without the consultation of Muhammad's family and over the material disinheritance of Fatima. Fatima is nonetheless seen as a continuous part of her father by the new political leadership. (Djebar 1991: 77) She is said to be the one who most resembled the Prophet through her language, "elle devient, par son lyrisme qui se déverse lentement, la poétesse de leurs remords . . . ." [she becomes, through her lyricism that slowly emerges, the poetess of their remorse] (Djebar 1991: 80) She is a force of unease at the tentative and early stage of political Islam due to her status, being the Prophet's daughter, and due to her relentless protest. "Fatima représente le doute, leur doute. Elle vivante, elle seule héritière par le sang et par la personnalité de l'homme Mohammed, elle incarne l'interrogation constamment ouverte sur le bien-fondé de cette succession!" [Fatima represents doubt, their doubt. Alive, she is, through blood and personality, the only one to inherit of the man Mohammed. She embodies the constantly open questioning of this succession] (Djebar 1991: 85) Abou Bakr, the new Caliph, manifests this in his unwillingness to pressure Ali to pledge allegiance to him as long as Fatima is besides him. (Djebar 1991: 78)

In her vehement attack, she, who is his sole inheritor, appeals to her double filiality, being his daughter and married to his cousin. (Djebar 1991: 80) Fatima implicates the new caliphate in doing away with the Islamic revolution: "*O vous qu'on appelait modjahiddines, c'est la loi de la djahilia que vous prétendez m'appliquer!*"[11] [O you who are called *Mujāhiddīn*, it is the law of pre-Islam that you pretend to apply to me!] (Djebar 1991: 81, emphasis in the original) It is an attack that Fatima launches not against the choice of Abu Bakr, the dear friend of her father, but against the caliph "celui qu'on a désigné calife hors la famille du Prophète . . . ." [the one who has been designated successor from outside the Prophet's family.] (Djebar 1991: 85) Fatima insists on safeguarding a role for herself in the spiritual and political consolidation of Islam, a role guaranteed by the revolutionary impetus of Mohammad's vision.

The other refusal that Fatima will launch is on behalf of herself this time. (Djebar 1991: 78) Fatima in effect is refused her share of inheritance due to Abou Bakr's narrow interpretation of Muhammad's ambiguous words: "Nous, les prophètes, aurait dit Mohammed un jour, on n'hérite pas de nous! Ce qui nous est donné nous est donné en don!" [We, the Prophets, Mohammed would have said one day, one does not inherit from us! What is given to us is given as a gift!] (Djebar 1991: 79) This interpretation proves decisive not only to the fate of Fatima but also to the entire Islamic community. Abu Bakr thinks that the family of the Prophet can neither inherit materially nor claim power of temporal succession. Fatima, following her father's move to grant women the right of inheritance, understands her father's words to mean that prophecy itself cannot be inherited. (Djebar 1991: 79) The symbolic disinheritance of Fatima, as Djebar foregrounds it, will initiate a whole tradition of dispossession, reverting Islam's progressive steps to pre-Islamic times in regards to women. Fatima's resistance marks the revolution of Islam and its ensuing struggle to be one around the question of inheritance.

> Fatima . . . pourrait aller plus loin encore, elle pourrait dire: "La révolution de l'Islam, pour les filles, pour les femmes, a été d'abord de les faire héritier, de leur donner la part qui leur revient de leur père! Cela a été instauré pour la première fois dans l'histoire des Arabes par l'intermédiaire de Mohammed! Or, Mohammed est-il à peine mort, que vous osez déshériter d'abord sa propre fille, la seule fille vivante du Prophète lui-même!" Fatima, la dépouillée de ses droits, la première en tête de toute une interminable procession de filles dont la déshérence de fait, souvent appliquée par les frères, les oncles, les fils eux-mêmes, tentera de s'instaurer pour endiguer peu à peu l'insupportable révolution féministe de l'Islam en ce viie siècle chrétien! (Djebar 1991: 79)
> [Fatima . . . could have gone further, she could have said: "The revolution of Islam, for the daughters, for the women, was first of all in granting them inheritance, in giving them a share of what comes from their father! This has been instituted for the first time in the history of the Arabs, through the intermediary of Mohammed. But hardly had Mohammed died that you dare to disinherit his own daughter, the only living daughter of the Prophet himself!" Fatima, stripped of her rights, the first at the head of an interminable procession of girls whose real disinheritance, often by brothers, uncles, and even sons, will be blocked to dam up little by little the unbearable feminist revolution of Islam in the seventh Christian century!]

Fatima's rebelliousness creates a rupture in a continuous line of patriarchal authority, and in the power structure of the *Ummah,* by instilling doubt through her complete refusal to accept the Caliph's power and her own disinheritance. She who rivals her father with her gift of speech "symbolizes the violent conflict among Muslims which will culminate in the schism between Sunnis and Shiites" and "her status as a non-son casts doubt, for many Muslims, on her legitimacy as an heir." (Woodhull 1993: 41) Fatima becomes one in a series of "women in movement," politically excluded and economically dispossessed, but subject of her own voice.[12]

Even after the death of Fatima, the feminine opposition continues, as Djebar relates. It continues as an inherited legacy through her daughters Oum Keltoum and Zeineb: "l'une et l'autre plus tard haranguent les foules, pour défier la lâcheté . . . quand Ali sera tué, quand Hossein sera martyrisé . . . Opposition que reprendront, presque à chaque génération et plus d'un siècle encore, d'autres filles des filles et des fils de Fatima." [Later, one and the other will harangue the crowd to defy their cowardice . . . When Ali is killed, when Hussein is martyred. Opposition which they will take up again, almost with each generation and more than one century still, other daughters of daughters and sons of Fatima.] (Djebar 1991: 299) As evident from Fatima's legacy, women who become "women of the verb," and hence subjects of their own voices, pay a terrible price for their attempt at change.

In the collective memories of Muslims, however, the importance of Fatima is relegated to the role of the mother while Aïcha is eternally deemed the "child bride." While both are probably the most revered women in Islam—Fatima as the daughter of the Prophet and Aïcha as the "mother of believers"—Djebar in this text points out that their complex identities as women are easily parted with in the early chronicles as well as in the contemporary practices of Islam. Djebar asks: "Les sources se taisent-elles vraiment toutes? Pourquoi Fatima n'apparaît-elle chez les chroniqueurs qu'une fois mère de Hassan et Hossein? Comme si l'amour filial, assumé à ce degré d'intensité, rencontrait, tout comme la passion, un mouvement spontané de retrait . . . de silence!" [Are all the sources really silent? Why does Fatima appear only once in the chroniclers' account as mother of Hassan and Hussein? It is as if filial love, assumed at this degree of intensity, encounters, like a passion, a spontaneous movement of silence and retreat!] (Djebar 1991: 62)

The accounts of Fatima and Aïcha frame the text as Djebar moves from Fatima to Aïcha: from the voice of public protest, 'parole de la contestation,' to the voice of transmission, 'parole de la transmission.' She sets the stage of political Islam in Medina, one where male dominance is solidified but overshadowed by female doubt: "Tandis que Omar ibn el Khattab . . . annonce à tous qu'il gouvernera les Arabes 'comme le guide du chameau dans le désert,' deux pôles de la présence féminine se maintiennent: Fatima morte dont la voix hante encore les rues de Médine, à l'opposé, Aïcha . . . évoque l'Absent devant un parterre enfantin pour l'instant." [While Omar ibn al-Khattab announces to all that he will govern the Arabs "like a camel guide in the desert," two poles of female presence are maintained: the dead Fatima whose voice still haunts the streets of Medina. Opposite her is Aïcha who evokes the Absent one before an audience of children for the moment.] (Djebar 1991: 299) They become the two important constellations of "women of the verb": "celle de la fille mystique sur un versant nocturne, celle de l'épouse sur le point de devenir femme de pouvoir et de rayonnement, sur le versant d'aube." [that of the mystical girl on a night slope, that of the wife about to become woman of power and radiance, on the slope of dawn] (Djebar 1991: 299)

Aïcha's work of transmission is political, forming an alternate history of Islam and safeguarding her own voice: "elle voit son destin se dessiner: . . . nourrir la mémoire des Croyantes, entreprendre cette longue patience, cet inlassable travail . . . Préserver, pour toutes les filles d'Ismaïl, parole vive. Vivre ainsi ancrée en soi-même, tous les jours de sa vie à venir, immobile certes, mais gonflée d'une parole à jaillir." [she sees her destiny taking shape . . . to nourish the memory of the believers, to undertake this long, patient, tireless work . . . to preserve, for all the daughters of Ishmael this living word. To live anchored in herself, all the days to come of her life, immobile certainly, but filled with a word about to spring forth.] (Djebar 1991: 294) Aïcha who is not even twenty when the Messenger dies, begins her political education in the presence of her father, the first Caliph.

Aïcha who safeguards memory works to contest the stories told and rendered formulaic by the men around the Prophet, offering her own vision of the past. Djebar sees her task to be somewhat analogous. Aïcha will eventually serve as a major source for the *Ḥadīth* and a crucial link in the chain of transmission. But as she lives, she is aware of the confining of her narratives to an audience of children by the companions of the Prophet, "eux, les bavards, les déjà si sûrs de leurs anecdotes . . . 'les oublieux aussi,' qui vont substituer leurs souvenirs bornés, n'ayant rien saisi des nuances" of the Messenger's words. [they the talkers, already so sure of their anecdotes . . . the forgetful also, who will substitute their limited memories, not having seized any of the nuances.] (Djebar 1991: 300)

Djebar locates Aïcha at the margins yet within the confines of the center. She seems implicated in a power structure that Fatima has refused altogether: "Si un jour, à force de nourrir la mémoire, Aïcha cette fois d'âge mûr . . . se levait? . . . Si Aïcha, un jour, décidait de quitter Médine? . . . loin de Médine, retrouver alors le vent, le vertige, l'incorruptible jeunesse de la révolte!" [What if one day, by force of nourishing memory, Aïcha this time of a ripe age . . . rises? . . .What if Aïcha one day decided to leave Medina, . . . far from Medina, to then find the wind, the vertigo, the incorruptible youth of the revolt!] (Djebar 1991: 301) The implication is that Aïcha's latter accounts will be incorporated in the chronicles because they are already recuperable by the existing power structure. Djebar leaves the account of Aïcha with open questions, but already there are insinuations in the text that Aïcha will participate or at the very least seek to participate in this power structure, that her word "serves organized religion, remaining anchored as it does in Medina." (Woodhull 1993: 29)

As she foregrounds her discourse of transmission, Djebar entertains the possibility of Aïcha leaving the Medina and in a sense joining Fatima, the one who rejected all forms of instituting traditions. Such a desire already announces its impossibility within the bounds of Medina, though it would result in "an Arab-Muslim woman who both speaks out and who has recourse to direct action." (Geesey 1996: 49) Instead, Aïcha, one of many wives, will face not the co-wives, as Djebar indicates, but Fatima. "Silence, six mois durant, entre les deux femmes car le pouvoir soudain oscille entre femme et fille. Qui est vraiment l'héritière? Elle, Aïcha, se voulant peu à peu porte-parole des huit autres mères des Croyants?" [Continued silence between the two women for six months due to the sudden oscillation of power between wife and daughter. Who is really the one to inherit? She, Aïcha, is seeking to be little by little spokeswoman of the eight other mothers of Believers?] (Djebar 1991: 289) Djebar's text ends before the struggle between Aïcha and Ali unravels, one in which Aïcha will fail. Both women in fact will fail in their polar oppositionary stances, but this will be borne by history rather than by the narrative which insists on the irreconcilable aporetic tension of impasse and possibility.

Aïcha raises doubt for the Islamic community as well but of another sort. Having lingered behind after one of the battles looking for a necklace she lost, she was brought back by a handsome, young man who found her after everyone has left. While the Qur'an itself, which demanded that four witnesses be found to claim adultery, dissipated such doubt, a stance in favor of women, the ramifications still resound today. The ambivalence regarding women's sexuality and "virtue" solidified the practices of veiling and confinement that may already have predated Islam. For, while Islam did much to improve the status of women, the conception of woman itself remained problematic.[13]

Fadwa Malti-Douglas points to the link established between woman's voice and sexuality: "With the raising of Joseph's specter, the crucial link is effected between woman's verbal meddling and the crime of sexual aggressiveness, so essential to the relationship of the Islamic Joseph with women . . . All of woman's incorrect or aggressive behavior becomes subsumed into the Joseph story and unbound sexuality." (Malti-Douglas 1991: 52) Djebar's creative reading of the Islamic story places hope on women and their ability to deliver Joseph and to deliver Algeria. For in this rendition, Joseph before being summoned by the ruler demands vindication of innocence from the women. (Djebar 2000)

While Djebar recognizes that the power of these early women of Islam is, to a large extent, "genealogical," implicit is a suggestion of equality between men and women borne out by her treatment of Fatima, one that begins to disintegrate with the struggle of Aïcha's will to power. (Zimra 1993: 127) Women's rebelliousness, however, remains intact and takes many forms, from seeking inclusion in a social order that excludes them (Fatima's struggle to receive inheritance from her father) to their desire to usurp power and lead differently (Aïcha). (Djebar 1991: 43)

Hagar: Legacy of Struggle and Survival

If as Sonia Lee argues, Djebar's project is to foreground the discourses of transmission as the real subject of her novel, then there would be no need to trace these "women in movement" back to Hagar.[14] Undeniably that is a significant part of what Djebar attempts in her narrative. However, Djebar in the epilogue traces this female heritage not only back to the early women of Islam but to the biblical figure of Hagar.[15] Djebar significantly subtitles her work "*filles d'Ismaïl,*" [daughters of Ishmael] establishing the perspective of narrative from the viewpoint of women as well as locating the inheritance of women as subject to paternal law and as subject to disinheritance.

Djebar's division of this second section of the epilogue into two parts—"voix d'hier" [voice of yesterday] and "voix d'aujourd'hui" [voice of today]—links the past to the present to illustrate how the past still impacts the present. The story is also related through voices, since again the emphasis is on women being subject of their own discourses; for the narrator recounts from a woman's perspective, "elle dit" [she says]. The voice of the past relates poetically the story of Hagar as if to announce a beginning, one of confronting one's fate and actively resisting: "*Agar l'expulsée, parce que la première accouchée. /Agar dans le désert avant que ne jaillisse la source, que ne pousse le premier palmier, Agar bien avant que la Kaaba ne soit construite par 'l'Ami de Dieu' revenu sur les lieux où a grandi son fils.*" [Hagar the expelled, because she is the first/Hagar in the desert before the source surges, before the first palm tree pushes forth, Hagar well before the Kaaba is built by "The Friend of God" who returns to the place where his son has been raised.] (Djebar 1991: 302) But this emphasis on women's subject position has its limitations since Hagar resists in order to physically survive. For her to invoke Hagar as a figure of resistance is to point to a painful history of women's submission.

She relates the story of Abraham's desertion of Ishmael and Hagar as it is incorporated in Islam. "*Ainsi rapporte Gabriel à Mohammed—qui sur ce point, modifie la Genèse—Abraham accompagna Agar et l'enfant, au moment de l'abandon, jusqu'au site de La Mecque, entre les deux collines de Safa et Merwa. /Puis Abraham partit. /Les voici seuls, immanquablement; la mère et l'enfant. / . . . /Ismaïl a soif; Ismaïl va mourir.*" [Thus recounts Gabriel to Mohammed—who at this point modifies Genesis—Abraham accompanied Hagar and the child until the moment of abandonment, at the site of Mecca, between the two hills of Safa and Merwa, then Abraham left. There they are inevitably, mother and child/Ishmael is thirsty/Ishmael is going to die.] (Djebar 1991: 302) In a delirium, Hagar searches for water, desperately traversing the two hills, going back and forth in a rhythmic movement that survives to this day by reenactments of the pilgrims to the Ka'abah. "*Elle va, elle vient, dans les transes et le blanc de l'effroi. / Ismaïl a soif; Ismaïl va mourir.*" [She goes, she comes, in transes and white fright/Ishmael is thirsty; Ishmael is going to die.] (Djebar 1991: 302) It is a re-enactment not only in the physical gestures of hurling back and forth between the two hills of Safa and Merwa, but an enactment of the expulsion of Hagar, the repetition of Ishmael's repudiation of his first wife commanded by his father Abraham who already repudiated his first Hagar on the injunction of the second wife Sarah. And all other Islamic repudiation of women follows. And this hurling back and forth, this frenzied dance is one of rhythmic displacement, the dance of a divided self, engendered from contradictions and paradoxical space. It is Hagar's dance of survival and the displacement of voice through the body. As Djebar relates, it is a reenactment that takes place for each Moslem once in a life time or once every year, "*l'unique théâtre/ pour eux et par eux/s'ordonne/la seule fiction islamique.*" [the unique theater/for them and by them/is ordered/the only Islamic fiction.] (Djebar 1991: 305) It is precisely the frantic dance of Hagar that is the added story by Islam. It is this dance that stages the fiction and this fiction that allows a voice to emerge through the body. "*L'enfant, dans un désarroi . . . gratte de ses doigts le sable, sous l'oeil du soleil . . ./Quand enfin l'eau jaillit/enfin une source/enfin une musique/de commencement. /Agar, danseuse de la folie désertée, Agar entend/Agar s'arrête.*" [The child in distress scrapes the sand with his fingers/under the eye of the sun . . ./When finally water surges forth/finally a source/finally music/of commencement/Hagar, dancer of abandoned folly, Hagar hears/Hagar stops.] (Djebar 1991: 303) This is not only the supposed beginning of the sacred spring of *ZamZam* that runs in Mecca to this day but is also the commencement of possibility.

In the voice of today, Djebar names Hagar as legacy of disinheritance for contemporary women of the Arabian desert: "'*Filles d'Agar', dit-elle/ dit toute femme dans le désert d'Arabie/qu'elle soit rebelle, qu'elle soit soumise à Dieu, / 'En quoi suis-je, en quoi sommes-nous toutes d'abord filles de l'expulsée . . . d'abord descendantes de celle . . . avant de nous savoir filles d'Ismaïl.*'" ["Daughters of Hagar," she says/says every woman in the desert of Arabia whether she is rebel or submitted to God/In what am I, in what are we first of all daughters of the expelled: first her descendents before knowing ourselves daughters of Ishmael.] (Djebar 1991: 303) Djebar wants to seek the maternal source for the legacy of Ishmael who ultimately repeats the repudiation of his father Abraham. When Abraham returns, it is said, after twenty years, he orders his son, in turn, to repudiate his first wife and to keep his second. Djebar juxtaposes this history/repetition of repudiation with the injunction of the Qur'an that charts the history of the Arabs with Ishmael in order to link together the authority of the sons of Ishmael with their submission of women: "*Laissons les fils d'Ismaïl ('ils ont autorité sur vous!' rappelle le Coran).*" [Let the sons of Ishmael be ("They have authority over you!" the Qur'an reminds] (Djebar 1991: 304) Again a re-writing of Genesis but one that stays faithful to the submission of women (and men) to the paternal law.

The predicament of Hagar and her daughters as one of displacement and dispossession, embodying both emigration and abandonment, is already figured in her name. Djebar notes that the Arabic name 'Hājar' shares the same root as 'hégire' which suggest migration as well as "hājirah," which denotes insolence. (Djebar 1991: 304) Hagar also carries in her name and in her body the spirit of struggle if not revolt.

Djebar imbricates this cultural legacy with a menacing present in an indictment against contemporary Arabia and Algeria. "*Abraham, sur ses pas, revenu.*" [Abraham has retraced his steps] (Djebar 1991: 305) The violent legacy of Abraham, authorized by a blind paternal faith turned law, is in the continual displacement and dispossession of Hagar.[16] Danielle Shepherd's comment on *L'amour, la fantasia* is appropriate as well for Hagar: "La femme se voit ainsi sans cesse appelée à vaincre les lois de la nécessité et à progresser malgré le destin." [Woman sees herself called upon ceaselessly to vanquish the laws of necessity and to advance in spite of destiny.] (Shepherd 1996: 188) The struggle of Hagar embodied in her frenzied dance is to survive and the need for survival still remains.

To survive is, potentially, to sustain and guard a collective memory in a continuous struggle. And it is women for Djebar who safeguard a cultural heritage. Specifically, it is the female ancestors who, despite their confinement, were successful in their work of transmission. "Les femmes, et surtout les aïeules, protégées par la claustration, ont donc servi à conserver intact l'héritage du passé, transmis aux générations qu'elles contribuent à former et qui, malgré leur évolution, maintiennent avec elles des liens de solidarité que la modernité n'atteint pas." [Women, especially the ancestral ones, protected by cloistering, have thus served to conserve the heritage of the past intact, transmitted to the generations that they have contributed to forming, and who, despite their evolution, maintain with them relations of solidarity that modernity has not touched.] (Clerc 1997: 95) Thus it is to women that Djebar turns in her book, *Loin de Médine,* placing them at the center of a cultural heritage, in order to revive a past against all fundamentalist constructions. She ends *Loin de Médine* with a "hymn" to the power of life despite the silencing and effacement of women, and despite the blind paternal legacy to sacrifice one's own future and kin.

Heritage, Writing, Home

As in her other works, the notion of heritage that emerges is one that no longer posits a dividing line between a dead past and a living present, a past that is given forth to the present. Rather cultural heritage coexists with the present, "héritage de sédimentation transhistorique." [heritage of transhistoric sedimentation] (Djebar cited by Clerc 1997: 64) For Djebar, heritage is specifically a body of writing where the two are linked in a complex manner. She conceives of writing as that which is disinherited, as "*matière bâtarde,*" [bastardly material] placing the patrilineal authority which is always divided against itself in question. (Djebar, 1993: 16)

Access to writing in turn becomes denied to women precisely because of the inheritance it would grant them. "L'expulsion coranique," one critic points out, "coïncidera avec le droit conféré aux femmes d'avoir une part d'héritage et de gérer leur biens matériels: c'est alors qu'on les fera s'absenter' de l'écriture pour les empêcher de faire respecter ces droits nouveaux et d'être cause de 'fitna' (querelle) parmi les mâles qui palabrent." [The Qur'anic expulsion will coincide with the right conferred upon women to have a share of inheritance and to manage their property: it is for this reason that they have been absented from writing, to prevent them from respecting these new laws and from becoming a cause of conflict among men who chatter.] (Clerc 1997: 66) Writing made sacred has served as another form of exclusion and disinheritance for women. In the name of Islamic law, women are secluded from writing, thus denying them any voice or expression of self. Djebar in an interview elaborates: "*On se sert de l'écriture sacralisée pour immobiliser le corps de la femme, pour, dans la pratique des générations mortes, lui enlever son héritage de fille ou de veuve, que l'écrit pourtant garantit.*" [one has used the sacred writing to immobilize the woman's body, to take away the inheritance of the daughter or widow, in the practice of the dead generations, an inheritance that this writing nonetheless guarantees.] (Djebar 1993: 8) Such exclusionary efforts are not always successful, for women do access writing even if it is through their bodies to write their silence.

While writing may be for Djebar a way of guarding against silence, it also situates things anew and grants them new meaning. In Djebar's works, women's writing becomes a betrayal of the father. For writing allows a certain possibility of experiencing power for women, beyond their infantilizing existence. "Provocation à la virilité triomphante des hommes, dont le pouvoir créateur de la famille, et organisateur de la société, se trouve ainsi bafoué par une capacité d'exister en dehors d'eux." [Provocation at the triumphant virility of men, the creative power for family and for social organization, which is undermined by the capacity to exist apart from them.] (Clerc 1997: 66) Djebar establishes writing as transgression not only in this work but in her other works as well. Not only does writing allow women freedom and the opportunity to be included in a public sphere where they can challenge male discourses and representations, but women also "[acquire] the power to operate the sign instead of being its object." (Gafaiti 1996: 813) Djebar calls attention to a heritage of women writing that spells out transgression and sacrifice: "Zoraidé, 'la première Algérienne qui écrit,' ressent dans sa chair le prix à payer de 'misère et d'incertitudes' pour son audace d'avoir pris la plume contre toutes les interdictions [du père]." [Zoraidé, the first Algerian to have taken the pen against all prohibitions (of the father) feels in her flesh the price to pay in misery and uncertainty for this audacity] (Clerc 1997: 122)

In her focus on the absenting of women, Djebar continues from her other work where she focused on the absenting of women from the history of Algeria in *L'amour, la fantasia,* from its public life in *Ombre sultane*, and here from the Islamic legacy. She tries to redress these absences paradoxically in writing in French. (Crosta 1996: 54) In *Le Blanc de l'Algérie* she connects white to silence, to absence, and to the space of non-writing. Thus, her project of "resurrection" is inextricably tied with writing. "Djebar explique la présence d'une écriture *sur* les femmes mais aussi les effets d'une non-matérialisation d'une écriture *des* femmes." [Djebar explains the presence of writing on women but also the effects of a non-materialization of a writing of women.] (Crosta 1996: 55) Henceforth, writing, like memory, in Djebar's work is inevitably gendered.

As Djebar has shown in *L'amour, la fantasia,* and as she demonstrates here, women have to revert to writing to empower themselves, especially when writing is a source of power in society. As Hafid Gafaiti argues, working against what he calls a "dominant critical discourse, both in Europe and the U.S., on orality in [Djebar's] production,"[17] Djebar not only points to Algerian oral culture to assert the role of women but equally emphasizes the North African written tradition. Djebar insists that the relegation of women to oral culture is not historically accurate: "Car il s'agit bien d'un 'retour' à la langue écrite . . . la culture arabe repose sur l'enseignement (et donc l'écriture lue et recopiée) du Livre; alors qu'au Maghreb, il y a une des plus anciennes cultures écrites, avec les femmes comme détentrices privilégiées de l'écriture, l'alphabet tamazigh des Touaregs.'" [It is a question of a "return" to a written language . . . Arabic culture rests on the teachings (and thus the writing read and recopied) of the Book; whereas in the Maghreb, there is one of the oldest written cultures, with the women as privileged holders of the writing, the alphabet Tamazigh of Touareg.] (Djebar cited by Clerc 1997: 65)

Djebar's project that seeks to foreground the role of women as "women of the verb" is embedded in a historical project. In all the work of Djebar, the process of reclaiming identity is through the work of history. As she indicates in one of her interview, "history figures as a quest for identity. It concerns not only the identity of women, but also that of the country as a whole." (Cited in Gafaiti 1996: 814) Elsewhere, Djebar reiterates that it is only through history that one can claim an identity. (Clerc 1997: 58) The writing of history remains, however, foremost writing. Writing through history allows for nothing less than the possibility of home for Djebar.

The project of Djebar is to create a language that allows her to express what history has repressed. Expression comes to inhabit writing as a result of its public censorship. And woman as the "unhoused" is woman as danger. (Green 1996: 117)

Political Poetics

As a result of her earliest works, Djebar has long been criticized for not being "political" enough. In this work, Djebar shows that the "cultural always enfolds the political." (Zimra, 1993: 119) She further demonstrates that the relation between the poetic and the political, while necessarily complex, remains possible. As Woodhull relates,

> We encounter the familiar association of femininity and poetic language with an intractable alterity that necessarily challenges power and eludes formulation in a politics. But because female rebelliousness takes a variety of interrelated forms in *Loin de Médine*—'uncontrollable freedom,' but also action and speech directed toward economic justice and political empowerment for women—its figuration in fact challenges the relegation of poetic practice to a sacred space divorced from politics. In a new and provocative way, Djebar's novel restructures relations between poetics and politics, calling into question French critical norms while simultaneously revaluing Islamic tradition. (Woodhull 1993: 43)

In the interview with Zimra, Djebar proclaims *Loin de Médine* to be "a response" to contemporary Algeria and "an answer back" to early Islam.[18] Political engagement is henceforth inextricable from moral ones. This inextricability ironically repeats the gesture of the Islamic fundamentalists but to different ends.

> For several years I had been an uncomfortable witness of the fundamentalist rise in public life . . . I told myself that the only kind of response of which I was capable, *as a writer*, was to go back to the *written* sources of our history. I wanted to study, in great detail this specific period that the fundamentalists were in the process of claiming for themselves, deforming it in process from the standpoint of facts as well as the standpoint of intent. *Médine* became this interruption in my own work, a piece written at one sitting, so to speak, in eagerness to enter this particular debate. (Zimra 1993: 122-123)

Djebar recuperates the fundamentalist move by appealing to Islam at its foundational moments only to subvert that very gesture. In locating her narrative at the originary moments of political Islam, with the dissension over material, spiritual, and political inheritance that ensues right after Muhammad's death, Djebar is also making a *fundamentalist* gesture. But she makes it to suggest that these originary moments were always open to contestation.

The Work of Vigil: Esma as the Figure of Healing

The work of the writer becomes an act of vigilance. More generally in her work, this act involves redressing the Algerian government's policy of "Arabization" and the fundamentalists' global Islamization by recalling "Algeria's denied or silenced multicultural, multiethnic, multiglossic past." (Zimra 1996: 828) This vigilance is not only critical; it also involves healing. Djebar attempts to address the wounds inflicted by gratuitous death and historical inequities. It is to come to terms with the unsettling remnants of colonization that continued with the liberation sons. (Clerc 1997: 169) Healing for her then is an act of writing that seeks home, "un dedans de la parole," [a within of the word] "seule patrie féconde désormais." [the only fertile homeland henceforth] (Djebar 1995: 275-76)

This strategically follows the spirit of the Qur'an, where a body of writing carries a promise of healing. It is not surprising, therefore, that Esma, "the healer," (Djebar 1991: 210) becomes a privileged figure in Djebar's *Loin de Médine*. She is not only a figure that stands "far from Medina" being doubly immigrant to the Medina and doubly apart, as wife of Abou Bakr, step-mother of Aïcha, and friend of Fatima, she will also be the possible meeting point as well as separation point between Aïcha and Fatima. She resides on a yet invisible border "frontière qui . . . s'approfondira, amènera progressivement dissension, puis violence à Médine" [a border which deepens, leads progressively to dissension, and to violence in Medina]. (Djebar 1991: 231-32) Esma supplants the traditionally problematic female figures of Fatima and Aïcha as exemplary, as "la seule, à nouveau, à subsumer les contradictions . . . qui vont apparaître; la seule à les dépasser." [the only one, again, to subsume the contradictions that will appear, the only one to surpass them] (Djebar 1991: 219). Djebar points to the possibility of overcoming the impasse in the symbolic figure of Isma; however, she, remains a vision for healing rather than for transformation, a transformation necessary in the struggles of Fatima and Aïcha, possible in the aporetic tension itself.

As Djebar returns to the origins of Islam to contend with religious fundamentalism and to reveal how visions of home are always already gendered, divided, how aporetic impasses could lead to alternative outcomes, Darwish returns in the following chapter to the early moments of Arabic poetry to chart a vision of home that defies its nationalist exclusions.

Notes

1. The Book of Genesis inaugurates this link of transgression and homelessness throughout the stories; any perceived transgression against the deity is punished by exile. Islamic revelation shares this Christian notion of wandering to some extent. If Satan was the first outcast, Adam and Eve were soon to follow, as Biblical and Islamic traditions would have it. Note the old inheritance from Genesis that specifically links Eve [and hence women] with moral failure in sharing Satan's spirit of wandering in the idyllic Garden of Eden. The original transgression of Eve is to eat from the tree of knowledge (of good and evil). (See Genesis 3) In Islam, Adam shares equal blame, however, when they together eat from the forbidden tree, a tree that is significantly not named. (See the Qur'an 2:34-37)

2. Islam, which sees itself as a continuation (and completion) of the monotheistic religions, believes that it shares that same revelation that stood before the "people of the Book." It inherited that writing again and declared itself the last of the religions if not the most definitive, for it is the only one that insisted that once the writing is written it cannot be changed, safeguarding any "tampering" with the revelation. The Qur'an not only acknowledges the other monotheistic revelations, it continuously dialogues with their writings.

3. *Ḥadīths* are sayings around the deeds and words of the Prophet and his companions. Transmitted orally, they were then written down after his death. According to Leila Ahmed, the *Ḥadīth* included a significant number of female accounts of their experience, revealing a society where women were active participants in the discussions taking place. Although the texts of the *Ḥadīth* were written by men, the sources of the accounts were oftentimes women. Aïcha alone apparently accounted for a sixth of the *Ḥadīth* corpus. (See Ahmed 50-51)

4. It is not until the reign of the third Caliph, 'Uthman, that the Qur'an acquires the authoritative and final version that we have come to know today. The *Ḥadīth* as well was authenticated three centuries after the Prophet. (Geesey 44.)

5. The subtitle of Djebar's *Loin de Médine* is *Filles d'Ismaïl.*

6. Even while Muhammad lives, the account of a Yemenite queen that launches the narrative of Djebar, inaugurates a series of effacements against women. Her rebellion is carried out against her new husband in the name of Islam and is eclipsed in the accounts as soon as it is carried out. (*LM* 27) Djebar names another rebel, Nawwar, who does not stop short of militarily challenging the Prophet himself for prophecy. The followers and supporters of Muhammad have to militarily stifle these voices, for the logic of monotheism prevails heavily and institutes that there can only be one last Prophet. She who awaits Gabriel fruitlessly is forced to flee to Damascus. More compelling yet is the adolescent Selma who is taken a prisoner of war when her father, chief of his tribe, launched a failed revolt against Muhammad. She is later converted to Islam. (*LM* 35) Selma, Djebar relates, does not hesitate to fight. (*LM* 37) In battle, she dies at the hand of Khalid bin al-Walid, Muhammad's most renowned warrior. Djebar adds to this list, Sadjah, of Christian origins, who aspires not only to religious primacy but to temporal leadership as well. While it is related that her force was her eloquence, her command of the rhymed verb, She is less strategic politically, however. She leads an army attempting to forge an alliance with Mosailima, remembered as the false prophet or "le prophète du Yemama." She is tricked into a false marriage with the handsome Mosailima, forgetting to ensure

her valor and the validity of the marriage through a dowry. She in her turn returns home and later, we are told, joins the Islamic faith in all obscurity. (*LM* 49)

7. Fatima's other sisters who die before their father are strong figures as well: one is remembered for saving her father's life and the other one stands apart for her impassioned love for her husband, a passion which delayed her conversion to Islam for a long time.

8. *Abtar* in the sense of having no direct male descendants.

9. Abou Jahl was a staunch opponent of Islam before his death, but his whole family converted to Islam afterwards.

10. Mohammed's paternal stance is singular in an Arabic cultural heritage given the father-daughter relations before and after his time. Most extreme perhaps is the fatherly spirit of the pre-Islamic poet-king, Imru'u al-Qais who, reacting to having no male sons, would kill his daughters whenever they were born. His wives began placing their newborn daughters with Bedouin tribes to protect them. He, in turn, upon discovering this, "would ride to one or another of the tribes, and, upon seeing a group of young girls playing, would offer his riding animal to whichever of them could match his verse with another verse on the same rhyme and meter. The girls would all become quiet, except for his daughter, who would take up the challenge. After she recited her verse, he would kill her." (Malti-Douglas 42).

11. Note that *Mujāhiddīn* are those who partake of the *jihād,* and *jāhiliyah* is the time period before Islam, literally denoting ignorance.

12. Women are "in movement" in the sense that they resist being fugitives to confinement.

13. Fedwa Malti-Douglas traces a "misogynist vision in Islam" back to the Qur'an, specifically to the story of Joseph. The seduction scene that misfires between Zulaikha, the Egyptian ruler's wife, and Joseph, argues Malti-Douglas, etches all women with an uncontrollable sexuality. What survives in the popular imagination is not the political challenges that early women have posed but rather a vision of their propensity for "excessive" sexuality. As it is related in the *Qur'an,* the ruler's response to his wife's lie is "Indeed your guile is great." The second-person pronoun is in the feminine plural in the Arabic, indicting all womankind. This Qur'anic phrase will reverberate throughout the Arabic-Islamic literary and cultural traditions. Had the story of Joseph ended there, one would agree with Malti-Douglas about the misogynist implications. But the scene of Zulaikha's banquet, where she invites the women and shows them Joseph in order to distance any unfavorable judgment upon her, points to the limits of that assertion. Having placed knives in front of the women, they all inadvertently cut themselves upon seeing Joseph. The banquet scene indicates that Zulaikha's response to Joseph is not an individual shortcoming but is duplicated in the women's actions, making a point about the excessive beauty of Joseph and the behavior of the wife becomes more understandable.

14. Lee argues that Djebar foregrounds language, the discourse of transmission, "as the real subject matter of Djebar's novel." (Lee 60) While Djebar is following the model of *Ḥadīth,* she is doing so to make some more controversial claims about the place of women in Islam and not only for the sake of performing this discursive paradigm.

15. The biblical account relates that Abraham had a son with his servant, Hagar, whom Sarah saw as a rival for the inheritance of Isaac. Upon her injunction, Abraham led Hagar and Ishmael to the desert to be abandoned and displaced. The Islamic rendition of the future father of the Arabs points to how he was left with his mother in desolate Mecca by Abraham. Dying of thirst and watching Hagar at a loss, Ishmael inadvertently discovers the spring of *ZamZam.*

16. Djebar's indictment of Abraham's legacy is more explicit in *Vaste est la Prison* where she writes: "*Les Égorgeurs d'intellectuels . . . se dressent, quelques-uns déterminés, transformant leurs propres enfants en moutons de l'Aïd, pour la grande fête du sacrifice d'Abraham, ne ressentant même pas une once de l'angoisse du prophète biblique.*" [Those who slit the throats of intellectuals . . . transform their own children into sacrificial lambs for 'Eid, the great feast of Abraham's sacrifice, and they feel not a hint of the anguish of the biblical prophet.] (Vaste est la Prison 237)

17. Gafaiti indicates, "in Arab-Muslim culture, the body, from birth, is textually given. Thus a newborn child, sipping from a bowl of water infused with scripture (traced with a vegetal ink), literally drinks sacred passages from the Koran." (Gafaiti 813)

18. The riots in Algeria began over the price of bread and culminated in a state of siege. A violent conflict has ensued since due to tensions already present from a corrupt military dictatorship run by the single party FLN. The *Front Islamique de Salut*, or Islamic Salvation Front "had become the only alternative . . . and won the national elections by a landslide . . . The government promptly declared the elections null and void. Outraged FIS sympathizers and women's groups, convinced that an FIS-controlled government would scuttle women's rights, took to the streets." (Zimra, When the Past 120)

Chapter Three

Poetic Survival: Post-Beirut Poetry of Mahmoud Darwish

"I learned all the words and how to take them apart so I can form one word, homeland."
—Mahmoud Darwish, *Dīwān*, volume two, 327.

"I am a poet of the homeland."
—Mahmoud Darwish, cited by Shakir al-Nabulsi, *Majnūn al-Turāb*, 220.

The poet, who addresses himself to the song and who recognizes himself as the inheritor of many civilizations that have passed through his land, defines his literary project as one of writing home.[1] The extent of incorporation or rejection of literary heritage in the poetic reconfiguration of home will be explored. Darwish defines his poetic project as one of *genesis*, linking poetry, history, and monotheistic myth as impetus for his vision. The turn to pre-Islamic and Andalusian moments of Arabic literary heritage is one that insists on less prevalent motifs in tradition, desire rather than loss, on a journey that is no longer nostalgic, and on a return no longer turned to the past but is an infinite movement toward the future.[2] Poetry itself is figured as home. Home is no longer connected to land or people but to the possibility of a poetic gathering of voices. And poetry henceforth is a staging of a plurality of voices. Darwish's poetry unfolds a desire to forge new collective forms and to establish poetry as a space of survival. In this search for form in order to safeguard a collective voice, the stage of the "epic song," from *Ḥiṣār li-Madā'iḥ al-Baḥr* (Siege for Praises of the Sea, 1984) until *Limādhā tarakta al-Ḥiṣāna Waḥīdan*? (Why Have You Left the Horse Alone?, 1995),[3] lyric emerges as one facet of discontinuity. In this chapter, we will mainly focus on *Ḥiṣār li-Madā'iḥ al-Baḥr*, found in volume two of his *Dīwān*.

Poetry as Heritage

While Darwish avoids definitions of poetry, he nonetheless states that he considers poetry to be a horizon and an inheritance. He sees his poetic experience in continuity with an Arabic poetic tradition.

> Poetry is that which we do not know, that in which the interweaving of prose and poetry intersect on the threshold of presence. And poetry may be simply the search for the poetry (*shi'rīyah*) of reality. But what is this *shi'rīyah*? . . . My experience is a continuation and not a rupture . . . My poetic reading of reality is developing, from transporting it to the text to enmeshing the text in its *nashīd*, without reality being the text and without the text being reality. (Darwish 1989:162-63)

In this brief pronouncement, Darwish locates poetry at the threshold as movement, a continuous questioning that inhabits the poem-song, *nashīd*. Poetry then not only interrogates the "real," it is also a questioning of the poetic. It is a quest for that which remains unspoken. In this context, it is important to note that the Arabic word *nashīd* etymologically signifies as a noun "poem-song" and as a verb the search for a lost object. Thus his attempt at *inshād*, his inheritance, is a double effort to sing and to search for what is absent: "And here is the *nashīd* pushing us for another search." (Darwish, 1984: 5)

Furthermore, Darwish insists on the sensory and musical aspects of poetry, which is a holding on to its pre-Islamic conception where poetry is metered and rhymed. And it is this musicality of poetry that may distinguish Darwish's poems from those of contemporary Arab poets. Darwish is well aware of this: "I consider myself a modest poet but I am strong in rhythm (*īqā'*) and this is what I have taken from the Arabic heritage." (Rahman 1996)

Darwish's heritage, however, is not limited to an Arabic one. One critic suggests that Darwish's command of the *nashīd* is attributable to the influence of the Torah on the poet. (Shanti 1986: 156) This will be made evident in our readings of *Ḥiṣār li-Madā'iḥ al-Baḥr*. Darwish himself proclaims his indebtedness: "the influence of the Hebrew language [that] comes from far in history, from the Torah . . . The Torah contains pages filled with poetry as well as mythical and epical constructions." (Cited in Shanti 1986: 156) Even with the Judaic tradition, Darwish's stance toward literary inheritance is one of development and continuation rather than rupture: "Conserving that which has vitality in the old is conserving the beginnings in order to continue the movement." (Darwish cited in Nabulsi 1987: 221)

Neither the stance of "worship" nor "disbelief" in the old is feasible. Although a participant, this makes Darwish critical of the Arabic *ḥadāthah*, or "modernism," movement in literature and poetry.[4] Two generations of modern Arabic poets emerged around two literary journals—*Al-Shi'r* with poets such as Adonis who were more interested in translations and experimentation with language and *Adab*, around which gathered Darwish and other Palestinian poets concerned with the movement of history and with innovations in meter. (Shanti 1987: 140) Darwish situates himself within the Arabic literary heritage in a progressive fashion: "I am a product of an ancient and rich dialogue, but I have a personal tone. As each poet adds something, there is in my poetry a conclusion of sorts of the history of Arabic poetry, both classical and modern. Whoever comes after me will include me in his ending."[5] (Yeshurun 1997: 124) While this continuity may be more an expression of desire, he nonetheless points to the limited vision of the modernists who call for a rupture with tradition. He cites al-Mutannabi of the tenth century as an exceptional poet who challenges the facile modernist claims of its contemporary proponents: "he sums up the history of Arabic poetry before him, during his time, and after him. He is more modern than us, because his poetry still resists the rhythm of our times." (Yeshurun 1997: 124)

Following Adonis, the contemporary Syrian poet and leading figure of modernism in Arabic poetry, he identifies his heritage as plural. Adonis affirms that the Arabic heritage of poetry is diverse; it "does not have one identity, creatively speaking, an identity of the similar and the familiar but rather it is varied, distinct . . . And if it can be said that there is a unifying identity, at this level, then it is a an identity of the plural . . . and the unity of the different, the many." (Adonis 1981: 138) Arabic critical discourse has tried to give Arabic poetry a unifying identity through meter and rhyme and has traditionally defined Arabic poetry as "rhymed words that are metered." As Adonis argues, this formalist unity is rendered superficial as soon as one delves into the poetry of the past. For Adonis, and Darwish as well, the plurality of an Arabic heritage of poetry is what gives it force, importance and richness. The difficulty of contemporary debates around Arabic poetry of attributing an "identity" to heritage is evident in the necessary, nebulous and provisional move Adonis is forced to make when he locates Arabic heritage in "the world that forms it, the vision that it unveils, and the horizons that it opens to sensibility and thought." (Adonis 1981: 138)

Specifying the character of Arabic poetry through meter and rhyme clearly has its shortcomings since Arabic poetry relies on Khalīl meters, codified in the eighth century by Khalil bin Ahmed, which determined the character of Arabic poetry through meter and rhyme until the last few decades. Rhythm has been traditionally created through the use of *'urūḍ* (prosodic or metrical divisions) or *taf'īlah* (foot of a verse meter or measure), which were made rigid by sheer force of practice, according to Adonis.[6] While some poets like Adonis see certain rigidity in the conception of Arabic poetry along *'urūḍ*, Darwish finds a treasure: "No other language possesses sixteen different meters like Arabic." (Yeshurun 1997: 125) Adonis insists on the historicity of these meters. He points to the fact that the definition of Arabic poetry as meter and rhyme began to be challenged in the tenth century with al-Suli's defense of the ninth century poet Abi Tammam. "With Jirjani [famous literary critic], there began a leaning toward doubting that only rhyme and meter could be standards for distinguishing between poetry and prose and to making the poetic language, or the way that language is used, a standard for this distinction." (Adonis 1981: 139) This does not necessarily mean that Adonis wants to do away with meter and rhyme, but he does not want them to be the sole consideration for what is Arabic poetry. He cites the examples of Abu Nawwas (750-810) and Abi Tammam (805-845) as two poets who were modern in relation to pre-Islamic poetry even though they continued to use the monorhyme and the meter, i.e. the formalist aspects of the *qaṣīdah* (a poetic form from pre-Islamic Arabia that recounts events from the life of the poet and his tribe with motifs of journey and desire).

This brings us to defining the relationship of the modern Arabic poet to his heritage. Adonis relies on the linguist Ferdinand de Saussure's distinction to make his analogy: the poet is defined not by the way the ancients said poetry (*langage* or *kalām*) but by the distinct Arabic language that he has inherited (*langue* or *lisān*). So if there is a unity in heritage it is the unity of langue (*lisān*) not the unity of langage *(kalām* or the personal, distinct use of *lisān*). Put differently, Adonis's notion of language is that it is not within the poet's possession, "it is not his language except to the extent that he is able to remove the influences of others on it . . . The poetic language does not speak except when it is separated from what it says, when it is rid of its weariness, and when it takes itself out of itself. Poetic language is always a beginning." (Adonis 1978: 78) This conception of poetry as a beginning is one that Darwish shares; in the case of Darwish, his poetry addresses the biblical Genesis that has charted visions of home and of identity.

The linguistic dispossession of the poet creates, therefore, longing for the fulfillment of language. For Adonis, the poet is a continuation of that heritage in his *langue* but this continuation, in order to be effective, has to rupture with the *langages* of previous and contemporary poets. Hence the relation with heritage is not one of repetition but one of dialogue. Darwish's stance toward heritage is one of dialogue as well, but while Adonis locates the specifics of dialogue in language, Darwish locates them in the lyrical aspect of poetry.

Poetry as Genesis: Desire for Poetry is Desire for New Beginnings and New Forms of Survival

Darwish chooses the song, breaking away from his earlier poetry where the acclamatory style tended to predominate: a rupture in his own poetry that is coterminous with the continuity he has with an Arabic lyric tradition. The song is necessary for while it embodies loss, absence, and the unknown, it is for Darwish "at the threshold of presence," "without reality being the text and without the text being reality." (Darwish 1989: 162-63) In the song, where absence and loss seem intrinsic as will be discussed later, there is fragility and sadness that Darwish seeks: "In despair sometimes there is the strength of hope." (Cited by Nabulsi 1987: 664) Despair ensuing from defeat is poetically charged for Darwish. It is affiliated with poetry as a necessary component for those silenced. "Despair approaches the divine poet, takes him to the beginning of writing, to the first word. It contradicts the victors' power of destruction, because the language of despair is stronger than that of hope. The language of Troy has not yet been spoken, and poetry is the beginning of the word." (Yeshurun 1997: 154-55)

Despair becomes a founding moment for writing, since it is able to gather (Darwish, 1973: 159) "the necessary debris . . . the primary elements of creation. And this force, this impetuosity, reverses roles, and despair finds itself in a position of force . . . it gives us force even if such force is fictive." (Beydoun 1997: 31) It is this possibility in poetry, where the ones who lost are able to draw force from it, which is the lure of poetry. His proclaimed project then is a rewriting of the beginning, a *genesis*, which alludes to contemporary defeats and the defeat of lost civilizations and cultures upon which the writing of the word by the victor is predicated.

Conceiving of his poetic project as *genesis*, Darwish situates his work within a monotheistic legacy, for he is responding to the Biblical Genesis, its poetic influences and mythic impact on history. The song thus envisioned allows Darwish to reconcile the poetic and the historical. Addressing the relation between the forms of poetry and history, Darwish states: "Poetry cannot reconcile itself with force, because it is inhabited by the duty to create its own force, founding a vital space for the defense of rights, of justice for the victim. Poetry cannot find a common ground with History except on this fundamental basis." (Hadidi 1997: 78) History then becomes his sole poetic preoccupation given his project of genesis. (Hadidi 1997: 74) This is because Darwish considers that it may be possible for poetry to testify, in the form of history. (Rahman 1996) Moreover, poetry itself is inhabited with a bygone temporality and a space of loss. "And poetry . . . remains incomplete if it does not resonate of echoes of the far past." (Beydoun 1997: 31) The question is: how is poetry in a privileged position to create this "vital space" for the victim? How does poetry testify? These are questions that we will address in reading his poetry. But already, Darwish points out the importance of poetry for poetic survival. For Darwish, "a people without poetry are a conquered people." (Yeshurun 1997: 154) It is precisely the fragile force of poetry that allows for a space of possibility for the silenced. "Poetry can be of little efficacy, but its force comes from recognizing human fragility." (Beydoun 1997: 47)

Darwish links poetry to history by defining the desire of poetry as wanting to write the beginning of things. Not only does the poet seek his Book of Genesis, one that would be in dialogue with the cultures that have passed through his land, but also this desire is fundamental to the poetic drive. "There is no poetry without genesis." (Jarrah 1997: 173) Darwish poetry seeks to "return to the initial narrative, to the first place." (Beydoun 1997: 45) But he recognizes that the beginning of things is exile and absence for those defeated. "I have a project for a 'Book of Genesis' that could very well be a 'Book of Exodus.'" (Beydoun

1997: 46) Whereas the biblical exodus is a "return to the promised land," Darwish's exodus is the first banishment.

As it is conceived collectively, genesis is close to epic. The "epic" that Darwish is trying to historicize is still open to struggle. He is trying to wrench it from historical closure, so that it leads to future possibilities. He characterizes his last works as constituting a project of an epic song that he hopes to continue, where "history will be a stage for poetic spaces . . . where peoples . . . can roam with no boundaries, and the search for the constituents of identity [will be] within the rules of mixture, confrontation and cohabitation of identities. I am searching for a locus for the *nashīd* in an open historical space." (Hadidi 1997: 81) The testing of poetic boundaries for Darwish is inextricably linked with his questioning of identity. While Darwish insists on the question of identity, he also insists on the deferment of articulating it: "Poetry must always ask the question without answering it." (Yeshurun 1997: 157)

In guarding an epic memory of home, in writing Palestine, there is, however, always the danger of absenting again in writing. As it has been written by Palestinian poets and writers, Palestine, Darwish argues, has been absented and displaced by its fixed discourse of patriotism and nostalgia: "I am disconcerted by the absence of place, of its veritable attributes, in a poetry that pretends to celebrate it. I don't find in Palestinian poetry the flora and fauna, the landscape, in other words the real Palestine." (Badr 1997: 103) This absenting of Palestine in writing may not be simply for the lack of descriptive power, as Darwish suggests, but may be inherent in the condition of writing, as I elaborate further. Nonetheless, it is significant that, for Darwish, Palestine needs to become "myth" for the Palestinian writer who needs to "import his language to concrete reality in order to transport it in the reality of words." (Yeshurun 1997: 164)

Darwish differentiates between myth of the Old Testament and myth which is yet to take shape, in the context of the Palestinians. "With the disappearance of our country, we found ourselves relegated to pre-Genesis. And our poets had to write our proper Genesis from this myth of the other." (Beydoun 1997: 27) The problem is that another has already written Palestine, and this writing has become sacred and made undeniable. Darwish wonders about the possibility of writing a less mythical narrative: "The problem with Palestinian poetry is that it was put in place without the appointed forces, without historians, without geographers, without anthropologists; it had to equip itself with all the necessary baggage to defend its right to exist." (Beydoun 1997: 27)

Needing to recover and preserve the past, Darwish believes there is still place for epic poetry since the voices of the defeated are absent and have never been heard, hence his quest for "the Trojan poet." (Yeshurun 1997: 153) The absent Trojan poets embody the threat faced by the Palestinian poets, whose own past is called into question: "we live in a moment of History where we appear to be deprived of a past. One of the fundamental aspects of epic writing is to recapture a past that risks cutting itself definitively from its prolonging." (Beydoun 1997: 28) Darwish then attempts to situate his lyric within the space of "epic" in order to safeguard a poetic survival for the retreating past: "We find ourselves today in a hybrid place, in a median point between the historic and the mythic. Our situation, our existence even, retreats." (Beydoun 1997: 27-28)

In this median locus between history and myth, there can be no contradiction for Darwish between lyric and epic in this project of "epic lyricism," as the modern Greek poet Ritsos first designated it. For Darwish, epic is lyric enfolding history. In his poetry, he brings together epic as the genre of homeland, following the tradition of the *Iliad*, the *Odyssey*, as well as the *Aeneid*, and lyric as the genre of loss in the tradition of Sappho and Horace. Darwish valorizes lyrical epic texts because they speak to collective predicaments of struggle, loss, "and are preoccupied with universal themes including the tragic perception of history and the expression of a collective conscience in the face of loss and mourning." (Hadidi 1997: 87) The epic, which gathers both the past and the present and directs them toward the future, arguably makes Darwish remain within a national register without being limited to its formulation of identity. The clear privileging of the epic over the mythic has to do with epic's open struggle and form whereas myth is and has been historically closed: "the notion of destiny does not exist as long as the conflict is open. This is precisely what makes our texts epic and not mythic." (Hadidi 1997: 80)

Threatened Desire as Intrinsic to the Song

Darwish's task to write the beginning of things, which he defines as the desire of poetry, and which is simultaneously his longing for the homeland, is inextricably linked with his lyrical endeavor. To pose the question of this ancient mode is to necessarily get entangled in desire. As Darwish puts it, "he who does not desire does not sing." (Darwish 1983: 222) Desire in his poetry is akin to that of the Sufi where the intermingling of loss and desire figures loss "not as nostalgia or regret but as a horizon, (*bu'd*)." (Rahman 1996) And if we follow the legacy of the orphic, desire and loss are intrinsic to the song. Maurice Blanchot writes in "Orpheus's Gaze":

> Only in the song does Orpheus have power over Eurydice. But in the song too, Eurydice is already lost, and Orpheus himself is the dispersed Orpheus; the song immediately makes him "infinitely dead." He loses Eurydice because he desires her beyond the measured limits of the song, and he loses himself, but this desire, and Eurydice lost, and Orpheus dispersed are necessary to the song, just as the ordeal of eternal inertia is necessary to the work. (Blanchot 1982: 173)

Blanchot locates the particularity of the song in being a site of power and loss. The song that grants Orpheus power over Eurydice is also that which "infinitely" kills him. Desire is necessary for the song, for its excess—desire extending beyond the "*measured* limits of the song"—is what creates loss. (My emphasis) The song, predicated on the double loss of Eurydice and of Orpheus, cannot contain desire, which is always excessive, or retrieve the loss. There is a compelling belatedness in the song: Eurydice is lost and Orpheus is "infinitely dead." This temporality of "always already" is absenting, rendering presencing or re-presenting impossible. Orpheus's quest for Eurydice in the world of shades, which is an attempt to presence her, fails because of that critical, instantaneous, transgressive gaze that refuses re-presentation for the sake of the song. It is in effect a failure to re-present Eurydice who is shrouded and concealed "[u]nder a name that hides her and a veil that covers her." (Blanchot 1982: 171) For Blanchot, failure is not a lack of success as he puts it; it is "in . . . beginning all over again." (Blanchot 1982: 243)

The musicality of poetry, although fleeting, makes it endure, granting it a certain permanence.[7] Not only does Orpheus infinitely die, but he is also fragmented to pieces while his floating head continues to sing. This "Orpheus dispersed" is also necessary for the song, since the scattering of his disembodied voice ensures the survival of the song. Lyric in this formulation is the disembodied voice on a continuous journey. The poet responds to the loss in his attempt to sing. Thus poetry's identity is its attempt, albeit failed, to redress this loss. This failure is precisely what leads to the continuation of the song due to the movement of desire. The song then is the movement of desire and this space of the search and of the loss.[8]

The siege of the city of Beirut has initiated an examination of the role of writing among writers and poets. In an interview, "A Pressing longing for Beirut," Darwish points to the transition in his work: "What I wrote before Beirut was derivative. The experience demands a new kind of writing, because what happened in Beirut is more than just the ordinary experience of people's history."[9]

Darwish's poetry not only follows the orphic in marking desire but also in announcing this desire as a threatened longing. "We restrain the longing in us, for it is not for us to reveal it, if for no other reason than this, that it is a threatened longing."[10] What threatens desire? In both cases it is desire itself, the desire to make present what has been absented and that absents the desired a second time. Darwish's entire poetic corpus faces the absence of the homeland and its impossible attainability. The poem is then necessary for the poet who "builds on sand what the wind carries/from battles and desires." (Darwish 1994: 90) It is a locus of desire where the loss is double, that of the homeland as well as that which supplants the homeland. "No, there is no harbor for me/to say there is a home" (Darwish 1994: 55)

Darwish forces an interruption in the song, which requires repetition in order to safeguard desire. This interruption is necessary for foiling desire in its very intense appearance. The poem also grants the poet power over it in his ability to interrupt the repetition to which the song is inclined, from the caesura he forces in his poem[11]: "and sing of the fields in which sun and heart run and never tire . . . and Desert/ /and desert! From one thousand years to the light I came." (Darwish 1994: 91)

More significantly, the threatened desire is a result of the task of writing. The poet is always in exile according to Blanchot because the poem is exile. (Blanchot 1982: 235) When the poet submits to poetry, he is exiled from the demands of daily life and from what connects him to reality and power. Darwish accordingly writes: "and poetry is exile when we dream and then forget when we awaken where we were." (Darwish 1994: 463) More importantly, the poetic condition is destined to be within error. "Error is the risk which awaits the poet . . . Error means wandering, the inability to abide and stay . . . In this absence of here and now what happens . . . recurs without cease; it is the horror and the confusion and the uncertainty of eternal repetition." (Blanchot 1982: 238) The poet who commits himself to writing risks the world that he knows and the certainty that he thinks he lives.

Exile is in a sense the "space of literature," the space of withdrawal which offers solitude for the writer wandering in an inaccessible desert and which spares him the demands of the everyday but denies him the power derived from that. The desert, as Darwish figures it as well, becomes both the refuge for poetry and the threat it poses for the poet. The work demands ruinous desire and that the writer delves in weakness in order for a work to come to being. And while it is necessary for Orpheus to look back and face the essence of the night as the other night, as Blanchot puts it, in order to safeguard the song, Darwish confronts not the temporal otherness of the night but the spatial otherness of the crypt as a locus of no-where. Hence the figuring of the desired (and poetry as locus of desire), as we will see, as a crypt, inaccessible, hidden, yet providing a refuge and protecting this longing.[12]

Andalusia as the Utopic Nowhere: Between a Crypt and a Desert

In the midst of political turmoil and continual change of boundaries and sovereignties, Arabic poets and writers, including Darwish, have often defined their identity in relation to an Arabic literary heritage. In fact the only continuity with the past that they can claim is a literary one through language. This is why the turn to Andalusia is important. Andalusia is seen as an analogous situation of loss. It invokes the return and speaks of the loss of the past.[13] It also recalls the pre-Islamic nomadic song that begins with lamenting a deserted site. Andalusia replaced the deserted sites and then Palestine took its place, especially in the popular Arabic poetry of the fifties and the sixties where Andalusia is also seen as a golden cultural and literary moment.[14] Darwish, however, questions a simple, continuous link of identity between Palestine and Andalusia as many Arab writers have often claimed, as they lamented Andalusia as a lost paradise.

Andalusia, a heterogeneous, cultural encounter of strangers, has a complex configuration in his poetry. "Andalusia is not the lost paradise," but rather the future and a point of intersection. (Rahman 1996)

> In every poet there is a loss or an absence. In every poet there is an Andalus. Otherwise how do we interpret the sadness of poetry and its thrust into two contradictory directions: the past and the future. And *poetry is the search for an Andalus* that is possible to recall, able to be presenced. From here grows the

> mysterious happiness, not in reality, but from creation, when the words are able to capture the impossible. (*Libération* 1991: 11, my emphasis)

Andalusia is this possibility of presencing which is the possibility of writing, since poetry for Darwish is "this search for an Andalus," which is the essence of the *nashīd*. In another poem, Darwish asks: "Was Andalusia/here or there? On earth . . . or in the poem?" (Darwish 1994: 476) The question points to the essential literary construction of Andalusia.

And yet Andalusia is this impossibility as a return:[15] "I cannot go to Cordoba." (Darwish 1994: 92) For Darwish, Cordoba is simultaneously the past, the displaced home, the disconnected identity, and the loss. But it is also the desire for a future. This rupture with the past is the foreclosure of any possibility of the "return."[16] In an enigmatic verse, Darwish writes: "I remember that I will dream again of the return." (Darwish 1994: 90) The remembrance is of the future rather than the past and is bound to its own present. There is no past tense. The tenses call attention to the constructed nature of the recollection and to the selective memory of the "I." The return that is conjured is offset by remembrance and dreaming and is therefore distanced and negated. The "I" that remembers the market places of Andalusia does not know the path to Cordoba. The "I" simply remembers that it cannot recall. But it claims to recall, in order to recognize, the necessity of constructing a memory. The double repetition of "strange," "desert," "white," as well as the plural refrains, establishes rhythm and inscribes a textual memory.

Memory, nonetheless, is important as an illusion of restoring continuity. Crucial in any formulation of the homeland, memory is foregrounded as an impossible recollection. Darwish wants to claim instead "the last smoke," since it is this trace which in its "presence" embodies the passage of disappearance and absence. "The beginning is not our beginning, and the last smoke is ours." (Darwish 1994: 89) This smoke, the passage of disappearance of the fire that was, the trace, and the invocation of the gods of poetry in their absence that the poet can claim in writing and not the genesis that was denied to him, that is denied to every poet.

The impossibility of Andalusia as a return, figured as a rupture with the past, bears with it other dislocations. In "Crypts, Andalusia, Desert," the poet marks a rupture with the poetry of the former poets, with his earlier poetry, and with the poem. "And believe my short journey to Cordoba./ And my separation from the sand and the early poets, and from trees that were no woman." (Darwish 1994: 89) The short journey to Cordoba, which serves as a mini refrain to the rest of the poem, may be read as the former continuity he believed he had with the Andalusian poets. But it is in verses such as "trees that were no woman" that Darwish perhaps separates himself from his earlier poetry which evoked organic images of the woman as the land and the homeland and which served as his national allegory. Furthermore, Darwish begins by dissociating himself from the poem itself, marking a rupture between the poet and the poem. "So you continue your lyric in my name." (Darwish 1994: 89)

It continues in his name, but it is not really his. "The beginning is not ours," disclaims that the lyric is in any sense originary or can lay claim to the past. But this continuation, repetition of the beginning, is within a summoning that is beyond the individual poetic self. In order to be lyrical, the poetic voice has to forget itself. This movement of forgetting is a retreat and is anticipated. Following the orphic, lyric demands disappearance: "To encounter Orpheus is to encounter this voice which is not mine, this death which becomes song, but which is not my death, even though I must disappear in it more profoundly." (Blanchot 1982: 156) Darwish performs this "secret identity" between death and song at the end of his poem where disappearance—not surviving—becomes song. But disappearance is not an experience that begins and that comes to an end according to Blanchot. And in this poem the disappearance neither begins nor ends since the poetic voice proclaims, after not surviving, the loss of the string in the crypt, and hence the search begins again in the song. This movement of disappearance becomes paradoxically the survival of the song.

> And wait for me little by little so I can hear the sound of my blood
> cross the street that explodes
> (I almost survived)
> —You will not win!
> —I will walk
> —To where my friend?
> —To where the doves have flown clapping the wheat
> to uphold this space by a chaff that waits.
> So you continue your lyric in my name
> and don't cry, my friend, for a string lost in the crypts.
> It's a song
> It's a song!

Darwish creates another level of meaning for return where it is no longer a response to the long travel but becomes a going toward the future. The return is eternally deferred and belated. (Rahman 1996) "And why do you want to journey to Cordoba?/—Because I don't know the path. Desert and desert." (Darwish 1994: 90) It is figured as an absurd journey.

> They opened the lonely door of confinement so I came out.
> I found a path so I walked.
> Where do I go? To the issue I said: I'll teach my freedom how to walk, she leaned on me,
> I straightened up, and straightened her up
> and I carried her
> over my back like they carry countries on camels and lorries, and I walked. (Darwish 1994: 92)

It is the singularity of the journey that has tied the Palestinian poets to Andalusia. "Nor do they ride to Andalusia/singularly." (Darwish 1994: 91) It is a journey through time that cannot be borne. "We travel like other people, but we return to nowhere as if travel is the path of clouds/ We have a country of words. Speak speak so we may know the end of this travel." (Darwish 1994: 331) It is only through language that there is possibility for an end to travel and a possibility for homeland. The homeland is built from words, and any notion of belonging needs to be constructed poetically. Writing is this detachment from the self, from language, and from the world.

Darwish invokes the older poetic theme of the pre-Islamic desert journey to mark his Arabic heritage and look to the open-endedness of the future. He marks the journey as a passage that may not lead anywhere and that has already begun. "I'd travel again on the roads that may or may not lead to Cordoba." (Darwish 1994: 325) Though the desire for the past remains, it has no place in the journey. The wandering of the ancient poets is tied to no space. It neither originates nor attempts to arrive at a specific destination. But the journey is now a lonely wandering: "Drink from my wine and do not leave me on the road of years alone, a worn willow tree." (Darwish 1994: 325)

Darwish is close to the Sufi tradition in how he formulates the journey (*raḥīl*), in the sense that he is not as concerned with the arrival as he is concerned with the path. "Do not fear this desert from us/ . . . we do not come to stay nor do we pass to return." (Darwish 1994: 240) This formulation of journey wants to insist on the "errance" and the wandering. The poet recognizes that poetry, like "errance", creates its own path. The valorization of the pre-Islamic poetic motif of the journey over the Andalusian notion of the return changes the shaping of the home by rejecting a presumed accessibility to the past. It also valorizes the movement of desire over loss. The homeland in this construction is no longer a project or a fulfillment of a destiny as it has been articulated in nationalist narratives and his earlier poetry. Rather, it is an echo mediated through desire and loss.

Having ruptured with the "past," Darwish encrypts it as if to keep its death alive but as an impossible access or return. "It's effortless and difficult this egress of the doves from the wall of language, so how do we pass to the small orange grove." (Darwish 1994: 89) Although the return to the homeland is conjured in the conventional image of the land of oranges, its access is rendered impossible. It is easy to read the past as one constructs it, but it is very difficult to read the past without re/construction; it is unreadable like the "egress of the doves from this wall of language." The title of Darwish's poem already encloses Andalusia spatially between crypts and a desert. In its singularity it juxtaposes the crypts but slips into them rhythmically. It is as if the crypts recall Andalusia, which in turn recalls the desert, an empty space that is marked but marks nothing. His poem announces itself as a crypt, one that implies in the poem a *topos* of death. "Do you die a lot?/ And I live a lot, and I hold my shadow like a ripe apple/ and the long road wraps itself around me/Like a noose of dew." (Darwish 1994: 91)

Throughout the poem, Darwish speaks of enclosed spaces of death such as the crypt, the cell, the enclosed wall, and the vault. The desert, an open space, is cryptic as well since it is a space of loss where there are no boundaries or clear passages, a space that resembles itself: what is seen tomorrow appears to be what was seen yesterday. The future then, in this space at least, is always past.

Both the desert and the crypt are defined by their inaccessibility: "Don't hide like the homeland." (Darwish 1994: 93) The homeland then is that which conceals itself and which resists access. This poem does not name Beirut, the supplanted homeland, but transplants itself in time and space to Andalusia. By not naming it, the poem encrypts it. Once it is encrypted it cannot be left; it becomes a journey that the poet bears with him.

What remains is the poem, which is encrypted just like a homeland or as a homeland: "It's effortless and difficult this ingress of the doves to the wall of language, so how do we bide before the lyric in the crypt? Desert and desert." (Darwish 1994: 89) Darwish locates the lyric in the crypt, and the reader is situated before it. It is language that leads Darwish to wonder about the position of the reader who has to address and come before this lyric. He wants to insist on the question of the inaccessibility of the lyric via language. The encryption of the poem preserves it so any reading of the poem is bound to misidentify it. In Jacques Derrida's reading of Paul Celan's poetry, he announces the crypt as "secret, the passage uncertain, and the poem only unveils this secret to confirm that there is something secret there, withdrawn, forever beyond the reach of any hermeneutic exhaustion." (Derrida 1992: xv)

The crypt is then the only threshold of presence and absence that offers safe refuge for a poet who even his exile he had to lose: "I lifted down my freedom like a sack of coal and escaped to the crypt;/ does the crypt resemble my mother your mother? Desert and desert." What space can the poet claim after the loss of a supplanted homeland except the space of the poem? (Darwish 1994: 92) Poetry is the closest thing to granting a sense of belonging for the poetic voice that poses it as a question, evident in the emphasis on the mother: "Did I choose my mother your voice?"

The poem becomes a date in its attempt at recollection, in its monumental markings. "One thousand years" dates the separation of Andalusia from the poem. In its inscription in the poem it may be creating an event rather than preserving a historical reference. Derrida suggests that this does not deny its readability or its connection to an event: "a date likes to encrypt itself in order to become readable, to render itself unreadable in its very readability." (Derrida 1992: 390) For no true witnessing is possible. The poetic "I" that defines itself as a "*shahīd*" (*shahīd* implies *shāhed,* martyr and witness in Arabic) is aware that true witnessing is predicated on death. This again reinforces the impersonality of the poetic voice: "they will steal you like me a martyr/ . . . And wait for me little by little so I can hear the sound of my blood/cross the street that explodes/ (I almost survived)." (Darwish 1994: 93) But these markings reveal their own penchance for effacement.

He defines the loss, toward the end of "Crypts, Andalusia, Desert," as the loss of the string in the crypts. The string is allegorical for the melody or the lyric that one associates with it, a lyric that cryptically bespeaks a desire for home. This desire for a homeland is a desire for refuge: "We come from countries that have no countries/ . . . So give us a wall so we can call . . . /Beirut is our last shelter/Beirut is our last star." (Darwish 1994: 198) The place of origin is not named, undeniable yet impossible. The demand for a fragment of a home expresses exasperation at one's strange predicament. It is Beirut that the poetic voice wants to mourn and not the lost home, as if to seal the latter's loss. The poetry privileges desire over loss so that there is no nostalgia in proclaiming it. Reconsidering loss, the voice proclaims: "What do we leave except this prison?/What do prisoners lose?/We walk toward a distant song." (Darwish 1994: 205) Neither the past nor the loss is valorized in relation to the present. "I don't look back/so that I won't remember that I passed through this land." (Darwish 1994: 482) Loss here is protected, guarding the lyric. For Darwish ends right after declaring the loss by an affirmation of the song where there is rhythmic harmony between the Arabic words "crypts" and "song." (*aqbiyah*, *ughniyah*): "and don't cry, my friend, for a string lost in the crypts./ It's a song/ It's a song!" (Darwish 1994: 94)

The song becomes the only belonging possible not only poetically but politically as well, assuming the collective voice of a displaced and threatened community. "Our crypt is dug so we sleep like ants in the small crypt/as if we were secretly singing/Beirut is our shelter/Beirut is our star." (Darwish 1994: 195-96) The poetic voice points to a suspension of identity, to a threatened desire of belonging, to the difficulty of claiming a common identity. The collective singing done in secrecy is qualified by an "as if" which makes the claim for a collective identity, grounded in the song that is predicated on the loss of Beirut, further removed and based only on the confines of this singing which has to be done in secrecy. The song is made manifest as concealment. The "assertion" of identity is also enunciated as a secret. So while there is the claim to a common identity, the basis for that claim is not revealed as if to further protect it.[17] There is only a shelter, a place of refuge in lieu of a home. Hence the distressed emphasis on the singularity of the shelter in the refrain: "Beirut is our only shelter/Beirut is our only star." (Darwish 1994: 197)

Throughout "Crypts, Andalusia, Desert" there is stress on the lack of permanence; for instance, in the collapsing wall which recalls the wall of language and which in turn recalls language's failure. "Sing of the similarity between a question and another question that follows it/so that one collapse may protect my collapse from a final collapse." (Darwish 1994: 90) The poet as well is the one who "builds on sand what the wind carries/ from battles and desires," who constructs nothing fixed but desire; his fragile construction threatened by impermanence and erasure is carried away by the wind. Like smoke, sand is that which fleetingly preserves a trace on its way to effacement.

In another poem, "Sand," Darwish writes of the preoccupation of the desert poet in his poems who searches for the traces of his beloved in the desert: "It is sand/ spaces from woman and thoughts." (Darwish 1994: 609) Pre-Islamic desert poetry begins with the poet stopping and lamenting the deserted abodes, demarcating the desert through the places where the woman passed and voicing his desires. (Nabulsi 1987: 356-357) Even the structure of the pre-Islamic *qaṣīdah* can be read on the basis of the poet's relation to the woman as absence, because she is the one who stops the poet on the deserted abode (*aṭlāl*) and who, by her absence, leads him to remember with sadness his past with her. Her departure leads him to travel in her trace and describe everything connected with that journey (*raḥīl*) in terms of events. This stopping, more than being necessarily nostalgic or a mournful, is a confronting of absence.

And sand is spaces of thoughts following a long tradition where Arabs used to read the sand, seeing it as traces.[18] The reader of the traces, called storyteller, the one who recounts events from what he reads in the sand, was able to identify much about the traveler from the way he stepped on the sand. So sand has a memory of sorts, hence the essence of reading predicated on the fragmentation and impermanence of traces that threaten to disappear. (Nabulsi 1987: 356)

The Song, the *Nashīd*, and the *Qaṣīdah*

The rupture with the past is coterminous with the persistence of the search for the absent, which is a continuance of the *nashīd*. So while Darwish mourns his separation from the earlier poets, he is simultaneously aware of the continuation of the heritage of poetry through the *nashīd* or lyric, "so you continue your lyric in my name." It is naming the *nashīd* as continuation, something that has already begun and continues even after the individual poetic voice is silent. In this poem, Darwish begins in continuation, with the first word of the poem "So" performing this, as if the poetic voice is engaging a dialogue that has already begun. This beginning of the poem also announces the withdrawal of the poetic "I", so that the lyric is also not claimed by the "I" but belongs to the interlocutor who has already begun it. The impersonality of the poetic voice is reinforced when the poetic "I" claims an "ancient heart." (Darwish 1994: 93)

Moreover, it is suggested that other poets continue the *nashīd*. The *nashīd* may take the collective effort of several poets, and it thus emerges as a collective song. In modern terms, it is often associated with nationalist songs that are recited in groups and with collective acclamations. But Darwish names it a song that is related to a people without an effective home. (Rahman 1996) "The long *nashīd* . . . founds a land which cannot contain one pace, and which opens a horizon that cannot contain one idea." (Darwish 1981: 4) The *nashīd* in his work is associated with the communal (*qawmīyah*) song and not the national (*waṭanīyah*) *nashīd* in particular; it is connected in various ways to the journey. In addition to being named as a journey, it is also a way of bearing this displacement. "Crypts, Andalusia, Desert" is about a *nashīd* and is a *nashīd* itself.

Darwish's poetry distinguishes between *nashīd*, *ughniyah*, or song, and *qaṣīdah*. Both the song and the *nashīd* are open-ended; while the song (*ughniyah*) is the "announcing" of an individual but distant voice, the *nashīd* is a continuation of the lyric. (Rahman 1996) The poem that begins with the continuation of *nashīd* ends by affirming ughniyah, the individual song: "It's a song!" Darwish's affirmation of the song in his poetry as the only belonging possible, as the threatened memory that insists on desire in remembering the loss, has to begin again and to continue for new songs to emerge so that the *nashīd* may continue.

Furthermore, the *nashīd* for him is the voice of the *qaṣīdah*, which he defines as a dialogue, containing a plurality of voices. (Rahman 1996) The poetic voice in this poem shifts from the speaker to the recipient and switches between the rhythmic and the textual in the dialogue that structures it. The shift in the use of the personal pronouns "I" and "we," according to Darwish, usually indicates a turn from the lyrical toward the epic. This use of the "we" is illusory: "A poet never accepts to be a part of a collective voice. He makes himself modest and leaves the 'us' speak . . . The poetic voice is not in a chorus . . . The 'I' is a central element in poetry, the 'I' creates the 'You', the 'They', and the 'Us'." (Yeshurun 1997: 133)

Lyric is the only remnant continuous with an Arabic heritage of poetry via the songs of Andalusia and the *qaṣīdah.* Adonis points to the oral origins of pre-Islamic poetry where poetry was *nashīd*, transmitted not through a pre-Islamic book but through memory: "Pre-Islamic poetry was born a *nashīd*, I mean that it developed through listening, a song not writing." (Adonis 1989: 5) But memory and the act of *nashīd* had the status of the book in both disseminating and conserving the poetry. The song is different from the *nashīd* since it usually follows from the poem, composing music to the metered words. For Adonis, *inshād* is one form of song. (Adonis 1989: 7-8) And poetry was often recited/sung by the poet himself. Predicated on listening, the art of this oral poetry was not just in what it said but how it said it.

In what it said, pre-Islamic poetry was one of testimony, according to Adonis, since it did not seek to change things or to follow them but simply to describe them. What it depicted is a collective existence, and it sought a dialogue with that reality.[19] "The pre-Islamic poet used to say . . . what the listener already knew: he said his customs and habits, his battles . . . in this, he did not say himself as much as he used to say the group, or \that he did not say himself except through saying the group. He was the singing witness." (Darwish, 1989: 6)

Darwish is perhaps the modern day "singing witness," who dialogues with his varied heritage and who considers the song to be at the heart of poetry. He, for instance, considers Lorca, whom he names in his poetry, to be exemplary since he resisted the exclusion of poetry from song: "Lorca used to sing." (Darwish 1994, *'ĀbirūĀn*: 175) Poetry is predicated for him on hearing and not on seeing. "Did we forget that this delicateness and this absence are the home of poetry which has no home? Did we forget this eternal happy marriage between poetry and music?" (Darwish 1994, *'Ābirūn* 174)

If the song is "a lone flute" then the *qaṣīdah*, whose origins are unknown,[20] is an orchestra of sounds. Most critics of Arabic poetry look at the etymology of the word, "*qaṣīdah*," to mean intention. Derived from the verb "*qaṣada*" which means to aim or to intend, critics have long wondered about its intention. Adonis, however, reads it in relation to its form: "*Qaṣīd* is the *mashtūr* (divided or fragmented). It is said: *qaṣada al-'ūd*, i.e. broke it in half, or *shatarahū* (divided it) into halves. So the naming, in this sense, does not come from the intention of saying, but from its form, which is *taqṣīd*, i.e. *tashtīr* (fragmenting)."[21] Explanations of the designation "*qaṣīdah*" remain controversial.[22] While much about the intentions and the form of the *qaṣīdah* is being debated, its continued importance cannot be denied.

Jayyusi writes in support of the persistence of the *qaṣīdah* form, attacking the proponents of free verse who argued that the old form was fragmented, limiting, and monotonous: "this is a poetry meant to be read aloud, subject to modulations of rhythm and tone, to changes in tempo and gear, to variations in the mode of address. None of this considerable elasticity was noted by the detractors of the form in the fifties and sixties." (Khadra 1996: 7) The flexibility of this form consists in the following: While the meanings and even objectives of the *qaṣīdah* are determined by convention, the way they are put together in a poem is left to the poet; and while there was a substantial variety in the meters and rhymes available "once chosen, they could not be varied," since a *qaṣīdah* is "a poem in monorhyme and monometer." (Sperl 1996: 10)

Traditionally it is the two hemistich verse, monorhyme, and length that were considered the most important elements of the *qaṣīdah*. (Sperl 1996: 47) The unity of the pre-Islamic *qaṣīdah* derived from the unity of hemistiches, unity of line, unity of rhyme, and unity of meter. The *qaṣīdah* with its distinct unity of rhythm and monorhyme was accused of fragmentation due to the special care given to each *bayt* or verse which lead the lines to be independent of each other—and this is in turn due to lyrical necessity, the fact that the poem will be heard and that the rhyme (*qāfiyah*) is specifically musical. (Adonis 1989: 13) According to Jayyusi it is the formal features of the *qaṣīdah* that made it persist so it is not gratuitous that the *qaṣīdah* is commonly defined by its form.

Jayyusi claims that there has been little change over the centuries in the *qaṣīdah* or Arabic poetry: "for all the enormous changes in diction, metaphor, and other poetic elements, such as the introduction of complex symbolism in Sufi poetry, the elements of rhythm, meter and, to a large extent, syntax, together with the basic Weltanschauung of the poets themselves, the *qaṣīdah* underwent little radical change over the centuries." (Jayyusi 1992: 319) The most important change is in Andalusian poetry, where the nostalgia in Andalusian poetry is more concrete when present, directed to a specific event or place.

Some changes in the *qaṣīdah* by the "new poetry" include replacing the unity of the line (*bayt*) with the whole poetic composition, dispensing with the transitional sections and the conventional aims such as that of the panegyric (*madīḥ*). Major changes are in meter and rhyme: metrical unity is achieved in the single foot (*taf'īlah*) rather than the line and free internal rhyming replaces the monorhyme. (Hafez 1996: 107) Also there is a change in language, from the referential to the inward looking, from an expressive and descriptive function of language to a creative one. Sabry Hafez writes: "Despite these changes, the deep structure of the modern poem continued to conduct a profound dialogue with the classical *qaṣīdah* form." (Hafez 1996: 107)

Poetic Displacement

The preoccupation with home has to do with a historical loss of a native place and with a particular treatment of poetic place. Place has a paramount status in Arabic literary heritage. The absence of place except as place-desert or place-errance relegates the poet to the space of the poem, because the desert is a space of absence. According to Adonis, place for the pre-Islamic poet is time which changes and creates loss; it is the place-*matāh* or wandering. From this the poet attempts to make of place a refuge and is full of regret when he sees things disappear, destroyed, absent. Place becomes another hidden-secretive language in the pre-Islamic *qaṣīdah*. The poet confronts place, because it represents the accidents of life, in order to prove his mastery over his fate. This desire for mastery becomes paramount in the face of loss. (Adonis 1983: 15) Place then not only attracts since it can fulfill the expectations of mastery, but it also threatens due to the surprises of failure. The pre-Islamic poet who resorts to brave work as outlet to his predicament also directs himself to the desert, in order to understand it and conquer it. The desert, however, does not yield but is a place of change and absence. (Adonis 1983: 14-15)

The poem embodies this absence of place, and in its displacement of the poet from his reality becomes his belonging. It is in its repetition that the poem saves the poet and itself, transforming the forces of change into eternal repetition of beginnings. In pre-Islamic poetry the *qaṣīdah* provided a supplanted home and a sense of belonging. It not only spoke of wandering, absence of a fixed place, it was also the space to express longing for what is absent. It is noteworthy that in Arabic, place (*makān*) is derived from *kānā* (to be, to exist, to take place). Intrinsic to being then is place but as the infinite "between": "We are here between the stones and shadows a place." (Darwish 1994: 355) But this "here" is on the threshold. This spatial in-between draws place and being together toward the poem. In "'. . . Poetically Man Dwells. . .'" Heidegger reads the entitled, partial verse of Holderlin as the compatibility of dwelling and poetry since "[p]oetry is the original admission of dwelling." (Heidegger 1971: 227)

> The godhead is the "measure" with which man measures out his dwelling, his stay on earth beneath the sky. Measure-taking gauges the between, which brings the two, heaven and earth, to one another . . . The taking of measure is what is poetic in dwelling. Poetry is measuring . . . The measure consists in the way in which the god, who remains unknown, is revealed as such by the sky. (Heidegger 1971: 221-223)

Paradoxically, however, it is poetic language and writing that safeguard a notion of place for Darwish.

In his last works, the word "homeland" is one of the least recurrent words. This is in contrast to his early period where he addresses it in profusion. His later works reveal a richness in the *topoi* of homeland, whereas other Palestinian poets, who preceded Darwish, such as Abu Salmah and Abdel Rahim Mahmoud, referred to the homeland conventionally as lost, raped, and wounded. Darwish however transforms the homeland into a *qaṣīdah*: "My homeland is my new *qaṣīdah*." (Darwish 1994: 108) Just as poetry is named as an estrangement, so is home: "The homeland is this estrangement." (Darwish, 1993: 156) And just as poetry is figured as a journey so is home, "my homeland, my suitcase." (Darwish 1994: 58) This homeland is possible through an echo, mediated already through loss: "we call you/the echo returns a homeland." (Darwish 1994: 115) These "distant countries/countries without trace" are only possible in writing where their trace is written. (Darwish 1994: 83) "And travel led me to travel/ and I don't see a country there." (Darwish 1994: 107) The homeland is throughout figured as absence in a poetry that absents it again but which at least inscribes it as absence: "the absence of countries that I shape in language." (Darwish 1994: 299) The creation of homeland becomes the work of the poet: "the countries between my hands are the work of my hands." (Darwish 1994: 382)

The *qaṣīdah* harbors poetic exile in the void that emerges between home and exile: "I have no harbor/ to say I have a home . . . No land below me so I can die as I wish/ and no sky." (Darwish 1994: 55-57) This exile is not only the poetic one that Blanchot speaks of but also the historical one of losing one's country in an age of nation-states. This is why Darwish wrote, in relation to the Palestinian poet Rashid Hussein who took his own life in New York City, "He who has no home has no exile." (Darwish 1994: 'Ābirūn 196) Again a link is made between poetry and home, between the political exile of home and the poetical one: "Rashid Hussein choked in the smoke of his own poetry . . . He did not find poetry . . . So he put fire to the recorded tapes of his poetry and he choked." (Darwish 1994, 'Ābirūn: 196) Darwish recognizes the many possible exiles in the twentieth century. "Exile can be in language or in poetry, both as refuge and exile." (Rahman 1996) In the absence of the physical home that historically created exile for Darwish and the Palestinians, there is another exile. "Should I find refuge in the *qaṣīdah* / and it is the one that opened onto my freedom my exile in you." (Darwish 1994: 315) Darwish faces a plurality of exiles: from the physical home, from the physical refuge, in language, in cultural and literary heritage, and in the poetic condition.

Adonis specifically comments on the exiles that the Arab poet faces, where the "origin" is exile both in language and in myth, which is to say the origin bespoke absence for the Arab poet:

> I write in a language that exiles me . . . a mother exiles her son, poetically, from the moment he takes form in her womb: that is the symbolic image to the relation in reality between the Arab poet and his language. And if we take what the Torah says about Hagar and Ishmael, and what the Qur'an recalled, then maternity and paternity, in addition to language, bore everyone [Arab] . . . in exile. (Adonis 1993: 13)

Following the Judaic tradition, Islam founds another beginning in this origin and yet another exile: "it took language out of its exile on earth and made it inhabit the homeland of revelation (*waḥī*): the sky." (Adonis 1993: 14) The followers of the prophet tried to apply this revelation, and this prophecy turned with practice to dogma, to orthodoxy that took form and is perpetuated until today: "We can say that Arabic poetic life, was from the beginning an exile of words and an exile of system (*niẓām*). And the Arab artist knew, past and present, various types of exile: surveillance, censorship, displacement, prison, death." (Adonis 1993: 15) *Niẓām* is exile for Adonis because it sets up borders and prohibitions, displacing the individual from a private space to the public sphere. So the other becomes a way out, a future directing the self toward the unknown: "The other was always present in the Arabic experience of creativity (*ibdā*'). In the language that the Arabic writer writes in, there are many other languages, ancient and modern. And Arabic, poetically, is a gathering in the form of words." (Adonis 1993: 15) The double absence that the Arab writer lives is that of himself and that of the other, and he lives between two exiles, an interior and an exterior one. This leads Adonis to ask: "How can I speak about freedom, democracy, and human rights and . . . I am not present to myself and for myself, and I am not present for the other? How can I speak when my being (*wujūdī*) is itself exile, and it is exile in . . . the established regime?" (Adonis, Qur'anic 18) And yet the poet, ironically, remains the one whose belonging gets tested before anyone else and who suffers the consequences of writing an identity outside the expected parameters. (Adonis 1993: 70)

Adonis contextualizes the state of contemporary Arabic poetry by tracing its demise with canonical Islam. Adonis argues that what has competed with poetry in Arabic societies was not philosophy but religion, since in its original denotation, poetry, before Islam, is prophecy "but without teachings." (Adonis 1993: 61) With Islam, revelation dismisses poetic inspiration and replaces it as the only source of knowledge. (Adonis 1993: 60-61) Poetry's new role is to glorify the truth that Islam proclaimed. (Adonis 1993: 66-67)

The role of poetry has been under interrogation by Arab writers and poets. In the political crises that the Palestinians and the Arab World in general have been facing, poetry was expected to play a role. In "Beirut," the poet asks: "—Do you think our *qaṣīdah* came to naught?" / . . . / we demand a falling harmony from the stone but it does not come/ and the poets have ancient gods." (Darwish 1994: 208) The belatedness is one form of this questioning of poetry and is attributed to the disjointedness of the modern world. The mode of despair that often characterizes the latter poetry of Darwish takes the form of belatedness: "The last train stopped at the last station. And there is no one to save the roses/ The *qaṣīdah* is no more able than the smolder of the sea was." (Darwish 1994: 335)

The power of poetry is deemed questionable: "A country gathers the ruins of my song/ what use is my song?" (Darwish 1994: 274) And yet the demand for poetry in times of crises remains. The crisis in the period of the siege of Beirut in 1982 is perhaps more about how to write rather than whether to write. Darwish wants to redefine the "political" especially when it is associated with poetry: "What threatens literary writing the most is the daily aspect of the 'political.'" (Cited by Nabulsi 1987: 9) Darwish writes: "The notion of political poetry has been confused with the notion of the event, isolated from the historical context." (Darwish 1987: 34-35) At the time that Beirut was under siege, the intellectuals were asking for a *qaṣīdah* that would somehow upset the balance of power. They expected a *qaṣīdah* then, for if it came later it would not be of use. Darwish comments that the idea of the poet writing his silence would have been enough to kill him at that time. (Darwish 1987: 35)

Darwish's dilemma in writing is expressed in his poetry when he declares:

> For thirty years
> he writes his poems and forgets about me
> . . .
> every death an image,
> every journey image. Every country
> image. Enough I said.
> We died thoroughly.
> Where is my humanity? Where am I?
> He writes his poems and builds a crumbling world around him. (Darwish 1994: 284-85)

The poetic condition transforms a world that is disintegrating in reality into another death in poetry. And yet not to write would lead to complete effacement: "What would happen . . . if we left death without witnessing and without beauty . . . What would happen if this absurd despair in our life was left without a creative force to transform its signs to hope?" (Darwish 1990: 76) He names the case of Khalil Hawi, the Lebanese poet, who literally killed himself so that, in the words of Darwish, "he would not see anything and would not testify to anything." (Darwish 1990: 81) The unbearable responsibility is for him to write and to testify in the silence of poetry. For Darwish, the poem is also necessary not only as a refuge but also as a cultural existence that cannot be refuted especially when the Palestinians' collective claims for self-determination have long been contested.

The *qaṣīdah* becomes poetic survival. It cryptically safeguards the homeland in its absence. Darwish is aware nonetheless of the limitations of poetry. "Difficult is poetry, not because its truth has not been evident yet, but because it has not been able to prove its necessity . . . nevertheless, we continue writing poetry from the moment that one needed to break his solitude from this world, and since he felt the need to deepen his solitude in it." (Darwish 1985: 215) The latter stage of Darwish's poetry shows the move toward the *qaṣīdah* as a long poem with a dramatic construction and multiple voices. It allows him a dialogue with his literary heritage and to guard a reservoir of the past. His poems increasingly develop a more mythic time with a receding narrativity. They move toward "epic" while emphasizing the continuity of the lyric. (Nabulsi 1987: 236-240) His later work reveals an attempt to move beyond a national allegory and toward a historical project, one that charts a new beginning and border lyric while allowing space for a collective voice. His poetry is henceforth a marking of desire and its unattainable object, inaugurating the home as poetic writing but also as a desert of wandering.

As with Djebar, he sees possibility in the tension of the aporetic. Like Djebar, also, Darwish has turned to the early "origins"—in his case that of the Book of Genesis, pre-Islamic poetry, and Andalusian poetry—to insist on *nashīd* as a perpetual search for home in an open historical struggle. Through his vision of *nashīd*, he creates a poetic vision that heralds a new beginning as an aesthetic and historical necessity.

Notes

1. Please note that all translations from the Arabic are mine, unless otherwise indicated.

2. See Barbara Harlow, "Palestine or Andalusia: the literary response to the Israeli invasion of Lebanon," *Race and Class* 26 (1984): 43.

3. Interestingly, Darwish only considers his writing after the Beirut siege in 1982 to be poetic. This was expressed in a personal meeting with him which took place on April 9 and 10, 1996 in Ramallah, West Bank and which corresponded with Darwish's first visit to the "West Bank." It was his first "return" since the early seventies to Palestine.

4. The debate on modern Arabic poetry is around the forms and meanings of poetry as well as the relation between poetry and "reality." See Helit Yeshurun, "Je ne reviens pas, je viens," in *La Palestine comme métaphore: Entretiens*, translated from the Arabic by Elias Sanbar and from the Hebrew by Simone Bitton (Paris: Actes Sud, 1997), 130. Darwish is more protective of the Arabic poetic heritage within the "modernist" movement and insists on the musicality of poetry in rhythm and rhyme. For Darwish, "modernity" in poetry has to be a natural continuation of an Arabic poetic tradition, and any real development of Arabic poetry has to work from within the history of Arabic poetry. Meter for Darwish was never an obstacle to developing the *qaṣīdah*. He expresses his fear that those trying to destroy *wazn* in the *qaṣīdah* are not familiar enough with the Arabic language. See Mahmoud Salih al-Shanti, "Khuṣūṣīyāt al-Ru'iyah wal-Tashkīl fī sh'ir Maḥmūd Darwīsh," [The Particular Vision and Form of Darwish's Poetry] *Fuṣūl* 4-7 (October 1986-March 1987): 143. Adonis's concern, on the other hand, is with language which for him only expresses itself and the promise of the real rather than the "real": "the value of the poetic work does not lie in the extent of it being 'real' or 'true', i.e. in the extent that it is 'representative' or 'reflective' but lies in its ability to make language say more than it says ordinarily, i.e. in creating new relations between language and the world." Adonis, "Fī al-Shi'rīyah," [On the Poetic] *Al-Karmel* 38 (1990): 144.

5. Darwish expresses his indebtedness to his "paternal" influences: the Palestinian poets Abu Salma, Ibrahim Touqan, and 'Abdul Rahim Mahmoud. In his earlier poetry, he is no less influenced by Arabic poets such as Nizar Qabani, Amal Danqal, Mohammed Mattar, Badr Shakir al-Sayyab, Abdel Wahab al-Bayati, Adonis, Salah 'Abd al-Sabbour.

6. The Arabic meter is based on the number of musical units: one long syllable and one short.

7. An example of the endurance of musicality is the poetry of the Andalusian Ibn Zaydoun. It succeeds in being remembered "by heart," perhaps more than any other Andalusian poetry. See Salma Khadra Jayyusi, ed., *The Legacy of Muslim Spain* (New

York: Brill, 1992), 343. But poetry itself as heritage was considered able to grant identity to the Arab poet. Until perhaps recently, poetry has been the preferred literary mode. Al-Jahiz states: "every nation resorts to a special form to chart its achievements and preserve its characteristics and the pre-Islamic Arabs resorted to rhymed and metered poetry to preserve its identity." See Sabry Hafez, "The Transformation of the Qasida Form in Modern Arabic Poetry," in *Qasida Poetry in Islamic Asia and Africa: Eulogy's Bounty, Meaning's Abundance,* edited by Stefan Sperl and Christopher Schackle, volume two (NY: E.J. Brill, 1996), 101. The etymology emphasizes this special status. In the words of al-Jahiz (d. 869) "*Dīwān al-'Arab,*" the register of the Arabs, granting Arab poets a special social status. The Arabic word for poetry, "*shi'r*, is derived from the verb denoting a special kind of knowledge. Hafez argues that viewing poetry as the literary genre needed to mediate reality explains why classical Arabic poetry reappeared in the neoclassical movement of Arabic poetry as an important component "of the quest for national identity at the turn of the century." (Hafez 1996: 102) Sperl adds that in pre-Islamic times where there was little permanence in life, "it was their one and only lasting expression of communal memory and identity." Stefan Sperl and Christopher Shackle, "Introduction," in *Qasida Poetry in Islamic Asia and Africa: Classical Traditions and Modern Meanings*, edited by Stefan Sperl and Christopher Shackle, vol. one (New York: E.J. Brill, 1996), 5.

8. Asked by *Libération* why he writes, Darwish responds that in writing poetry he is really conducting a dialogue with himself but admits that the "drive" for writing "is the desire to find a compensation for a loss that cannot be found outside of writing. When I lose love, the homeland, time, a beautiful scene, I recall it in writing." "'Libération': Why do you Write?," *Aswār* 11 (1991): 139.

9. Barbara Harlow, "Memory and Historical Record: The Literature and Literary Criticism of Beirut, 1982," *Left Politics and the Literary Profession*, edited by Lennard J. Davis and M. Bella Mirabella (New York: Columbia University Press, 1990), 192.

10. Harlow, "Memory and Historical Record," 192.

11. Blanchot names this necessary interruption "mastery," whereby the hand that does not write is able to intervene and interrupt the writing at the critical moment. Maurice Blanchot, *The Space of Literature*, translated by Ann Smock (Lincoln: University of Nebraska Press, 1982), 25.

12. Darwish speaks of the crypt as a suspended space, "closed and at the same time open, a place where strangers gather, meet, and talk, a refuge" (Rahman 1996) In a sense, it is a place of possibility and hence it is not surprising that he links the crypt with Andalusia.

13. A notable example is the poetry of King al-Mu'tamid, Ibn Abbad of Sevilla (reigned 1068-1091), who recites: "Would that I knew if ever again I shall sleep with a stream behind me and a garden before me." James T. Monroe, ed. and trans, *Hispano-Arabic Poetry* (Berkeley: University of California Press, 1974). I have modified the translation slightly.

14. See Yeshurun, "Je ne reviens pas, je viens", 118. The significance of Andalusia is evident in such works of Darwish as *Aḥada 'Ashara Kawkaban* [Eleven Stars] which was written in memory of the five centuries since the expulsion of Jews and Arabs from Spain and the accidental arrival of Christopher Columbus to the Americas. *Eleven Stars* can be found in volume two of Mahmoud Darwish's *Dīwān,* [Complete Collection of Poems] two vols. (Beirut: Dār al-'Awdah, 1994).

15. Darwish no longer attempts to posit a space of return in turning back as he has done in his earlier poetry. Earlier he wrote: "I will not leave/-Mother await us at the door. We are returning." (Darwish, *Dīwān*, vol. one, 114)

16. Critics such as Barbara Harlow indicate that the "return" is a prevalent theme in Andalusian poetry. See Harlow, "Palestine or Andalusia: the literary response to the Israeli invasion of Lebanon," 43.

17. Darwish's predominant poetic voice in the poem is the collective "we." He defines the identity of the "we" further on as *sabāyah*. *Sabāyah* are women who are carried off in war by the victors. The condition of the people is gendered. The status of being *sabāyah* and then being handed back points to a loss of "honor" and "identity" that has happened in the meantime.

18. See Shakir al-Nabulsi, *Majnūn al-Turāb: Dirāsah fī Shi'r wa Fikr Maḥmūd Darwīsh* [A Study of the Poetry and Thought of Darwish] (Beirut: al-Mu'assassah al-Arabīyah lil-Dirāsāt wal-Nashr, 1987), 356. Adonis reviews the etymology of the word "*fikr,*" or thought, and finds that it is on the side of the heart and not the mind. It means making *al-khāṭir* in something, and *al-khāṭir* is what occurs to one's heart. But the mind in its original etymology is from the side of *akhlāq* (manners, decorum), that which prohibits. *Fikr* then is a mixture of intuition and contemplation. Adonis, *Al-Shi'rīyah al-'Arabīyah* [Arabic Poetic], second ed. (Beirut: Dār al-Adāb, 1989), 71.

19. Adonis, *Muqaddamah lil-Shi'r al-'Arabī* [An Introduction to Arabic poetry] (Beirut: Dār al- 'Awdah, 1983), 25. Adonis, however, is quick to relegate a defining character to one period. In pre-Islamic poetry, there were after all the *Ṣa'ālīk* poets who did not share this common experience and did not seek to partake of this communal existence.

20. The "beginnings" of Arabic poetry have often been located within the time frame of the sixth century to the thirteenth. An oral tradition in its beginnings, the poem was transmitted from poet to reciter and transmitted through generations, from one reciter to another. The poem, performed before an audience, was usually combined with music. The poet's expected role was to praise tribal virtues. There were, however, vagabond poets, *Ṣa'ālīk,* such as al-Shanfara, who rejected and were rejected by their societies. Since the early development of Arabic poetry was not preserved, we find examples of both the short, monothematic poem (*qitā'*) and the multi-sectional, polythematic *qaṣīdah*. The latter was especially valued by early Muslim rulers and became a standard for the study of the classical Arabic language. Seven (and later ten) were chosen as *mu'allaqāt,* as the most illustrious collection of early Arabic poetry.

21. See Adonis, *Shi'rīyah,* 12. Poetry was considered by the history of Arabic criticism as *sina'a* (making) or *shu'ūr* (feeling, knowledge).

22. While the received view is that the structure of pre-Islamic *qaṣīdah* is fragmented, some argue that the choice and ordering of the various parts are intended to illustrate the contrasts in community life. The various parts consist of: *naṣīb* or erotic prelude within the context of *aṭlāl,* a section describing a poet's arrival at a deserted encampment, a transitional section describes the *raḥīl,* departure or the desert journey, and then *gharaḍ,* the purpose of the poem which is often to bolster the community through praise of its virtues. Various segments of the *qaṣīdah* gradually evolved into distinct genres such as hunt poems, wine poems of which a notable example is the poetry of Abu Nawwas.

Part II

The Reconstitution of Home through Language

Chapter Four

The Language of Home and the Fragmented Heritage: Assia Djebar's *L'amour, la fantasia*

"Everything is clearer
and nearer to us
than the words we choose
to speak of it."
—Adonis, *Al-Kitāb* 53.

"I have become to myself the country of destitution."
—St. Augustine, cited in *Fantasia: An Algerian Cavalcade* 216.

"*L'Amour, la fantasia* est ainsi une double autobiographie où la langue française devient le personnage principal."
—Djebar, "Le Discours de Francfort pour le prix de paix"

In *L'amour, la fantasia*, Assia Djebar writes of her desire to redress the absence of home: "I do not claim here to be either a story-teller or a scribe. On the territory of dispossession, I would that I could sing."[1] Djebar's prose seeks literary forms that can face dispossession, and that can carry this threatened longing for home and the promise that lies within it.[2] This valorization of lyrical poetry corresponds to Darwish's quest for "divine prose," a sense of the limitation of their individual endeavors. However, the two writers seem to call attention to the siege of narrative: mythic narratives turned to history, death-dealing narratives, and narratives yet unborn. In *and our faces my heart, brief as photos*, John Berger distinguishes between poems and stories:

> Poems, even when narrative, do not resemble stories. All stories are about battles, of one kind or another, which end in victory and defeat. Everything moves toward the end when the outcome will be known.
> Poems, regardless of any outcome, cross the battlefields, tending the wounded, listening to the wild monologues of the triumphant or the fearful. They bring a kind of peace . . . by recognition and the promise that what has been experienced cannot disappear as if it had never been . . . The promise is that language has acknowledged, has given shelter to the experience which demanded, which cried out . . . Poems are nearer to prayers . . . In all poetry words are a presence before they are a means of communication. (Berger 1984: 21-22)

For Berger, but also for Darwish and Djebar, poems are ultimately "wagers on lastingness." (Steiner 1991: 57) In addition to their particular temporality, they also partake of the physical nature of the human body. As George Steiner indicates, "the meaning of poetry and the music of those meanings, which we call metrics, are also of the human body." (Steiner 1991: 9) Djebar evokes the physicality and rhythm of writing to reinforce the link between writing and possession, even as she announces the ultimate limits of such possession. "When the hand writes . . . carefully bending forward . . . crouching, swaying to and fro...as in an act of love. When reading, the eyes take their time, delight in caressing the curves, while the calligraphy suggests the rhythm of the scansion: as if the writing marked the beginning and the end of possession." (Djebar 1993: 180)

Writing, for Djebar, is a threshold where possession may become possible in the inherent act of dispossession that is writing. The search for form points to the limitations of writing home, a writing that keeps taking place only to proffer its own materiality. It is nonetheless the physicality of writing that embodies possibility and rhythmically engulfs the maternal cry of welcome and of protest, of love and of violence that Djebar seeks to reveal.

Similarly, reading always proceeds "as if" in order not only to possess meaning and intelligibility from writing but also to mark the possibility of survival. Maurice Blanchot, in his reading of Kafka, entertains literature as possibility: "art can succeed where knowledge fails: because it is and is not true enough to become the way, and too unreal to change into an obstacle." (Blanchot 1995: 19) He writes:

> Art is an as if. Everything happens as if we were in the presence of truth, but this presence is not one, that is why it does not forbid us to go forward. Art claims knowledge when knowledge is a step leading to eternal life, and it claims non-knowledge when knowledge is an obstacle drawn up in front of this life. It changes its meaning and its sign. It destroys itself while it survives. That is its imposture, but that is also its greatest dignity, that same that justifies the saying 'Writing is a form of prayer.'" (Blanchot 1995: 19, emphasis is mine)

It is from this duplicity of writing (and its duality as disappearance of the maternal oral cry and its survival in writing) that Djebar begins, from the inherited "*cri*" already there in *écriture*.

Writing for Djebar remains that hand extended by the father, a borrowed one, a severed fragment from the past, one that cannot be completely claimed nor can it appropriate the present even as it seeks self-possession; it is always already both overtaken and violated. Following Djebar, one wonders where possession "beyond beginning and end" is demarcated within writing, also where her text begins and ends, where the boundaries are drawn between epigraph, epilogue, text, and pre-text. Not only does her work resist a founding moment from which to begin despite the profusion of dates, it also refuses closure.

This chapter considers the fragment as key to the reconstitution of home in writing and as a facet of discontinuity in the heritage of Djebar. Djebar gathers fragments of the past handed to her primarily by a paternal heritage that she translates through her own fragmentary writing. Writing through the fragment marks absence in her ventures of reconstruction and struggle against effacement of the maternal past. But while writing gives voice, this voice remains a "hieroglyph of a wild, collective voice." (Djebar 1993: 56) The fashioning of this voice in the project of reconstruction is what Djebar foregrounds as fiction. The fragment, as written remnant of an effaced past, allows for the possibility of testimony for Djebar.

The link of home to writing is exemplified in Djebar's inheritance of *écriture* as linguistic exile. This articulation of home already challenges its restitution by nationalist modes of reading. If we consider the French language that the father passes on to his daughter, and which allows her to write the forbidden love letters and later to read the fragmentary written accounts of the French chroniclers on the conquest of Algeria, then this heritage is not proper to the self. It is a heritage not in one's language and not in one's mode of expression. It is an unexpected inheritance of conquest and of violence that is given out lovingly to the female child by the father. It is also the father as symbolic order who is inherited with language. George Steiner suggests that language is always inherited along with the figure of the father: "our language inheritance is the father figure, the proponent figure of speech, which threatens to devour the autonomy, the novelty, the immediacy to ourselves (the idiolect) toward which our feelings, thoughts, and needs strive." (Steiner 1991: 108) The narrative of the gendered self is also that of a transformed language, one inhabited by exile and by the possibility of freedom, by disconnection and by solidarity.

Writing is demarcated as a forbidden inheritance for females by the social order of the father. And yet, Djebar suggests, it liberates in its unveiling, allowing one freedom of movement and the words inaccessible passages. It also allows for reconstructing the past, and hence for a glimpse of it in its disappearance. To probe the implications of a literary project that seeks reconstruction of home from the fragments of the past will allow us to delve into the enactment of writing as home for Djebar in a narrative of a particularly complicated identity.

Djebar not only fragments her text in her play of incorporating different genres, in her binding of love and war, and in her ambivalent use of the French language, Djebar's text is also a composite of intertextual fragments.[3]

L'amour, la fantasia as a Work of Translation

Djebar, as one herself, sees the historian as a translator who reads the past with the present in order to probe its discontinuities. Like Darwish, it is through a work of history that a different vision of home becomes possible. While Darwish brings together poetry and history, Djebar attempts to do so through a narrative that cannot be easily settled solely into fiction, autobiography, or testimony. Thus translation would disrupt rather than interpret the presumed continuity. Just like Walter Benjamin, she conceives of the past as fragmentary, accessible only through moments of crisis: "the past can be seized only as an image which flashes at the instant when it can be recognized and is never seen again . . . For every image of the past that is not recognized by the present as one of its own concerns threatens to disappear irretrievably." (Benjamin 1969: 225) The past is only accessed when the fleeting image is acknowledged, in other words, testified to as testimony. Likewise, translation's historicity enables a questioning of the status of the "original," where history is neither a recollection of a state before fragmentation nor a subjective consciousness of this fragmentation. It is translation as a fragment of a fragment that bears the tension of the necessity of witnessing and the impossibility of doing so. Benjamin's notion of translation as a broken fragment is useful for Djebar because it follows the logic of heritage rather than identity. It also presents the translator as a historian, one committed to the vanquished of the past and to those struggling in the present.

Djebar's *L'amour, la fantasia* is a work of translation (translating the fragments of the past into the present, the historical into the personal and the literary, the oral into the written, etc.).[4] The historical account of this text begins with the capture of Algiers in 1830 and extends to the War of Independence of 1954-62. For covering the War of Conquest, Djebar relies on her archival research and obscure fragments of eye-witness accounts written at the time by participants in the war who wrote either for publication or simply to their own families. The oral testimonies of the women who participated in the struggle form the basis for covering the War of Independence.

Her text more importantly performs itself as translation, as displacement.[5] In crossing borders of language, time, national cultures, genres, and strict gender demarcations, it crosses forbidden limits. But the limits themselves become the writing of imbricated borders. She interlocks fragment and narrative, history and translation, testimony and fiction. Inherited generic differences are destabilized if not undone by Djebar. The first "*roman*" of a quartet, *L'amour, La fantasia*, is simultaneously an autobiography, a historical narrative of the effacement of Algerian history under French colonization, a rewriting of French archives, and a transcription of oral testimonies by Algerian women. Her work announces itself, in an exemplary gesture of testimonials, as paradoxically a "fiction." Evading the posture of testimony for a moment in a "soliloquy," she ruminates:

> My fiction is this attempt at autobiography, weighed down under the oppressive burden of my heritage. Shall I sink beneath the weight? . . . But the tribal legend criss-cross the empty spaces, and the imagination crouches in the silence when loving words of the unwritten mother-tongue remain unspoken . . . language conveyed like the inaudible babbling of a nameless, haggard mummer . . . How shall I find the strength to tear off my veil, unless I have to use it to bandage the running sore nearby which words exude? (Djebar 1993: 218)

Implied in this narrative is the impossibility to speak from the "inside," in one's "mother tongue." What is being "testified to" is absence, as the burden of heritage. She nonetheless attempts to translate this silence in her venture of reconstruction. Testimony is unveiled as a duplicitous intervention. It is not the speaking subject that testifies but her language, the imposed French language handed to her by a father wearing a European suit and a fez, "little girl going to school for the first time . . . walking hand in hand with her father." (Djebar 1993: 3) Problems of testimony, reconstruction, narration, and writing are situated at the level of language as a symbolic system, which allows for naming, appropriation and representation, a language which, in attempting to witness, cannot escape the repetitive gesture of violence. "Le viol, non dit, ne sera pas violé." [Violation unspoken will not be violated] (Djebar 1993: 226) There is a central aporia: if one represents, one risks reproducing, however slightly, the gesture of violence. But if one does not speak, one risks effacing the traces. Djebar throughout foregrounds her role, posing her ventures of testimony as aporetic questions: "Are these the ghosts of the raped, flitting over the piled-up corpses? Is it the spirit of an unacknowledged love, felt only in an intuitive sense of guilt?" (Djebar 1993: 16) The distanced fascination of the writers who report the war for Paris is not only acknowledged by Djebar but perhaps shared as well. She asks: "what if this fascination also paralyzed the threatened camp?" (Djebar 1993: 16) And: "But why, above the corpses that will rot on successive battlefields, does this first Algerian campaign reverberate with the sounds of an obscene copulation?" (Djebar 1993: 19)

Not unlike the work of linguistic translation, Djebar's writing threatens the security of borders. Steiner reflects on the destabilizing force of the process of translation: "Translated into saying . . . the conceptual process, the deed of imagining can abolish, reverse, or confound all categories (themselves embedded in language) of identity and of temporality. Speech can change the rules under which it operates in the course of its operation." (Steiner 1991: 54) The passage of writing entrusted to the translator is not only unstable but is potentially also a violent one. The translator in Djebar's text who carries a letter of peace eventually dies from bearing the written words. "Any document written by 'The Other' proves fatal, since it is a sign of compromise." (Djebar 1993: 33)

Just as the written words are perceived as a sign of political compromise so is writing for women seen to compromise them.

Djebar in turn foregrounds her position as translator. "This language was formerly used to entomb my people; when I write it today I feel like the messenger of old, who bore a sealed missive which might sentence him to death or to the dungeon." (Djebar 1993: 215) For her to use the language of the "former enemy" complicates her work of testimony further and breaks down the frontiers of this passage of translation.

Djebar violates the prohibition against "laying bare one's self" and "attempting an autobiography in the former enemy's language" in order to carry out her project of reconstruction. (Djebar 1993: 215) To reconstitute the effaced horror of the Algerian past, she relies on the fragmented accounts written in letters by French fighters and observers. These accounts were written in the same French language that silenced the Algerians and which she now uses. Despite its wounds, French is nonetheless her access to these fragments and to writing. Her re-appropriation of these fragments allows her to reread the traces of a writing that has been erased. This further allows her to rewrite the story of Algerians centering on women. Her reading of these French accounts further destabilizes them, wrenching them from their previous context and from their process of effacement. To this French writing, she attempts to integrate oral accounts by women. The disjunction created between her fictionalized rewriting and the concealments of the letters reveals the fiction of these autobiographic letters and her own fictional reconstruction becomes perhaps a more significant historical narrative.

This narrative presents itself as a writing that interrogates and reflects on the act of writing, all the while aware of the fiction of referentiality and the confrontation with the other language.[6] The narrator who poses as a self-conscious "witness" does not refrain from mingling the personal story with the historical narrative of the Algerian people and making them indissociable. Nor is the past singular, it is the personal past of her childhood and the collective memory, the 1830 invasion of Algeria and the 1954 war of liberation.

The History of Love and Fantasia

The figure of the father represents plural and aporetic aspects of heritage, tradition and modernity, love and fantasia (warring), fragments of which could be reconstituted for a different vision of home.[7] The first part of the text, entitled "The Capture of the City or Love Letters," already imbricates love in the historical events of war. The early personal and historical accounts are brought together, inextricably. The dominant theme of love is depicted against fantasia. Love always there, precedes any warring as *amour* precedes *fantasia* in naming this text. It is a love that remains undisclosed, however. "It is as if these parading warriors . . . are mourning their unrequited love for my Algeria. I should first and foremost be moved by . . . the suffering of the anonymous victims, which their writings resurrect; but I am strangely haunted by the agitation of the killers, by their obsessional unease." (Djebar 1993: 57) Djebar is forced to share in this love, if only to simply identify her own love for Algeria.

Love is intertwined in a letter, in the written words. The father's love is relayed through the gift of writing and is expressed in writing.[8] At the same time, her father's prohibition is against writing love letters. It is paradoxically in the words of the "other" that she attempts to write this love: "Love, if I managed to write it down, would approach a critical point: there where lies the risk of exhuming buried cries, those of yesterday and as well as those of a hundred years ago."[9] (Djebar 1993: 63) This attempt at writing love would allow her to "exhume the buried cries" of the dead. Love is already there in writing as the ambivalent cry: "love is the cry, the persistent pain which feeds upon itself, while only a glimpse is vouchsafed of the horizon of happiness." (Djebar 1993: 107)

Djebar musters ammunition of many languages for women denied an intimate expression of love or desire: "French for secret missives; Arabic for our stifled aspirations toward God-the-father . . . ; Lybico-Berber which takes us back to the pagan idols-mother-gods of pre-Islamic Mecca. The fourth language, for all females, young or old, cloistered or half-emancipated, remains that of the body." (Djebar 1993: 180) Djebar asserts that the body is invisible without words. At the same time, writing serves as another veiling of the body, a veiling that makes the body invisible in its visibility. Writing in the language of the other also changes one's perception of and relation to the body: "Writing the enemy's language is more than just a matter of scribbling down a muttered monologue under your very nose; to use this alphabet involves placing your elbow some distance in front of you to form a bulwark; however, in this twisted position, the writing is washed back to you." (Djebar 1993: 215) Writing becomes veiling and unveiling in the appropriation of French. As Clarisse Zimra suggests, "[w]oman becomes a textual trope of absence, even when on display." (Zimra 1992: 70) And the body is also at stake in writing as it is unveiled. It is exposed in its enactment of love, in its cries as the writing recalls the voices of the past. Writing itself is as much about evading individual effacement as it is about the survival of collective memory.

> L'amour, ses cris ("s'écrit"): my hand as I write in French makes the pun on love affairs that are aired; all my body does is to move forward, stripped naked, and when it discovers the ululations of my ancestresses on the battlefields of old, it finds that it is itself at stake: it is no longer a question of writing only to survive. (Djebar 1993: 214)

The French language, which allows for a writing of love, is also for Djebar the language through which violence speaks. It is ambivalently constructed as one of violation and freedom, of home and exile. Her paternal inheritance of this language both liberates and exiles her. It liberates her from the confinement of a patriarchal tradition, but it exiles her from the women of her own culture. "French . . . the language that my father had been at pains for me to learn, serves as a go-between, and from now a double, contradictory sign reigns over my initiation." (Djebar 1993: 4) French lifts the burden of the inherited taboos, but it also implies dissociation from others of her tribe. "Once I had discovered the meaning of the words—those same words that are revealed to the unveiled body—I cut myself adrift." (Djebar 1993: 5) The image of cutting adrift in this discourse of liberation is indistinct from the ship, which recalls the invading French. Djebar further reminds us that the oral source of the French language for the colonized is violence; it is the language of law courts, of words of accusation, and of legal procedure. (Djebar 1993: 215) Writing in French becomes a way of inheriting this colonial violence as well as a way of resisting it. "Words that are explicit become such boastings as the braggard uses; and elected silence implies resistance still intact." (Djebar 1993: 178) This veiling allows her resistance, the ability to write under a pseudonym about the women in her country and about the war, as well as to "affirm" herself just like in the forbidden love letters written by the young women: "As if the French language suddenly had eyes, and lent them me to see into liberty." (Djebar 1993: 181)

Structural Fragmentation

Intertextuality structures *L'amour, la fantasia* along paternal figures, reflecting the plurality of heritage. (Donadey 1993: 107) Fromentin's words frame her novel, while the three main sections are divided into very short pieces and are introduced by an epigraph to each section. The first part opens with an epigraph from Barchou de Penhoën followed by an account of her father taking her to school. Ibn Khaldun opens the second part, while one of the epigraphs to the third part is from St. Augustine, and the other is from Ludwig van Beethoven. The third part, "Voices from the Past," is structured as in a musical composition, divided into five movements where each movement begins with a "voice" and ends with "embraces."

An ending fragment further follows each section. The first part, for instance, is concluded with a section entitled "Deletion." It is not only a structural fragment but it speaks of the fragment as well. This italicized fragment is embedded within an alternation of plain text and italicization of passages of poetry, an alternation that marks ruptures as borders for the personal and historical. It speaks of fragments in its turn where "faint images flake off from the rock of Time." (Djebar 1993: 46) Djebar seeks to capture these forgotten, "liberating" moments that Walter Benjamin has spoken of: "And for a fleeting moment, I glimpse the mirror-image of the foreign inscription, reflected in Arabic letters, writ from right to left in the mirror of suffering; the letters fade into pictures of the mountainous Hoggar in prehistoric times." (Djebar 1993: 46) The ephemeral image of Hoggar emerging from the fading letters is one of suffering and effacement already there inherited in the maternal figure as other. The image glimpsed of writing, already pointing to the absence of thing and to writing's own disappearance, is that of otherness, foreign but reflected in Arabic letters.

The difficulty of reading this writing that reflects the effacement of the maternal figure lies in the fact that it also requires impossible rigor and a certain vulnerability: "To read this writing, I must lean over backwards, plunge my face into the shadows, closely examine the vaulted roof of rock . . . lend an ear to whispers that rise up from time out of mind . . . Alone, stripped bare, unveiled, I face these images of darkness." (Djebar 1993: 46) Not unlike the task of writing, the process of reading unveils the reader as well. Djebar, who reads the divine command "Read" made in the cave as the Angel Gabriel unveiled the Qur'anic revelation to Muhammad, is exempted from the ritual of female veiling. When the familial matriarchs question her mother as to why the young girl is not veiled, the mother answers "she reads," which in spoken Arabic also means she studies. Reading provides for revelation, and for her it is that of her own body. This revelation is also mediated through the body.

> This language which I learn demands the correct posture for the body, on which the memory rests for its support. The childish hand . . . begins to write. "Read!" The fingers laboring on the tablet send back the signs to the body, which is simultaneously reader and servant. The lips having finished their muttering, the hand will once more do the washing, proceeding to wipe out what is written on the tablet: this is the moment of absolution, like touching the hem of death's garment. Again, it is the turn of writing, and the circle is completed. (Djebar 1993: 184)

Reading approximates prayer, a prayer that is incidentally a series of ritualized body movements accompanying Qur'anic recitals. Reading is performative, submitting to the command "Read" by reading it.[10] The repetitive move from reading to writing is predicated on erasure in Djebar's formulation; this erasure is what provides absolution, a protection not only for the reader but for the writing itself as well in its repetition.[11]

Heritage

Djebar encounters her heritage as fractured. It is divided between a paternal heritage where love recedes and a maternal heritage is in retreat: "How are the sounds of the past to be met as they emerge from the well of bygone centuries? . . . And my body reverberates with sounds from the endless landslide of generations of my lineage." (Djebar 1993: 46) Heritage is expressed in the familiar familial tropes. The beginning of her narrative juxtaposes the paternal father passing on to her the French language and the mythical mother in deletion. Another juxtaposition is placed between that same Hoggar and Abraham whose ballad is situated toward the end of the text.

"The Ballad of Abraham," a fragment of the overall heritage she invokes, points to the convergences and separations of paternal traditions inherited. This heritage offers her the opportunity for dialogue through song. "Tradition would seem to decree that entry through its gate is by submission, not by love. Love, which the most simple of settings might inflame, appears dangerous. There remains music." (Djebar 1993: 169) Music is perhaps that exceptional excess that is allowed a cultural space. It is also a response to longing, a possibility, and a "promise."[12]

Djebar offers a reading of the ballad of Abraham, seeing the primacy of love in that story. She also sees love in the story of Muhammad, a love rendered secondary to submission if not altogether irrelevant in traditional Islam. This primacy of submission is valorized in traditional considerations of the figure of Abraham. The paradigmatic father, father of Arabs and Jews, he dispossesses and exiles one son as well as acquiesces to sacrifice his Isaac.[13] But Ishmael is forever the remainder, and in the texts of Djebar he is connected to music.[14] It is the submission of Isaac that made it compelling for her. "I loved the simplicity of Isaac's song." (Djebar 1993: 171) But the story was never that simple as it has been passed on, since it valorizes submission over love and points to that threatening possibility of foreclosing one's future for one's past. Djebar locates a discontinuity and attempts a new reading of this story.

Her narrative is framed with the father, whether it is her Algerian father, the literary fathers of St. Augustine and Ibn Khaldun, or the French figures such as Fromentin or Pélissier. It is an inheritance usually bestowed on males, which she is aware of being privileged to receive. One of the epigraphs to the third part is from St. Augustine who, after five hundred years of Roman occupation of his homeland, writes his own biography in Latin. Both father of the Catholic Church and of the western autobiography form, he, like Djebar, writes his story in the language of the other. (Djebar 1993: 241-42) "And his writing presses into service, in all innocence, the same language as Caesar or Sulla," writers and generals of the successful 'African Campaign.'" (Djebar 1993: 215) She inscribes her work in this heritage that precedes an Arabic one.

Another great figure that she claims for her heritage is the famous historian Ibn Khaldun, who opens the second part "The cries of the fantasia." He also writes his autobiography in the dominant language of the other, that being Arabic. In opening this section, there seems to be an implicit comparison between the violence of the Arab conquerors and the violence of the French occupation.

> As with Augustine, it matters little to him that he writes in a language introduced into the land of his fathers by conquest and accompanied by bloodshed! A language imposed by rape as much as by love . . . Ibn Khaldun is now nearly seventy years of age: after an encounter with Tamerlane—his last exploit—he prepares to die in exile in Egypt. He suddenly obeys a yearning to turn back on himself: and he becomes the subject and object of a dispassionate autopsy. (Djebar 1993: 216)

Djebar claims the lineage of St. Augustine and Ibn Khaldun not only because they wrote in the language of their conquerors and did violence to writing, but also because they are fathers of the forms of autobiography and history, which she employs. She names them as her own, fellow compatriots, so as not to be exiled. For Djebar proclaims that speaking of one's self outside the language of the ancestors exiles one. But the language of the ancestors when it is written is always a borrowed one. (Djebar 1993: 178)

She in turn also claims the French language, the writing of the French chroniclers. Inheritance becomes simultaneously liberating and dead weight. It is a language that she not only masters but also exploits poetically so that it yields beautiful passages around her own disinheritance. "The French language could offer me all its inexhaustible treasures, but not a single one of its terms of endearment would be destined for my use." (Djebar 1993: 27) Commenting on the voluminous amount of print written by so many fighting men and on the fact that linguistic representation is itself violent, she writes: "And words themselves become a decoration . . . words will become their most effective weapons. Hordes of interpreters, geographers, ethnographers . . . will form a pyramid to hide the initial violence from view." (Djebar 1993: 45)

Djebar recognizes that she bears an inescapably ambivalent heritage. "For my part, even when I am composing the most commonplace of sentences, my writing is immediately caught in the snare of the old war between two peoples. So I swing like a pendulum from images of war (but always in the past) to the expression of a contradictory, ambiguous love." (Djebar 1993: 216) Aporia inhabits the heart of the intimate self. Her narrative as well alternates between present and past where her account of the French and Algerians are brought together and are intertwined.

Djebar announces another father figure who is strategic for mediating her move from "fact" to "fiction." The 19th century painter Eugène Fromentin, the official painter of the conquest of Algeria, is important for her literary intervention as she relies on his travel notes in her rewriting: "I intervene to greet the painter who has accompanied me . . . like a second father figure . . . Fromentin offers me an unexpected hand, the hand of an unknown woman he was never able to draw." (Djebar 1993: 226) Djebar wonders about the effect of this hand on the painter who spent more time writing than painting: "Is it the feel of this object in his hand which transforms him from a painter of Algerian hunting scenes into the writer depicting death in words? . . . As if the story passed on to him could only find its final form in words." (Djebar 1993: 167)

Djebar repeats the recounting of this fragment from Fromentin's travelogue, which tells of him picking up a severed hand of an unknown woman and throwing it away. This is the unexpected hand that she takes from him. In this repetition, Djebar adds: "Fromentin picks up out of the dust the severed hand of an anonymous Algerian woman. He throws it down again in his path. Later I seize on this living hand, hand of mutilation and of memory, and I attempt to bring it the *qalam* [pen]." (Djebar 1993: 226) This retrieval of the hand from Fromentin, which is severed, then rejected, then re-appropriated by Djebar as the instrument of writing, enables her to rewrite the story of the mutilated Algeria. Djebar's gesture of picking up the hand becomes an act of testimony by writing the Arabic traces and by attempting to liberate the gendered through inscription. The borrowed hand, a significant recurrence and frame of this novel, is a starting point for writing and for possession, since it is through the hand that one appropriates the world. And yet the hand being severed is also testimony to the inability to narrate what resists narration.

The novel opens and closes on another fragment, a citation from Fromentin's, *Une année dans le sahel*: "A heart-rending cry arose—I can hear it still as I write to you-then the air was rent with screams, then pandemonium broke loose." (Djebar 1993: 1) She, as well, is able to hear these intermittent cries through writing. The ominous last lines that close her novel are an oral reworking of Fromentin's citation: "I wait . . . foreseeing the inevitable moment when the mare's hoof will strike down any woman who dares to stand up freely . . . Yes, in spite of the tumult of my people all around, I already hear, even before it arises and pierces the harsh sky, I hear the death cry in the Fantasia." (Djebar 1993: 227) In this reworking of Fromentin's words, she links the "inevitable" future of Algeria to its past and present where violent warring and subjugation of women prevail over unspoken love.

Djebar also names Pélissier as part of her paternal legacy of writing and of violence. The narrator is "moved by an impulse" to express gratitude to the one that handed her the report, the "butcher-recorder": "After the . . . brutal killing . . . he is overcome with remorse and describes the slaughter he has organized. I venture to thank him . . . for having indulged in a whim to immortalize them in a description of their rigid carcasses . . . for having looked on the enemy otherwise than as a horde of zealots." (Djebar 1993: 78) Her expression of gratitude seeks to emphasize the threat of complete effacement without writing and recording. In rendering a tribute to their remorseful killer, however insincere she may deem it, does she not inescapably commit violence against the memories of victims? In the gesture of gratitude, does she not momentarily forget the victims in order to remember him? (Djebar 1993: 79) Yet it is her own tribe that falls victim to Pélissier's act. Her own act of reconstruction is revealed to be aporetic in its violent ambivalence and necessity.

Writing can potentially grant "voice," one that is not dissociated from what it hears: "one hundred years later . . . I find the strength to speak. Before I catch the sound of my own voice I can hear the death-rattles, the moans of those immured in the Dahra Mountains . . . they provide my orchestral accompaniment." (Djebar 1993: 217) Djebar recognizes that she ultimately shares in this long violent legacy even as she attempts to redress it.

The voice is also a cry that is always there in writing, in the violence of colonialism, in the imposition of the French language, as well as in the silence of the women. "I am alternately the besieged foreigner and the native swaggering off to die, so there is seemingly endless strife between the spoken and the written word." (Djebar 1993: 215) The play on *cri* and *écriture* undermines the dichotomy between orality and writing, and points to the dialogism between the oral and the written. For Djebar, writing is the other language; it is language as other. She is aware of the inherent contradiction in her project. She wants to represent the silence of women and of the dead. But how can one give voice to another long silenced or dead? She asks: "can I pretend to live these voices?" (Djebar 1993: 226) While she nonetheless attempts it through self-conscious fragmentation, and foregrounding of narrative, she simultaneously announces its impossibility.

Writing becomes a way to respond to and redress the amorous aphasia of her veiled and silent "sisters." (Djebar 1993: 142) It allows her to hear the women's silent cries of protest. "Writing does not silence the voice, but awakens it, above all to resurrect so many vanquished sisters." (Djebar 1993: 204) For the veil stretches beyond covering the face or body, it also covers the voice: "To refuse to veil one's voice and start 'shouting', that was really indecent, real dissidence. For the silence of all others suddenly lost its charm and revealed itself for what it was: a prison without reprieve." (Djebar 1993: 204) Djebar attempts to reclaim the cry/voice in writing.

Writing is also linked to self-affirmation for Djebar. "The half-emancipated girl imagines she is calling on his [the father] presence to bear witness: 'You see, I'm writing, and there's no harm in it . . . It's simply a way of saying I exist!'" (Djebar 1993: 58) But inversely the language in which she writes points to the disconnection between her reality and that conveyed by the language she uses: "the [French] words I use convey no flesh-and-blood reality. I learn . . . lists of flowers . . . that I shall never smell . . . In this respect, all vocabulary expresses what is missing in my life . . . I do not realize . . . that, in the conflict between these two worlds, lies an incipient vertigo." (Djebar 1993: 185)

Testimony

Djebar's work, preoccupied as it is with the figure of the father, is also grounded in the oral testimonies of the Algerian women. Some named, some unnamed, some close relatives, others compatriots, Djebar frames their stories with her own voice, as if to simultaneously render the distance of their voices from hers visible, and join hers with their own. At the center of these vignettes is "the ballad of Abraham" as if to locate a source for the tradition of gender exclusion. The stories all relate everyday struggle, personal and national.

Significantly, she ends her narrative on a fragment on Pauline Rolland, an 1848 French revolutionary who was deported to Algeria, before returning to Fromentin who frames her text. Although she is not Algerian, she nonetheless is claimed as an ancestor because of her struggle: "her true heirs . . . the chorus of anonymous women of today . . . could pay homage to her with that ancestral cry of triumph, the ululation of convulsive sisterhood!" (Djebar 1993: 223) Through this ending story, Djebar reveals a heritage imbricated not only in orality and writing but in cultural and linguistic terms as well. Pauline wrote of relating to and living with the women of Algeria, rich and poor; she was able to see them as sisters rather than as others, unlike her countrymen. The story of Pauline "finally sets free" the narrator allowing her to reconfigure her heritage so that her quest for identity is linked to a greater quest for solidarity.

She sustains the tension and ambivalence of inheritance to the end. The epigraph to the ending section, which the story of Rolland begins, includes two definitions of cry, *tzarl-rit*, a cry of misfortune and cry of happiness. The French words that she uses to conjure the voices of the women are the same ones that divide her from them. Djebar cannot access her heritage except through a language imposed, that which is written and which does violence to her retreating oral heritage. While this language may set her apart from the other women, it also reinforces the gender dynamics of reticence: "I cohabit with the French language: I may quarrel with it, I may have bursts of affection . . . If I deliberately provoke an outburst, it is . . . because I am vaguely aware of having been forced into a 'marriage' too young, rather like the little girls of my town who are 'bespoke' in their earliest childhood." (Djebar 1993: 213)

The third part of her narrative is especially testimonial as she relates the stories of the Algerian women in their own voices. When writing, Djebar insists on the necessity of the language of the other for witnessing. She problematizes the valorization of occulary testimony since the usual association of the notions of testimony and witnessing are with seeing, hearing, living and do not include writing. She not only includes but foregrounds writing. There is always an excess of what the witness can see or hear or live. "I . . . read as if I were shrouded in the ancestral veil; with my one free eye perusing the page, where is written more than the eye-witness sees, more than can be heard." (Djebar 1993: 209) She problematizes her role of "witness," pointing to its many limitations: "Can I, twenty years later, claim to revive these stifled voices? And speak for them?" (Djebar 1993: 202) This is no longer an immediate "eye-witness" account. But testimony [and narrative] is always necessarily retrospective and after the fact. In a sense it is impotent since the stakes are no longer the same when one belatedly testifies. "I, in my turn, write, using this language, but more than one hundred and fifty years later." (Djebar 1993: 7) So the problem of memory and language that underlie fictionality are there. This fictionality, however, is often denied in testimonial narratives.

Testimony reveals a double structure: the witness testifies not only to the perceived, lived, and heard of "event" but also to his/her own reliability. The witness is to testify essentially to his/her own ability to tell the "truth," and curiously to his own potency, to his/her generative power.[15] There is a sense of impotency for the witness in this belatedness. "What ghosts will be conjured up when in this absence of expressions of love (love received, 'love' imposed), I see reflection of my own barrenness, my own aphasia." (Djebar 1993: 202) Just like translation, the compelling need for testimony is accompanied by the foreknowledge of the failure to do so. Djebar connects the testimonial writing of the French officials to the love letters written by young Algerian women as being futile. These young women wrote because of their confinement; "they mark their marasmus with their own identity in an attempt to rise above their pathetic plight." (Djebar 1993: 45) The accounts of the French fighters depict "invaders who imagine they are taking the Impregnable City, but who wander aimlessly in the undergrowth of their own disquiet." (Djebar 1993: 45)

Djebar's text seems poignantly aware of how narration and representation cannot escape fictionalization and transformation of what one is trying to see. Claiming all generic identities, she claims also their fiction.[16]

Djebar recognizes that there are only traces of writing that she can work with and hence stays with them in rewriting the history as her story. But this "reconstruction" remains fragmentary in its excess, hallucinatory in its movements. Testimony is revealed as always fleeting and forgotten. (Djebar 1993: 116) It cannot provide a totalizing narrative, and hence the valorization of the fragment even in this paradoxical "narrative." Testimony for Djebar seems to be an inheritance, an exhumed memory that one inhabits and whose aftermath one lives. (Djebar 1993: 92)

Notes

1. See the original in Assia Djebar, *L'amour, la fantasia* (Paris: Éditions Albin Michel, 1995). First edition is that of Jean-Claude Lattès, 1985.

2. George Steiner, in his emphasis on music as granting "real presence," cites Pierre Jean Jouve, the French poet and essayist, who defines "the promise" as "the concrete universal of the challenging and consoling experience of the unfulfilled" and situates it in music. See Steiner, *Real Presences* (Chicago: University of Chicago Press, 1991), 19. For Steiner, literary texts are not unlike the musical composition. Steiner, *Real Presences,* 27.

3. This anticipates her other writing projects where she writes in an intertextual manner, retracing the other writing in its fragments and incorporating it in her writing. In *Loin de Médine,* she reads the historical accounts of the early Islamic century, those of Ibn Hashem, Ibn Sa'd, and Tabari, a period which begins with the death of the prophet Muhammad in order to "resurrect" these forgotten women that traverse the early (and later accounts of Islam).

4. She follows from the traditions of Arabic translations of the ancient Greek manuscripts, especially those commentaries of Ibn Rushd (or Averroes) on Aristotle, to reveal a notion of translation that allows for intertextuality rather than a limited notion of mimesis.

5. In Latin, *translatio* suggests displacement through its meaning of "carrying over".

6. Djebar implicates her own autobiographical project in the inherent contradictions and fictionality of language itself. Writing is also linked to the anonymity of the self in the venture of autobiography. "While I thought I was undertaking a 'journey through myself,' I find I am simply choosing another veil. While I intended every step forward to make me more clearly identifiable, I find myself progressively sucked down into the anonymity of those women of old, my ancestors!" Assia Djebar, *Fantasia: An Algerian Cavalcade,* translated by Dorothy S. Blair (Portsmouth, NH: Heinemann, 1993), 217. The project of autobiography itself resists the anonymity practiced by and required of an Arab woman.

7. Fantasia suggests the Arabic *fantazīyah* which signifies "ostentation" and which is associated with warring. It designates more specifically "a set of virtuoso movements on horseback executed at a gallop, accompanied by loud cries and culminating in rifle shots." See Dorothy S. Blair, "Introduction," *Fantasia: An Algerian Cavalcade*, n. p. It also alludes to an improvisational musical composition. It is in the third part of the novel where the musical references are most insistent and which is divided into five "movements."

8. The cultural transgression of the father, who at one point writes the mother and not the family, hence understood as an open declaration of love, is significant for her since love is articulated but in the language of the conquerors, a language paradoxically imposed and liberating. Her mother's transgression is by referring to her husband by his first name.

9. Djebar seems to make an implicit reference to the pre-Islamic *qaṣīdah* through the desert journey motif.

10. The Qur'an even etymologically suggests that which is to be read, placing the emphasis on reading rather than writing.

11. In Jacques Derrida's discussion of Freud's mystic pad, writing always attempts to safeguard itself. Derrida suggests: "the trace is the erasure of selfhood, of one's own presence, and is constituted by the threat or anguish of its irremediable disappearance, of the disappearance of its disappearance. An inerasable trace is not a trace, it is a full presence." "Freud and the Scene of Writing," in *Writing and Difference*, translated and introduced by Alan Bass (Chicago: The University of Chicago Press, 1978), 196-231. Whereas the layer of celluloid shields the wax paper, Djebar has many veiling techniques including her own pseudonym.

12. Steiner's central claim in his book is that "the experience of aesthetic meaning in particular, that of literature, of the arts, of musical form, infers the necessary possibility of this 'real presence.'" See Steiner, *Real Presences*, 3.

13. There is a tendency in popular Islamic beliefs to view Ishmael as the one that Abraham set out to sacrifice.

14. Djebar will connect Ishmael to music in *Loin de Médine*, as the possibility for a new beginning. See *Loin de Médine: Filles d'Ismaël* (Paris: Éditions Albin Michel, 1991).

15. Testimonials strangely foreground the sexuality of the witness, predicating the ability to testify with one's generative possibilities. See, for instance, Ghassan Kanafani's *Men in the Sun* where Abu al-Khaizaran the guide, the survivor, and witness, who is further associated with the Palestinian national liberation movement, is named and identified as castrated. *Rijāl fī al-Shams* [Men in the Sun] (Beirut: Mu'assassat al-Abḥāth al-'Arabīyah, 1963). See also *The Last of the Just* where Krémer, the sympathetic humanist, the witness from the window, has one testicle. André Schwarz-Bart, *Le Dernier des Justes* (Paris: Éditions du Seuil, 1959). It is also noteworthy that Deuteronomy rejects detesticled males as non-Jews; and those with one testicle cannot enter the house of God. "He whose testicles are crushed or whose male member is cut off shall not enter the assembly of the lord." (See Deuteronomy 23:1) One's ability to proliferate the continuity of the father through one's progeny and words is the implied measure of the witness.

16. Genre testifies to its own corpus of works and assumes that individual texts testify to their communality with other texts.

Chapter Five

Writing Absence:

Language, Rhythm, and Temporality in the Poetry of Mahmoud Darwish

"When I am alone, the light of day is only the loss of a dwelling place."
—Maurice Blanchot, *The Space of Literature*, 31.

"Every absence is my father."
—Mahmoud Darwish, *Dīwān*, volume two, 102.

"It is absence of countries that I form in words."
—Mahmoud Darwish, *Dīwān*, volume two, 299.

This chapter examines the writing of home in Mahmoud Darwish's recent work, *Limādhā tarakta al-Ḥiṣāna Waḥīdan?* [Why Have You Left the Horse Alone?] In addition to the structure and thematic of absence in this poetic work, absence is embodied more significantly in language, one that is primarily rhythmic. Language also embodies a temporality that looks to writing, a temporality that is spatially conceived between home and poem. It is a language invoked from the limits of an Arabic literary heritage where poetic writing was home. A peripheral, Sufi notion of language emerges as a discontinuous moment within this Arabic heritage in order to textually re-envision home against inherited and predominant textual delineations of it as land and people. This language allows the threatened desire of the poet to "testify" to the past in its absence and to the self in its dissociated state.

This work of Darwish is also important for situating narrative, autobiography, and biography within the framework of lyric. Darwish himself calls it "an autobiography that is both personal and poetic."[1] (Beydoun 1997: 59) It not only retraces the dispersal of self from loss of place to exile, but it also performs the poetic development of the poet, from influences to changing techniques. Darwish's work is one of testimony, of wanting to register events, a work of autobiography as well as a biography of place, stemming from his desire and fear to not let the past be "confiscated" but to try and "open the register of absence." (Beydoun 1997: 45)

Darwish, who in the words of Nabulsi "lights presence by absence," begins this work in a tone of crisis, invoking the ancient prophets and calling for new ones for this age. (Nabulsi 1987: 612) He begins from the end, from the fragments of a precarious present, in a hesitant turning back and looking over, surveying with longing as in a pre-Islamic poetic mode, the early place which has disappeared, seeing a ghost which he calls his own from the cracks of place. This ghost is not only of himself but is that of his paternal father who is identified with departure from that past place, of the literary forefathers who beckon him, as well as of the ancient prophets. The ghost is the looming paternal heritage that Darwish stages in order to dialogue with these haunting figures. The haunting is not only of the past and its failings but of the future and the limits of the poetic endeavor as well. This ghost is the poetic gaze itself. It is a witness, foregrounded as absence in its vigilant, ever dying gaze.

Thematic and Structure: Guarding against Absence

Before considering the Sufi tradition from which Darwish draws a conception of language, and before examining the mechanics of language as rhythm and temporality, an overview of this work of poetry is a useful starting point. Already on a thematic and structural level, poetic language is being foregrounded as that which paradoxically guards against absence.

Home is ever present in this work but as absence. The poems of *Limādhā tarakta al-Ḥiṣāna Waḥīdan?* [Why Have You Left the Horse Alone?] are a meditation on this absence and, paradoxically, a structuring of it. Divided into six parts, this volume begins with a separate poem that looks back on the first departure from "place" and moves as in a journey to other places. The early place becomes increasingly more remote. And with this displacement of place, there is a displacement of a self, one that is separated from others and from itself. The divided self bears an abyss of questioning, and his questions become nonetheless a way of reshaping his recollections. This poetic voice that seeks to rediscover what happened realizes that recollection takes place in a present that the poetic "I" does not possess; it can only rearrange the events from beginning to end. (Hamoudeh 1995: 45) And hence the act of recollection is predominated by a sense of siege, the poetic "I" looking from the critical present at the remote past and moving to the present. As Hussein Hamoudeh remarks, "recollection is achieved, if it is achieved, in the context of interrogating the use of recollecting, and gives the sense that it is confined within this act of recollection which presences and withdraws." (Hamoudeh 1995: 45) This journey embodies the world of absence from the first disappearance of place to a point where the poetic voice reviews this journey, including the beginning, to a stage of witnessing, testifying to absence. (Hamuodeh 1995: 44)

In the first poem "I see my apparition coming from afar," the poetic voice speaks from absence moving from his time to this beginning. He opens his work not only with the earliest moment of his life where he encounters the first place, but with the earliest moments of Arabic literary heritage, the *aṭlāl*, the pre-Islamic poetic mode where the poet stops in the middle of his desert journey to look upon the traces of the abode of his beloved, to face this absence. It is the poetic mode of overlooking which allows the poetic voice to speak from a higher standpoint (far in time and far in place) where he can survey and see the distant impressions of his world. But in looking back he is no longer himself. In being outside of things, he is closer to them by harboring the distant gaze, as if he just left the place, for seeing assumes distance. This poetic mode of overlooking allows him in the poem what it does not allow him in reality: "I look upon what I want, like a dwelling's lanai." (Darwish 1995: 11) What he sees is announced as absence and hence this turn to volition. Maurice Blanchot reflects, in a different context, on the poetic gaze:

> What fascinates us robs us of our power to give sense . . . Separation which was the possibility of seeing, coagulates at the very center of the gaze into impossibility. The look thus finds, in what makes it possible, the power that neutralizes it . . . preventing it from ever finishing . . . In it blindness is vision still, vision which is no longer the possibility of seeing, but the impossibility of not seeing, the impossibility which becomes visible and perseveres always and always in a vision that never comes to an end: a dead gaze, a gaze become the ghost of an eternal vision. (Blanchot 1982: 32, my emphasis)

This gaze turned ghost is one that cannot see and cannot stop seeing, so it turns to volition in its powerlessness. This volition of the self that is repeated throughout the poem is one that is clearly constructed in poetic language. It is the poem that allows for such a gaze determined by such a desire. Desire grows out of this absence that he chooses to see to ward off further disappearance not only of that past place but of himself as well. "I look upon sea gulls and lorries of soldiers/altering the trees of this place." (Darwish 1995: 11) It might also be that poetic language forces this turn back, drawing the poetic voice to the sight of this early obscure place, "so that the turning back may be accomplished" in him. (Blanchot 1982: 151)

The poetic voice in his position of *aṭlāl* chooses to look at the critical present and far into history to turn toward himself as image and apparition. "I look upon my apparition/coming/from/ afar." (Darwish 1995: 15) Darwish recognizes the image as image in the intangible turning back. This self encounters the division and the death that inhabits it: "I look upon my image running from itself." (Darwish 1995: 13) The self in its division is doubled as image and is in ceaseless movement. It is a gaze emanating from death. For, as Blanchot indicates, "[t]o see properly is essentially to die." (Blanchot 1982: 151) "I look upon my body fearful from afar." (Darwish 1995: 14) At the same time, seeing grants things seen their plenitude, when seeing things is not limited to one point of view. (Blanchot 1982: 151)

This dissociation of the self bears with it a language in the margins: "I look upon words no longer in *Lisān al-'Arab*."[2] (Darwish 1995: 13) In his turn to language, the poetic voice looks to the absence of words no longer in use. "I look upon my language after two days. It's enough absence." (Darwish 1995: 14) The threat of absence inhabits even his own language; not only is the self the image of the self but poetic language itself is the image of language. Blanchot asks: "doesn't language itself become . . . image? . . . not . . . a language containing images . . . but one which is its own image . . . which issues from its own absence, the way the image emerges upon the absence of the thing, a language addressing itself to the shadow of events . . . not to their reality." (Blanchot 1982: 34n) Image affirms the object in its disappearance. It sets a limit where personal intimacy is destroyed. (Blanchot 1982: 254) In establishing a limit at "the edge of the indefinite" an illusion is created about having control over absence. (Blanchot 1982: 254)

The image is mostly non-mimetic, it does not correspond with the "real" and does not copy it. And yet the image is material. Rather than considering image secondary, coming after the object, Blanchot, for instance, considers its distance not between the object and the image that follows but "in the heart of the thing": "The thing was there . . . and lo having become image, instantly it has become that which no one can grasp . . . but the thing as distance, present in absence, graspable because ungraspable, appearing as disappeared." (Blanchot 1982: 254-255) The image of the object is not its sense and does not provide an understanding of it. On the contrary the image of the object tends to withdraw the object from understanding by maintaining it in the immobility of a resemblance that has nothing to resemble. (Blanchot 1982: 260)

Blanchot compares the image to a cadaver or a damaged tool: the cadaver is absolute likeness but it resembles nothing and the tool that is no longer useful appears as image and as resemblance. The image is that which haunts, presenting itself as absence in its "cadaverous resemblance." (Blanchot 1982: 259) In its immobility it does not rest. "The place which it occupies is drawn down by it, sinks with it, and in this dissolution attacks the possibility of a dwelling place even for us who remain." (Blanchot 1982: 259) Darwish uses image extensively in this work. What draws him continuously to the image is perhaps its affirmation of objects in their disappearance.

The self that is compared to a dwelling ("I look upon what I want, like a dwelling's lanai") is linked to it through language, which "grants other beings their time, place, and outcome, and . . . meaning." (Abdel Haq 1992: 52) Language names things anew, and so it allows Darwish to establish a special language around the place to which he belonged. For instance, the mother is continuously associated with remaining whereas the father is associated with departure. But it is perhaps the language of the horse that becomes the most significant in this work. The horse linked with travel, remaining, dance, and music is most importantly associated with the question that the child poses and which entitles this work, "*Why have you left the horse alone?*." Through the paternal response, "for homes die without their inhabitants," he inherits a notion of home in its absence from the one who left. (Darwish 1995: 33-34) The horse becomes a way of resisting absence, not only for the father but also for the son in his poetic endeavor. (Hamoudeh 1995: 52) Through the dialogue with the father, the son who only recognized the departure sees how home inhabits a paternal heritage, a paternal failing, and cannot be dissociated from the question and the words between father and son. There is a dependence on this question in the form of dialogue throughout the work. The lack of clear answers allows for openings to pose the question again and again about the absence of home.[3]

And it is specifically the absence of home that preoccupies Darwish. "I look upon the wind searching for the home of wind/in itself." (Darwish 1995: 12) The search for home is no longer tied to place but to self in its movement. While the poetic voice in this poem looks onto the more mundane aspects of daily life that constituted a sense of familiarity and belonging such as seeing his friends carrying bread and wine in the evening, he shifts to the more critical events that transformed his life, the soldiers that altered the familiar place that he once knew and lead to its distancing from himself. These events force him to look upon his own literary heritage that presumably provides a sense of continuity in his own identity. But even this review provides him with a different reading of his heritage given what took place: "I look upon the name 'Abi Tayeb al-Mutannabi'/traveling from Tiberia to Egypt/over the horse of *nashīd*." (Darwish 1995: 12) It is a heritage of displacement both for the Arab and for the poet. And *nashīd* here is named as that lyric which bears journey and displacement. This leads Darwish's poetic voice to ask in exasperation: "I look upon a procession of ancient prophets/as they climb barefoot toward Orshalim/And I ask: Is there a new prophet/for this new age?" (Darwish 1995: 13) The ancient prophets, who in their departure too marked the history of this early place, loom over its present. It is an age in crisis that demands new prophets, and, by extension, new myths.

Absence permeates everything here: history, self, place, language, people, as he looks upon the ancient peoples of Persia and Rome in light of the new refugees. The compelling question of this poem in turning back and facing absence as well as facing his inheritance is "What will pass after the ash?" (Darwish 1995: 14) It is a poem that begins the work with death.

Blanchot indicates that many writers who are prompted by the fear of losing themselves turn to writing a journal in order to maintain a relation with the self. (Blanchot 1982: 28) While this is not a journal, it traces the self through time in the face of its fear of disappearance: "What must the writer remember? Himself: who he is when he isn't writing . . . But the tool he uses in order to recollect himself is, strangely, the very element of forgetfulness: writing."

(Blanchot 1982: 29) Hence it is a paradox of trying to guard against forgetting through the material inscription of effacement.

Blanchot describes this journal as a project of "overlooking" not unlike what Darwish's poetic voice undertakes. (Blanchot 1982: 29) *Darwish's Limādhā tarakta al-Ḥiṣāna Waḥīdan?* [Why Have You Left the Horse Alone?] is aware that an attempt to establish the "movement of writing in time" in order to have the security of the event is illusory. (Blanchot 1982: 29) According to Blanchot, the writer who does not know how to do anything but write is "no longer truly historical"; in writing a journal, he is trying to avoid "the extreme of literature, if literature is ultimately the fascinating realm of time's absence." (Blanchot 1982: 29-30)

As much as Darwish is facing this self in the absence of place he is equally facing the task of poetry. The poetic voice in remembering that distant, first place is not concerned with the faithfulness of what was as much as it is concerned with rebuilding those memories, fragile as they are, to ward off complete disappearance. (Hamoudeh 1995: 46) Inversely, as one critic points out, the writer also engages in effacements of his own, "as one of the techniques of writing in light of the daily effacement that the Arab faces . . . effacement here has no fixed bases but takes unknown paths where inner voices multiply and address the absent/ present voice." (Muhammed 1995: 42) As he looks back, the poetic voice often speaks from a threatened locus. "We looked toward the lorries and saw absence/ stacking selected things and pitching its eternal tent from around us." (Darwish 1995: 28) The connection between the child and place is henceforth ruptured, but the child inherits his father's burdened belonging to place: "As you used to carry me my father, I will carry this longing/ to my beginning and to its beginning/ and I will cross this road/ to my end and to its end." (Darwish 1995: 42) The connection between the father and son is further reinforced by their exile. (Hamoudeh 1995: 47) According to Muhammad, Darwish also transforms the real into myth by focusing on its details in order to destabilize the power that rules over it.

The burden of heritage where "everything begins anew" is now manifested in the mythical and troubled fraternal relations of Joseph and his brothers as well as Cain and Abel. The common paternal heritage that binds them together through writing is also the one that violently separates them.[4] The self here reflects on its relation with its other: "I am you in words. One book gathers us." (Darwish 1995: 56) And this "I" returns to itself and to its own siege: "absence was pushing me and I was pushing it." (Darwish 1995: 55 cited in Hamoudeh 1995: 47) Added absence from the disparate elements of the heritage he invokes: from Adam to Caesar, 'Anat to Hagar, Sumer to Egypt, Gilgamesh to Dhu al-Qarnayn, etc.

The dissipated self offers itself as testimony to what was and what is. (Hamoudeh 1995: 47) This testimony takes the form of an accusation and a defense, a judgment between himself and the others that "live his life instead of him." (Darwish 1995: 152) A certain responsibility is unclaimed: "and he says my words instead of me." (Darwish 1995: 152) This testimony, raised on behalf of the self and others, on behalf of a present time and a lost place conceals the first place where it becomes a memory. (Hamoudeh 1995: 50) And the self is completely divided between its present being and its absent identity. This self that began with reconstructing its past "as it wills," having no control over its reality, now moves to question the dream itself. (Hamoudeh 1995: 50)

Like Djebar, Darwish's testimony is connected to other events in history, linking his experience with that of others, all the while a testimony that is specific to his own experience. Whereas Djebar's effort of "resurrection," which she problematizes, renders the self inextricable from the collective, Darwish's testimony remains first of all on behalf of the self, even if this experience also belongs to the collective. This testimony remains lyrical as if lyricism cannot consider testimony to be adequate in itself but has to sing it in order to protect it from the shadows. (Hamoudeh 1995: 53) It unravels the world of absence of the self within a world of history and heritage.

Language and the Experience of Sufism

It is important to examine language in the poetry of Mahmoud Darwish in relation to what Arabic literary heritage also proffers. As Adonis has argued, Sufism, or Islamic mysticism, was a rupture in writing and thought from what preceded it and from its own cultural context. More importantly, it was a rupture because of its enrapture with language.[5] The experience of Sufism also allows us to see heritage not as past but as future. Munsif Abdel Haq, informed by his readings of the Sufi al-Nuffari, suggests that literary heritage may be considered as the "time of the written" rather than associating it with a closed past or the time of its writing: "Everything that we write until now escapes, by the act of writing the hegemony of the time of writing itself, in order to enter the time of the written, i.e. the time of heritage." (Abdel Haq 1992: 70) So even contemporaneous reading is already heritage since, written at a certain moment, it has escaped from that temporality to meet the reader. By being there and in a sense invoking its reading, the writing brings together the past to which it belongs (the time of its writing) and the present and future as possible times of reading: "This parting, double situation of heritage . . . situates it between the experience of writing and the experience of reading. Writing draws it to the past and reading draws it to the future. And between the past and the coming futurity extends the time of the written." (Abdel Haq 1992: 70-71)

The experience of Sufism as writing and as literary heritage still beckons to be read, especially that this experience of writing has remained without significant consideration until this century and contemporary efforts addressing it remain meager. Adonis is one of the few who reflect on it in relation to language and writing. And we consider it as a parallel experience to Darwish's writing of home, as a writing that becomes its own home. Adonis relates:

> Sufism founded a writing replete with subjective experience within a culture preoccupied with public, religious, and institutional knowledge. It remained, however, a writing . . . without a place. It is as if its writers were not living in a

> place but in their texts, as if the text for them is the real home. And it is as if the Sufi moves inside this text, and creates with it and in it the world of which he dreams. The words were hiding places for his passages, his horizons, and his symbols. (Adonis 1995: 115)

And these words are specifically poetic for Adonis. According to him, Sufism reverted to continuing what was there before Islam, when it turned to the language of poetry, i.e. linking the relationship of poetry to the unknown and to absence.[6] While Darwish would locate the poetic in the rhythmic, Adonis locates it in its language. It is a language for him where "everything in it is itself and something else." (Adonis: 1995: 23) For Adonis, it is a vision of language that was there and that has been oftentimes neglected.

> Our predecessors agree that most of language is *majāz* [image, metaphor, and interestingly passage], even though today we do not pay attention to the importance and correctness of this saying when we read a poem . . . in *majāz* we make images for things that appear to be themselves and at the same time other than themselves. *Majāz* takes the thing out of itself, and enters it into something else. And this is what al-Jahiz means when he says *tashbīh* (resemblance) is useful for otherness not sameness. This is where "strangeness" lies that *majāz* bears . . . it makes language say what it does not usually say. (Adonis 1993: 127-128)

Poetry for Adonis is the attempt through language to say what cannot be said. (Adonis 1993: 24) Another critic who considers Sufism and its enrapture with language is Abdel Haq. He claims that Language is not simply for discourse and dialogue. It is a horizon from which communication with the other, with the infinite, with the unknown is made possible."[7] The Sufi bears a dialogue with the other, a dialogue that positions the Sufi as listener to the words that writing allows to emerge. This dialogue is not mediated through a text but through the body. This dialogue cannot be instituting in its subjectivity. According to Adonis, it is a changing condition from moment to moment. So the knowledge gained cannot be taught or represented nor can it be gained through learning. Sufi writing becomes a history of the time of the dialogue between the self and the other. (Adonis 1993: 116)

The writings of al-Nuffari (mainly *al-Mawāqif* [Positions or Stopping places] and *al-Mukhāṭābat* [Discourses] take the form of divine invocations directed at the Sufi who in turn listens to those invocations and writes them. Nuffari's writing "is a story on the silence of the Sufi and his stopping of speech: he lives his experience as a listener only to what the other says." (Abdel Haq 1992: 54) The Sufi stops speaking before the divine since the condition of speaking with the divine is silence: "do not speak, for whoever arrives does not speak." (Cited in Abdel Haq 1992: 54) And here silence is specifically losing the ability for human speech. "The path of the Sufi is not the path to speech, but it is a path toward speaking, not human speech but divine speech." (Abdel Haq 1992: 54) The speaking that takes place between the self and the celestial other is not the conventional dialogue but more a listening to the issuing of language as divine speech that is directed toward the writer who "writes the desire of language to issue forth." (Abdel Haq 1992: 55)

The celestial other's relation to the Sufi is not a paternal one but one of detachment. It presents itself in the *mawqif* as intimate detachment: "I am closer to you from everything . . . and I am closer to you than yourself." (Cited in Abdel Haq 1992: 56) This reflects an affinity between the two natures: "it will bring together presence and absence. Its relation to the divine summons is its presence as self but . . . it [also has] to break its boundaries as self: its narcissism and language." (Abdel Haq 1992: 56) And the movement of presence and absence traces the movement of his writing, since the Sufi can only engage with it as language and not as thing. For he cannot apprehend it as he does other things, because it presents itself to him as language. Language here is that other in which the Sufi reads his own retreating self. He is therefore positioned as strict listener to this language, a language that commands him to be silent and to absent human speech. For the Sufi who has lost the ability for human speech has no recourse except to write his silence and register his absence. The Sufi achieves his own absence in losing his ability for human speech, a demand of a language that he is immersed in and that allows him access to the divine.

In writing his withdrawal, the Sufi is also writing the fulfillment of language. So the Sufi writes for the celestial other who enabled him to write. Listening is not only a response to the summoning of language, and one of the possibilities of silence; it is also a response to the absence of the self. "And whoever listens gets emptied, and whoever gets emptied was listening." (Cited in Abdel Haq 1992: 59) Listening then is the possibility that opens toward language.

Language and Darwish's Poetry

Darwish has oftentimes been called *mutaṣawwif* or Sufi in his writing. Describing his turn to writing, one critic comments that for Darwish "writing has become an ontological act to rebuild the situation of the poetic self in its time." (Muhammad 1995: 39) Darwish draws a parallel *mawqif* to al-Nuffari's in the poem "A Traveler Told Another," situating writing on the margins, a writing requiring nothing short of divine intervention to bring it to the fore. But writing is inextricably linked with the withdrawal of the self. And as with lyric poetry, the relation to language is primarily one of listening.

> I don't know the desert,
> but I grew on its limits words.
> The words said their words, and I went
> like a separated woman, I left as her broken spouse. (Darwish 1995: 110)

The desert is a space where nothing new is encountered, locating both language and self on its margins and situating writing in its errance. Moreover, the poetic voice is identified as a traveler, whose subjectivity is not fixed to a place nor presumably to itself but wanders the moment it sets its task to write. As with Djebar, language here is not in the possession of the writer; rather his subjectivity is dissociated from what it speaks.

> Language . . . is not the power to tell. For this language speaks as absence. Wordless, it speaks already; when it ceases, it persists . . . The poet is he who hears a language which makes nothing heard . . . It speaks, but without any beginning. It states, but does not refer back to something . . . like the meaning behind an expression, which would guarantee it. (Blanchot 1982: 51-52)

In this poem, which is framed as a dialogue as the title indicates, one traveler speaking to another, but which is more of a monologue with the self where the interlocutor is the other of the self, what the poetic voice keeps is the song in his desire for union with things, and with the past: "I did not keep except the rhythm/I hear it/and I follow it/and I raise it a dove/in the passage to the sky,/the sky of my song." (Darwish 1995: 110-111) The poetic voice only belongs to the song, which is a repetition of the impossible return, for what one traveler tells another is that "we won't return the way we left." (Darwish 1995: 110) The poet is further defined as the one who is able to hear this rhythm: "and I take the pulse of the alphabets in their echoes." (Darwish 1995: 111) Again his relation to language is one of hearing that belated and vibrating absence that is the echo.

The writer hears this interminable as speech and abides by its demand to the point of being lost in it. But to maintain it, the writer must interrupt it, hence making it "perceptible, [having] proffered it by firmly reconciling it with this limit. He has mastered it by imposing measure." (Blanchot 1982: 37) The song itself, also a space of contestation like Darwish's land, open and in movement, becomes this space that is inhabited by rhythm and that safeguards the poet's sense of belonging.

The poetic voice grants himself an identity only to write the movement of the withdrawal of its self:

> I am the son of the Syrian coast,
> I live it a journey or shrine
> between the people of the sea,
> but the mirage draws me east
> to the ancient nomads. (Darwish 1995: 111)

He is not able to live this multifarious identity. It is either a memorial for him, a sacred ruin of the past, or a journey, a perpetual search. While he is among the people of the sea, it is his wandering that links him to the ancient nomads, although his identity is not limited to them. "I forget who I will be so I can be/a people in one," (Darwish 1995: 111) This movement of identity is one that necessitates forgetting and that is aware that it is inhabited by a plurality of peoples. It is an identity that bears its heritage.

The poetic voice does not know the desert, the infinite, where he is visited by the unknown, and where it becomes the locus of a prophetic moment, a space of withdrawal, in Blanchot's terms.

I don't know the desert,
no matters how I visit its foreboding,
And in the desert the invisible said to me: Write!
I said: On the mirage there is other writing
He said: Write so that the mirage becomes greener
So I said: I'm short of absence
And I said: I have yet to learn the words
He said to me: Write so you will know them
and to know where you were, and where you are
and how you came to be, and who you'll be tomorrow,
put your name in my hand and write
to know who I am, and pass a cloud
in the expanse.
So I wrote: whoever writes his story inherits
the land of words, and possesses significance thoroughly!
(Darwish 1995: 112)

The inspirational command to write recalls the command bestowed on the Sufi and that given to the Islamic prophet to read. Implied is the plenitude of writing: though there is other writing the poetic voice is still chosen to write.

It is only through writing that one encounters language. While writing seems to be connected to the absolute—he has to write in order to situate himself, to know where he is and who he will be—it also requires a withdrawal of self. Placing his name beyond himself, in order to write, the self has to announce its own death in the name. This again will grant the poetic voice a certain knowledge about that which is beyond identity. It is a question of transformation: "in imaginary space things are transformed into that which cannot be grasped. Out of use, beyond wear, they are not in our possession but are the movement of dispossession that releases us both from them and from ourselves." (Blanchot 1982: 141) The transformation is to safeguard precisely through a language of absence: "'How,' says Rilke, 'how could one sustain, how could one save the visible, if not by creating the language of absence, of the invisible?'" (Cited in Blanchot 1982: 142; my emphasis)

In this poetic language, everything is announced and withheld. What does the poetic voice, transient as he wanders in the expanse, write? He writes: "whoever writes his story inherits/the land of words, and possesses significance thoroughly!" And this is what Darwish attempts in *Limādhā tarakta al-Ḥiṣāna Waḥīdan?* [Why Have You Left the Horse Alone?] He writes his own story in order to safeguard his inheritance. In writing, he is seeking an inheritance that will not dispossess him through this paradoxical medium, one that exiles and absents.

Writing supplants the previous grounding of the land, and it even replaces it as a contested space in the poem. Darwish compares land and language in many different places in his poetry: "whoever writes his story inherits the land of words." (Darwish 1995: 112) In comparing language to land, it supplants it as an essential grounding for being. Furthermore, the poet gives land the signification of language; "this way land becomes a special temporality with which the poet moves wherever he wants and anytime he wants . . . It is a creative time, represented in poetry, that puts all other times within it, and the poet then does not live in a place as much as he lives in time." (Samti 1995: 71) In turn, Darwish's homeland, borne by lyric, moves in infinite time, to its mythic moments and to deferred spaces.

The poet continues his departure even from his desert of wandering and this inspirational encounter that does not yield knowledge:

I don't know the desert,
but I take leave of her: peace
to the tribe east of my song: peace
. . .
to the *mu'allaqah*[8] that guards our stars: peace
to the people passing memory to my memory: peace
to the peace upon me between two *qaṣīdahs*:
a *qaṣīdah* written
and another whose poet died desiring! (Darwish 1995: 113)

Bidding peace to his cultural heritage and even to the peace he harbors in writing his poems, those written and those to come, the poetic voice is left to himself attempting to face absence:

Am I myself?
Am I there [. . .] or here?
. . .
I am you the interlocutor, it is not exile
to be you. It is not exile
to be the I in you. And it is not exile
for the sea and desert
to be the song of a traveler to traveler. (Darwish 1995: 113-114)

The encounter with writing, rather than granting identity, forces a series of question about identity and grounding. While it is forcibly an experience of exile, the self that dissolves in an "essential solitude" in its encounter with inspiration achieves almost a mystic unity in language not unlike the language of al-Nuffari.

In "Poetic Planning," Darwish opens the poem with a linking of language and self:

There was for the stars no role
except they taught me how to read:
I have a language in the sky
and on earth I have a language
Who am I? Who am I? (Darwish 1995: 99)

The question of identity is posed in the context of the two languages, suspended in between, in an abyss of questioning. The recurrent reference to stars in this poem and in the other poems in this work implies disorientation. Stars are specifically related to prophecy through reading. The disaster is this break from the stars, this suspension that is siege. This is where Darwish wants to locate poetry in this space of in-between:

The *qaṣīdah* is in between and it has the power
. . .
to return, with a cry of a gardenia, a homeland!

The *qaṣīdah* between my hands has the power
to command the affairs of myths,
through the work of my hands, but I
since I found the *qaṣīdah*, displaced myself
and asked her:
Who am I?
Who am I? (Darwish 1995: 102)

Language and self are linked again through the poem that echoes for this poetic voice a homeland, but only in a space of nowhere; what the poetic voice possesses between his hands comes about through his own work. Darwish brings together poetry and domestic affairs or daily living only to show the distance between them. He painfully points to the divorce of poetry from the "reality" of the everyday, and while he proclaims the power of the *qaṣīdah*, it becomes clear from the rest of the poem that the poem has no such power.

The *qaṣīdah* above, has the power
to teach me whatever it wishes
such as opening a window
and arranging my domestic affairs
between the myths. It has the power
to marry herself to me [. . .] time. (Darwish 1995: 100)

Already in placing it above he renders it far from daily events; and what it teaches is absurdly within the realm of the domestic. In a sense, he is proclaiming its powerlessness in the face of daily realities. At the same time, it is that which supplants home. Juxtaposed to the above poetic verses are affirmations of rootedness despite displacement:

And my father below carries an olive tree
of a thousand years,
she is neither eastern
nor western.
Perhaps he will rest from the conquerors,
and will incline toward me a little,
and will gather for me lily of the valley. (Darwish 1995: 100-101)

The father below is part of a reality in crisis. Carrying an olive branch of a thousand years links him to a land from its ancient times, refusing easy identification, yet he is dispossessed of that claim facing no rest from conquerors. The powerlessness of the poem is rendered more trenchant and wistful. Again he follows these verses by juxtaposing the self to the happy sailors, carrying longing sadness and harboring hope for the *qaṣīdah* as refuge, but one that escapes him.

The *qaṣīdah* distances itself from me,
and enters the port of sailors who adore wine
. . .
and who do not carry longing to anything
nor sadness! (Darwish 1995: 101)

In "A Rhyme for Muʿallaqāt[9]," Darwish further develops the relation of language to self, so that the only guarantee of the self becomes language.

No one guided me to myself. I am the guide[10],
I am the guide to myself between the sea and the desert.
(Darwish 1995: 115)

The self is between two spaces that resist borders and resist linear time.

No tomorrow in this desert
except what we saw yesterday,
so I will raise my *muʿallaqah* so that circular time will break
and the beautiful time will be born! (Darwish 1995: 117)

It is not a question of creating an identity, for identity is what always presents itself, and what others grant. The poetic voice wants to create his own time, space, and being through poetic language.

I am my language I,
and I am *muʿallaqatun* [. . .] *muʿallaqatān*[11] [. . .] ten, this is my language
I am my language. I am what the words said:
Be
my body, so I was for its tone a body. I am what
said to the words: be the crossing of my body with
the eternal desert. Be so I can be what I say!
No land over earth bears me, so my words bear me
ascending, parting from me,
and they build the dwelling of their passage before me
in my debris, in the debris of the enchanting world around me,
(Darwish 1995: 116)

This identification with language and with an Arabic, pre-Islamic poetic heritage is more specifically a desire to link language with being, for that harmonious unity between being and the words. If this being has no bearing on land, he hopes it will be borne by language, but the poetic voice is aware that there is a detachment that happens between language and being, there is a certain death that takes place in the encounter with language. If there is a harmonious unity between language and being, then it is momentary. Language then establishes its own being on the debris of the poetic self and his world: "my words bear me/ascending, parting from me, and they build the dwelling of their passage before me/ in my debris, in the debris of the enchanting world around me." (Darwish 1995: 116) This departure of language from the self recalls its departure from the others, and the self is left once again alone:

> [. . .] this language of mine is pendants[12] from stars encircling the embraces
> of the beloved: migrated
> they took the place and migrated
> they took time and migrated.[13] (Darwish 1995: 116)

"A Rhyme for Mu'allaqāt[14]" points to the suspension of poems, stars, disastrous reality, and of beings becoming.

> Will the echo expand, this echo
> this white, resonant mirage for a name
> which the unknown fills with hoarseness, and which travel fills with
> divinity? (Darwish 1995: 117)

A sense of siege is encircling and suspending this self.

> The sky sets a window upon me so I look: I don't
> see anyone besides me [. . .]
> I found myself upon its surface
> like it was with me, and my gaze
> does not leave the desert. (Darwish 1995: 117)

The gaze of the poetic voice is a passive one that cannot see except itself; it becomes an illusory way of effacing the threat of disappearance embodied in them: "from wind and sand are my steps/and my world is my body and all that my hands possess." (Darwish 1995: 117) The emphasis on the physicality of the body is an accounting of it and its parts as well as a linking of this personal body to a collective one. But the poetic voice is both in departure from its world, self, and the passage of the poem itself. "I am the traveler and the passage/gods look upon me and retreat, and we don't prolong our talks about what is to come." (Darwish 1995: 117) The encounter that the poem allows with the infinite or the invisible is announced as always in retreat. Although what is at stake is the future, it is not brought to discussion. The problem is instead posed as one of temporality: "so I will raise my *mu'allaqah* so that circular time will break/and beautiful time will be born!" (Darwish 1995: 117) The temporality of the poem is able to break the circular time that is entrapping him. It is also the circular time of his book. There is hope harbored here for the future, but who can exceed the past? The double gesture is continuously being made: this self fluctuates between being present and being emptied by travel, performing the temporality of the poem.

> Past is what I see
> for one a kingdom of dust and his crown. So let my language
> triumph over time the enemy, over my descendants,
> over me, over my father, and over disappearance that does not disappear
> this is my language and my miracle
> . . .
> and the sacred of the Arab in the desert,
> who worships what flows
> from rhymes like stars on his cloak,
> and he worships what he says
>
> it is necessary for prose then,
> it is necessary for divine prose for the prophet to triumph.
> (Darwish 1995: 118)

The poetic gaze that can only see the past is not prophetic. Language here is the only reality and the only possible triumph not only over time but also over the inherited way of establishing identity and the heritage of dispossession. And language is a way of guarding off disappearance "that does not disappear." The language of this poem, especially in this passage, recalls the language of the Qur'an in its rhythm and its words. The idea of language as miracle is one of the paramount claims of the Qur'an. As Adonis points out, (Arabic) language becomes divine with Islam adding even more import to a language that had its poetic weight in pre-Islamic times. The Qur'an claimed that its language was not poetry, and that its language was nothing like anything seen before. And in fact its language is often considered as such for its innovations, being neither prose nor poetry.[15]

And what is demanded in the ending enigmatic verses is specifically divine prose. Prose, in Arabic *nathr*, also means scattering, dispersal. It is necessary for prose in order for the prophet to triumph in an age of defeat, reflected in a history of great poetry. Prose in its dissemination is that which will guard against absence, as the other writing of poetry. Poetry as *Dīwān al-'Arab* (register of the Arabs) is connected to the ancient prophets and to a paternal heritage. This new age demands new prophets and new languages. Darwish in his continuous interrogation of why poetry and not other writing seems nonetheless to be establishing poetic language as the only guard against absence.

Language and Temporality

Writing imposes its own temporality, one that does not presence. This impossibility is beyond the temporal disjuncture between writing and reading, and the disjuncture between poetic saying and what it presumably represents. Absence in Darwish's formulation is beyond exile; absence means non-presence, distance, and wandering . . . Absence does not negate presence in the future and in absence we can presence that which can not be presenced." (Ghazoul 1986: 196)

But this future, perhaps already past and a recurrent absence, is plagued by a thematic of belatedness: "it is already too late" or "it is already past": "The train passed quickly/it passed me, and I/am still waiting." (Darwish 1995: 65) Darwish in an interview expresses the same sentiment: "Time passes us like a train. Events always precede us."[16] A creative dispute ensues then between memory and imagination in Darwish's poetry. Memory, connected to recalling the past, happens only in the time of the future in his poetry. One critic reads this temporality to indicate that "the poet will not arrive at his past, to his land, except after the passage of the occupier, and this occupier will not leave now, and may not leave in the future." (Samti 1995: 85) And so the arrival at the past is predicated upon the future. Darwish recalls the past or history through vision or imagination ("I see"). And image, when it is used, recalls the absence of the original. "I look upon Persians, Romans, Sumerians/and the new refugees . . . / . . . /I look upon my apparition/coming/ from/afar." (Darwish 1995: 15)

In this work, Darwish departs from linear time composed of past, present, and future to circular time which is infinite and multiple. (Samti 1995: 70) The turn to circular time in his later works is a turn to the temporality of writing itself, "folding on rhythms, song, monologue, dialogue, short sentences and long sentences and the varied poetic phrases." (Samti 1995: 73) The poet not only observes his time but also directs himself to the disappearing moments of history. In his poetic delivery, he anticipates and dreads linear time. This is in contrast to his early poetry where one temporality predominated his poetry, speaking narratively of the dream for the future. It speaks of one event from one perspective. The later poetry, however, provides a plurality of times, including mythical and historical time as well as the moment at stake. (Samti 1995: 73)

Some critics argue that time is subordinated to place in the poetry of Darwish, so that what preoccupies his works is not so much when as where. (Nabulsi 1987: 525) Darwish's poetic temporality may be more complex than that, where temporality becomes interconnected with spatiality.[17] For Darwish, temporality "includes looking toward the future and toward writing." The emphasis on the future is on its endless repetition from home to *qaṣīdah*, "as if this future became a [spatial] home for the poet, a temporary substitute for his homeland/place; it becomes this temporary substitute in writing." (Samti 1995: 78) Darwish writes: "I am who/said to the words: be the crossing of my body with/the eternal desert. Be so I can be what I say!" (Darwish 1995: 116) Darwish's poetry looks toward the future but as repetition "so that the past, present, and future become one temporality, that of the future." (Nabulsi 1987: 526)

In this work, the past awaits or sometimes becomes the "dream time": "Here is a present not touched by yesterday/ . . . / here is a present timeless/ . . . /here is a present/that has no place/ . . . /here is a present/passing." (Darwish 1995: 31) The poetic "I" reconsiders its potential time that it doesn't possess. There is no place for this desire, and so the poetic voice carries it in this circle of absence to the endpoint that begins anew. (Hamoudeh 1995: 48) The refrain of "Ishmael's Lute" is precisely that "everything will begin anew." (Darwish 1995: 45) But this beginning and end are not clearly demarcated but circular. In the last section, the relation with the past is ruptured: "the past went to the past quickly." (Darwish 1995: 151) A new temporality emerges: "the past tomorrow coming from a tea party." (Darwish 1995: 162)

The temporality of the future is one of anticipation: "Ishmael . . . sing/to us so that everything becomes possible near presence [*wujūd*—also existence, being]." (Darwish 1995: 47) It takes many forms in his poetry: through the present tense that is preceded with "will" (the Arabic *sawf* or *sīn*); through the conditional (if, whenever, while, dreaming); through exclamations (when); through command verbs; through time indicators (tomorrow, night, future); through dream and imagination (I see); as well as other expressions presented through the text (the beginning and end, end of night).[18] The temporality of verbs (such as "sing") consists in the movement. His poetic scene is also marked with travel, movement, and in observing the small details. This movement indicates a temporality that negates the fixity of things. The sentences that are verbal tend to predominate over the nominative, which leads us to claim that his poetic text leans toward movement. (Farouq 1995: 54) When he uses the present tense and precedes it with a word indicating a future time, he delivers it from its past and opens it toward the future. Whereas the name is fixed, it is the verb that creates movement and temporality in his poetic phrasing toward the absent future that may or may not come about. These verbs not only move the poetic phrases but the entire poem. Most of Darwish's verbs are in the present tense and are involved in introduction of the verse or poem, in dialogue, and in questioning. (Nabulsi 1987: 618) The past tense is used to establish an indirect dialogue within his poem. (Nabulsi 1987: 621)

The futuristic time is, as Samti points out, one "where its coming temporality multiplies and is in dispute," and where "the constructed poetic expressions are stressed in terms of time." (Samti 1995: 75) For instance, repetition becomes "an extended future verb," "a time that parallels history, which is outside physical time, it becomes parallel to the creative time which looks at time as a unity that the poet cannot change." (Samti 1995: 117) Perhaps the best example is the above mentioned not only because it is repeated but also because it bespeaks repetition: "everything will begin anew." (Darwish 1995: 45) Repetition destroys the present in its movement of over and over. Darwish also uses the command verb, often at the beginning of poems, in order to emphasize the present tense. But this command has no temporality; it is suspended as the possible in infinite time. (Samti 1995: 76) This way the present tense remains predominant and is directed toward a futurity. As one critic indicates, "most of Darwish's poems have no temporality because their present tenses are . . . futuristic and are not concerned with what happened but with what will happen." (Nabulsi 1987: 621) The command verb is connected to an absent interlocutor who presumably receives the command. It creates a certain drama that conceals the futurity since the command is operative until it is achieved. The future also cannot be apprehended except through questioning and desiring. (Samti 1995: 77)

Language as Rhythm

Language as rhythm in the poetry of Darwish consists not only in the incorporation of musical elements such as rhythm, rhyme, and meter but also in its overall emphasis on sound in the poetic utterance. Rhythm is also inextricably linked with the temporality of his writing. This is following the inheritance of lyric's ancient ties to music where al- Farabi, for instance, considered poetry and music to be originating from the same genre that is composition and *wazn* (or meter) as well as the balancing between movement and stillness. (Cited in Adonis 1989: 8) As Adonis points out, "rhythm is the basis for the pre-Islamic poetic saying, because it is a living force connecting the self and the other . . . The pre-Islamic Arabs distinguished themselves from other peoples in the poetic rhythm, in something central which is the *qāfiyah* [or rhyme]." (Adonis 1989: 21)

Whereas in pre-Islamic times the poet decided on meter and rhyme before he even said one verse, rhythm in contemporary Arabic poetry develops with the poem. The rhythm is no longer in the *'urūḍ* (prosodic or metrical) or *taf'īlah* (foot of a verse meter or measure) but in the verb: Rhythm, whose movement is in flux and changes from one moment to another, is constructed in time. (Nabulsi 1987: 646)

Rhythm for Darwish is fundamental in differentiating between poetry and prose, although he experiments sometimes with the "prose-poem." He believes that this differentiation needs to be maintained. Arabic poetry for him is a "musical treasure": "No other language possesses sixteen different meters like Arabic. The Arabic meter is based on the number of musical units: one long syllable and one short" (Yeshurun 1997: 125) Like many critics, Darwish himself is aware that the strength of his poetry lies in its rhythm and musicality. Arabic poetry in modern times is not primarily to be recited but to be read, albeit it gets incorporated into songs and is recited on many occasions. There is a difference, as Adonis maintains, between an oral culture of poetry and a written one. Darwish, while aware of this, maintains the emphasis on the listener in his poetry.

Rhythm is established in the poetry of Darwish through poetic meters, interior and exterior rhymes, and the arranged sounds of the text in melodic units. It is also established through syntax and textual signification. Moreover, the temporality of his poems is inextricably linked with his use of rhythm, as indicated above: "Rhythm is based on the idea of time, in movement and stillness, in presenting and deferring, and in presence and effacement." (Samti 1995: 80) There has been a transformation in his rhythmic use from his earlier poetry, so that now he uses a variety of metrics. (Darwish, however, uses predominantly *al-baḥr al-kāmil*, which has the effect of giving the sense of extended time without much change, of infinite time.) Moreover the new poetic language with its new rhythms employs repetition and refrain extensively. And he uses it sometimes to emphasize a certain time in order to contain the poem within that time. This repetition is of course based on deletions and additions to the same verse, and hence creates a rhythm. An instance of this is found in the variations of the refrain of "I look upon." He also uses the poetic sentence, a musical unity that occupies more space than does a verse or poetic line, and which is a new rhythm in contemporary Arabic poetry.

> I choose a cloudy day to pass by the ancient well.
> Perhaps it has been filled with the sky.
> Perhaps it has been flooded with meaning
> and the proverbs of the shepherd.
> I shall drink a handful of its water.
> And I shall say to the dead who surround it:
> Peace be upon you, those remaining. (Darwish 1995: 69)

The poetic sentence is not a rupture from the old rhythm but is born from contemporary times. Darwish also uses rhyme differently so that it is now interior rather than exterior. Moreover, contemporary use of rhyme, as Nabulsi indicates, "allows the reader to stop and move at the same time, whereas rhyme in the old poetry demands a stopping . . . From this the new rhyme depends on the musical sense and not on language." (Nabulsi 1987: 649) And it is rhythm that unifies his poems. An example of this is "Poetic planning" where there is a prominent external rhyme for the poem ending each poetic sentence. In addition to external rhyme, there is an internal rhyme and rhythm. This external rhyme is "*anā*," Arabic for "I". The ending words of each poetic phrase are chosen to maintain this rhyme. This poem is also a clear example of how difficult it is to translate rhythm. It is a poem where rhyme and meaning combine for rhythm to predominate.

While Darwish's poetry is not solely lyrical, lyric plays a significant role. Samti distinguishes between what he calls the lyrical in Darwish's poetry from the poetic. *Inshād* or lyricism has, furthermore, a distinct temporality: "it does not grant us real time but an illusory time . . . However, it does not have in the strict sense of the word a first spring, a center of expanding. Its noted origin is repetition." (Samti 1995: 83) Darwish breaks this *inshād* with *infi'āl* (state of being affected) so that the continuation based on poetry is more obscure.

Important for Darwish's rhythm is image, especially that Darwish uses a great variety of images in his poetry. Poetic images create a rhythm where the time of the poem is connected to home. Stressing its importance, Nabulsi states: "we cannot apprehend the poetic image outside the general rhythm of the *qaṣīdah*. The rhythm of the image is part of the rhythm of the *qaṣīdah*." (Nabulsi 1987: 656) Again this can be seen in "Poetic Planning" where the individual poetic sentence, in its image, rhythm, and rhyme, is fragmentary in meaning and derivative in rhythm.

> I don't want an answer here
> Perhaps a star will fall upon its image
> Perhaps the forest of chestnuts will rise
> and raise me toward the galaxy, at night time,
> and say: you will stay here! (Darwish 1995: 100)

Beyond calling attention to its use of image as in the second line, the words "here," "chestnut," and "I" all rhyme in Arabic, ending in *anā* or "I". They create rhythm through their image, placement, and repetition. However it is only in the general rhythm of the poem that it becomes clear that *anā* or "I," *hunā* or "here," *shajana* or "sadness," *waṭana* or "homeland," *zamana* or "time," words that end each poetic image, rhyme and create a rhythm where identity of self is linked in its rhythm to the time of the poem and to homeland and place.

Sound is also emphasized in the poetry of Darwish. The shaping of language, by repeating a word and its constituents in a similar context, depends on play with utterances, collecting fragments and establishing new relations between words. A good example of this is in "A Traveler Told Another."

> Am I myself? [A anā anā?]
> Am I there . . . or here? [A anā hunāllika . . . am hunā?]
> In every "you" I, [Fī kulli anta anā]
> I am you the interlocutor. [An takūna anāyā anta . . .] (Darwish 1995: 113)

Already in the word "there," "here" is enclosed; and in the Arabic "you" or "anta," "anā" or "I" is enclosed. In this rhythmic play, through sound, Darwish establishes new relations between these words. Not only does he intertwine identities and questions, rhythm performs the movement of home as errance, or as a search for home just like the pre-Islamic *qaṣīdah* had oftentimes the rhythm of the desert journey, the trample of the riding animals.

> I am from here. And here is I. Echoes my father: I am from here.
> And I am here. And I am I. And here is here. It is I. And I am here.
> And here
> is I. And I am I . . .
> . . .
> The echo sounded never here never here . . .
> And the shape of echo appeared a homeland here...
> so breach the wall of being, father,
> echo surrounding echo, and erupt:
> I am
> from
> here
> and here is
> here and I am
> I . . . (Darwish 1994: 394-95)

Darwish's poetry is ultimately rhythm. Elias Khouri, the Lebanese novelist and critic, writes: "Homeland which becomes in the *qaṣīdah* an address for the long travel is an act (*fi'l*) and not oranges or things." (Khouri 1982: 272) The critic Naim Araydeh, as well, looks at such verses as "the desire of the words to change its speaker" and claims that the word for Darwish is a new rhythm.[19]

"Poetry is a type of writing absence," notes Adonis, since it is a search for the unknown. It is an absence as movement and condition of writing. (Adonis 1993: 70) In his letters to the Palestinian poet Samih al-Qasim, Darwish shares this vision of poetry, as much as he is distant from Adonis. He writes to al-Qasim: "The poem surpasses its subject to be mesmerized with itself and its techniques." (Darwish 1990:36) Poetry, however, remains testimonial in *Why Have You Left the Horse Alone?*, for one who recognizes that testimony is impossible except through the silence of death in writing: "I am a witness and it is useful to know that for martyrs and witnesses there is one vocabulary in the Arabic language, so the witness is the martyr (*shāhed* [witness] and *shahīd* [martyr])." (Darwish 1990:36). As with Djebar, the work of testimony is a fundamental component of the reconstitution of home. Whereas both are aware of the difficulty of true testimony, each foregrounds this according to the literary form that the writer is using. If language testifies for Djebar; for Darwish, language charts another possibility for home.

Notes

1. All translations from the Arabic are my own, unless otherwise indicated.

2. Literally the "tongue of the Arabs," it is an authoritative Arabic-Arabic dictionary that provides etymologies of words and literary references.

3. Ramadan Muhammad argues that Darwish also dialogues with an absent text, which is political discourse. He offers the poem "Aḥmad al-Za'tar" as an example, where Ahmad is one of the names of the prophet Muhammad and Za'tar is the name of a Palestinian refugee camp in Beirut. These names are transformed from their historical signification and are rendered "mythic." Ramadan Basstтawissi Muhammad, "Al-Ḥadātha fī Shi'r Maḥmūd Darwīsh," [The Modern in Darwish's Poetry] *Al-Qāhirah* 151 (1995): 42.

4. Regina M. Schwartz, in her bold book, *The Curse of Cain: the Violent Legacy of Monotheism*, attributes these sibling rivalries to a process of identity formation that operates on a principle of scarcity and oneness pervasive in the logic of monotheism. "Scarcity is encoded in the Bible as a principle of Oneness (one land, one people, one nation) and in monotheistic thinking (one Deity), it becomes a demand for exclusive allegiance that threatens with the violence of exclusion." Regina M. Schwartz, *The Curse of Cain: The Violent Legacy of Monotheism* (Chicago: University of Chicago Press, 1997), x-xi.

5. Sufism is said to derive from the Arabic word for wool, *ṣūf*. The Sufis apparently wore wool for humility. Others attribute the name to *ṣafā'*, Arabic for purity.

6. Adonis considers Sufi writing, in addition to its expository aspect, as written in a poetic language that is metered but in prose. He also sees it as expanding the metrical forms, and that it resembles what is called today a "prose-poetry." Adonis, *Al-Ṣūffīyah wal-Surriyalīyah*, [Sufism and Surrealism] Second print (Beirut: Dār al-Sāqī, 1995), 22.

7. For Abdel Haq, the Sufi's preoccupation with language is exemplary: "No one was captivated with language as Sufism was to the point of madness. And what more mad than to destroy the self or absent it in order to issue forth language and fulfill it?" Munsif Abdel Haq, "Zaman al-Kitābah, Zaman al-Inṣāt," [The Time of Writing, the Time of Hearing] *Al-Karmel* 46 (1992): 52. *Ibdā'* or innovative creation for Sufism is not simply "the ability to break the familiar boundaries for using language but rather in breaking the self's ordinary relation with creative language. He does not write a new

language as much as he writes a new relation with language." Abdel Haq, 53. Furthermore, Sufi writing poses reading as a problem as we will see in the case of al-Nuffari's texts, not only because the reader will not be able to derive any knowledge from what is read but also because the texts of al-Nuffari, as Abdel Haq points out, refuse their readers. Al-Nuffari distinguishes himself from other Sufi writers because his writings, in addition to being non didactic or communicative, do not address an outside reader. Rather, his writings close upon themselves. Abdel Haq, 53.

8. Maurice Blanchot, *The Space of Literature*, translated by Ann Smock (Lincoln: University of Nebraska Press, 1982), p. 142.

9. *Mu'allaqah* is singular for *mu'allaqāt*. *Mu'allaqāt* are known as "suspended poetry"; they are the oldest collection of Arabic *qaṣīdahs* or poems. Believed to be seven, later ten, chosen as the best ones and written in gold, they were hung at the wall of Ka'ba, a shrine, in Mecca, hence their names which means to be hung or suspended.

10. The Arabic word "*dalīl*" which I translated as "guide" is rich in meaning and can mean the following: sign, mark, evidence, proof, testimony, witness, clue, key, index, reference, etc.

11. *Mu'allaqatun* is the singular, indefinite form for *Mu'allaqāt*. *Mu'allaqatān* refers to two.

12. The Arabic word for necklaces "*qalā'id*" can also mean exquisite poems.

13. *Hājar* and *hājarū* signify migration. Hājar is the first name of the first wife of Abraham who bore Ishmael, the presumed father of the Arabs. Hājarū signifies "they migrated."

14. *Mu'allaqāt* is plural for *mu'allaqah*.

15. See Adonis's analysis of the language of the Qur'an in *Al-Naṣṣ al-Qur'ānī wa Afāq al-Kitābah* [The Qur'anic Text and the Horizons of Writing] (Beirut: Dār al-Adāb, 1993).

16. Meeting with Darwish in Ramallah, April 10, 1996.

17. Abu 'Ala' al-Ma'arri is another, earlier example. He used the Arabic word "*dahr*" [temporality in the long sense, long time, era] in its spatial signification: "And even if Gabriel flew the remainder of his life/ from *dahr* he would not have been able to get out of *dahr*." Cited in Ali Shawk. "Ihtimāmāt Mithūlūgīyah wa-Istiṭrādāt Lughawīyah: Al-Qism al-Thālith," [Mythological and Linguistic Interests: Part 3] *Al-Karmel* 26 (1987): 6.

18. On the elaboration of the various forms, see Abdallah al-Samti, "Maḥmūd Darwīsh wa-Mawāqīt al-Qaṣīdah: Jamālīyāt al-Zaman al-Naṣṣī: Muqāranah Waṣfīyah Simyā'īyah," [Mahmoud Darwish and the Times of the Qaṣīdah: A Semiotic Comparison] *Al-Qāhirah* 151 (1995): 73-74.

19. 'Araydah calls the rhythm of "Qaṣīdat Bayrūt," for instance, the "sea rhythm," since it begins with a short rhythm and then expands gradually just like the movement of the sea. Beirut is named "sea," "war," "ink," "profit". The play in Arabic on the letters of the word "sea" in its association with Beirut is difficult to translate. Darwish takes the consonant letters of the word sea (b, ḥ, r) and plays on the variation of the letters to create *baḥr*, *ḥarb*, *ḥibr*, *ribḥ* (sea, war, ink, profit).

Afterword

"We live not just our own lives but the longings of our century."
—John Berger, *and our faces, my heart, brief as photos*, 67.

If the loss of home is a de-centered experience of fragmentation, the only way to redress homelessness is through solidarity as John Berger argues, and as the literary works of Assia Djebar and Mahmoud Darwish bear out. (Berger 1984: 57, 67) In the novels of Djebar that we considered, *Loin de Médine* and *L'amour, la fantasia,* it is with the female figures of Isma and Pauline that Djebar ends her respective narratives, valorizing them as sutures of contradictions, as women who privileged solidarity over identity, whether filial, national, or that of class, encountering them through writing even if that barely brings them to light. In Darwish's poetry, solidarity is implied in the dialogue of the poet with the other and with his heritage, in the collective poetic endeavor of the *nashīd.* Solidarity points a way beyond the impasse of the present.

While the work of both writers is addressed to language itself and recognizes how language may be the only home, the poetry of Darwish and the novels of Djebar also allow for a consideration of narrative in relation to poetry. Both writers point to the possibility and limits of the forms they use, foregrounding an inextricable link between the quest for identity and for form. Whereas for Darwish, it is poetic language that charts the possibilities for home through its lineage and ruptures with a poetic heritage of *nashīd,* as a double quest for poetry and for lost home, interrogating poetry's possibility of presencing that which can no longer be presenced; for Djebar, it is language as aporia that reflects the hybrid and fragmenting narrative of the divided self. The aporia manifests itself in a language of the other that narrates the self, a language transmitted through love and violence, a narrative that attempts to relate the unarratable. The aporia, like her autobiographical and testimonial narrative of fiction, is the necessary but impossible task.

> Language is . . . *potentially* . . . complete . . . holding . . . the totality of human experience . . . It even allows space for the unspeakable. In this sense . . . it is . . . the . . . only dwelling place that cannot be hostile to man. For prose this

> home is a vast territory, a country which it crosses through a network of tracks, paths . . . for poetry this home is concentrated on a single center, a single voice, and this voice is simultaneously that of an announcement and a response to it. One can say anything to language. This is why it is a listener, closer to us than any silence or any god. Yet its very openness can signify indifference . . . Poetry addresses language in such a way as to close this indifference and to incite a caring . . . Poetry can repair no loss but it defies the space which separates. And it does this by its continual labor of reassembling what has been scattered . . . Poetry's impulse to use metaphor, to discover resemblance, is not to make comparisons . . . or to diminish the particularity of any event; it is to discover those correspondences of which the sum total would be proof of the indivisible totality of existence . . . Apart from reassembling by metaphor, poetry reunites by its *reach*. It equates the reach of a feeling with the reach of the universe. (Berger 1984: 95-97, emphasis is in the original)

A new beginning for both authors lies in language, where possibility beyond the violent history can emerge. The originality of the word implies, as Berger suggests, a certain return to origin but also novel creation: "In poetry alone, the two senses are united in such a way that they are no longer contradictory." (Berger 1984: 98) Both authors, whether through poetry or narrative, seek new literary forms and articulations of self precisely through revision of heritage.

In language, a judgment is rendered, as seen in the literary periods addressed, the quartet of Djebar—*L'amour, la fantasia* (1985); *Ombre sultane* (1987); *Loine de Médine* (1991); *Vaste est la prison* (1995)—and Darwish's post-Beirut 1982 writing, approximately the stage of the "epic song," from *Ḥiṣār li-Madā'iḥ al-Baḥr* [A Siege for the Praises of the Sea] (1984) until *Limādhā Tarakta al Ḥiṣāna Waḥīdan*? [Why Have You Left the Horse Alone?] (1995). As John Berger writes: "language offers, obstinately and mysteriously, its own judgment when it is addressed as poetry. This judgment is distinct from that of any moral code." (Berger 1984: 98-99) It is one rendered by history; and one that poetry, as well as narrative, renders through its testimony. And more distantly, it is rendered by the language itself, the French language of Djebar and the distant lyric of Darwish.

Language poses as one of the features of comparison of the cultural production of the Maghreb to that of the Mashreq. While the literature of the Maghreb has been multilingual—mainly of Arabic, of French, and of Berber, the Mashreq has presented a seemingly monolingual corpus in Arabic literature. Increasingly its multilingualism is becoming visible with Arab writers writing in English, French, and Hebrew to name the most obvious ones. While Francophone literature has existed in Arab countries in the Middle East, the extent of it is nowhere near that of North Africa. The history of such a choice varies as well. The French mandates in Arab countries of the Middle East have not lead nearly to the effect of French colonialism in Algeria. This is in addition to the physical proximity of North Africa to Europe and to a long history of foreign domination. The question of language—its choice and its implications on identity have been quite theorized in the context of Maghrebian literature. For Darwish, it is unthinkable, emerging as he did as a poet of resistance in the sixties and experiencing the overtake of his homeland in his youth, to ground his identity in a language other than Arabic. Djebar, however, is writing after over one hundred and fifty years of French colonialism.

While both writers address themselves to a paternal heritage, the question of gender remains mostly symbolic for Darwish, although writers from the Middle East, both men and women have dealt with it in its social everyday aspect as does Djebar in her work. This may be partially due to the form. Djebar's vision remains unique, however, as she considers the plight of women through a dialogue with heritage.

What may also be a large distinction between Mashreq and Maghreb literature is the fact that on the international scene, in terms of awards and recognition, it is narrative that is mostly featured in Maghrebian literature, specifically francophone novels. Consider for instance the admittance of Djebar to the Académie Française in 2006 or Taher Ben Jelloun's Prix Goncourt in 1987. In the Arab Middle East, poetry remains vital as seen in the work of the living poets Adonis and Darwish, who are not only recognized in the region but internationally, more perhaps than any writer of narrative from the Middle East. Of the living contemporary Arab writers of Mashreq, they are the only possible contenders for the Nobel Prize.

Home, whether articulated in the Maghreb or the Mashreq, remains a desire and an estrangement, often irrecuperable. As it was in the biblical rendition of Abraham, home remains a deferral and cannot be dissociated from a paternal heritage. Home has been inherited as *disorder*, one that Abraham never succeeded in setting in order or where order has been violently imposed through exclusion and confinement. From its origins, disorder has been closely tied to conflicts of inheritance of home and of name. This is the heritage of paternity received as social and political order from the myth of Abraham filtered through the various traditional accounts. The sons and daughters of Ishmael seem to have been the true inheritors of this legacy of dispossession. The paternal figure in the work of Darwish and Djebar, as emblem of faith and submission predicated on the exile and sacrifice of the son, is re-examined to allow for home, hope, and future without exclusion, submission, or disappearance. Both of their literary ventures involve an attempt at reconstruction, a collective effort through narrative and poetry that would allow for new stories to emerge from the old myths. Darwish and Djebar foreground the way in which history has read the Abraham myth to result in nationalist and fundamentalist configurations of identity.

Perhaps for both Darwish and Djebar, Abraham is ultimately the site of contestation that remains, not only through the historical conflicts that are contemporaneous but also through the textual production. While Djebar increasingly links the legacy of Muhammad to that of Abraham, locating Islam within this fixed paternal heritage of sacrifice and dispossession, she at the same time recalls Hagar and her daughters as the body of struggle. The predicament of Hagar and her daughters as one of displacement and dispossession, embodying both emigration and abandonment, is already figured in her name. As Djebar returns to the origins of Islam to contend with religious fundamentalism and to reveal how visions of home are always already gendered, divided, how aporetic impasses could lead to alternative outcomes, Darwish returns to early moments of heritage to chart a vision of home that defies its nationalist exclusions. The figure of the father represents plural and aporetic aspects of heritage—tradition and modernity, love and warring, departure and becoming, dispossession and inheritance—fragments of which could be reconstituted for a different vision of home.

Each foregrounds the literary form that the writer is using: interestingly, Darwish and Djebar are attempting autobiographies in poetry and narrative respectively, mainly in *Limādhā Tarakta al Ḥiṣāna Waḥīdan*? [Why Have You Left the Horse Alone?] and *L'amour, la fantasia*. If language testifies for Djebar; for Darwish, it charts another possibility for home. Poetry itself is figured as home, as genesis, desire, survival, *nashīd* as perpetual search for home in an open historical struggle. Through his vision of *nashīd*, Darwish creates a poetic vision that heralds a new beginning as an aesthetic and historical necessity. Djebar's palimpsestic writing reveals in the fragments of the past a vision of solidarity.

Darwish and Djebar ultimately address themselves to two facets of the socio-political legacy of a paternal heritage: exile of the sons and exclusion of women as they manifest themselves in contemporary failures of nationalism and religious fundamentalism. In reading Darwish, Djebar would certainly evoke the faces of women and their daily realities, exploring gendered visions of home as both domestic and national, calling perhaps for the need of examining new configurations of the domestic space while Darwish would see Djebar's emphasis on women as a necessary and constitutive part of the human struggle for freedom. Both writers probe meanings of home in light of historical conflict, where home is itself is at stake and is constitutive of the conflict. Djebar who longs to sing recalls Darwish's dream of divine prose, connecting their aesthetic quests with their historical struggles for new liberating visions and social realities to emerge. Home is revealed as a process of becoming rather than one of departure. And so, home has never been so close.

Bibliography

Abbas, Ihsan. *Ittijāhāt al-Shi'r al-'Arabī al-Mu'āṣir.* [Trends in Contemporary Arabic Poetry] Kuwait City, Kuwait: Al-Majliss al-Waṭanī lil-Thaqāfah, 1978.

———. *Tārīkh al-Naqd al-Adabī 'ind al-'Arab: Naqd al-Shi'r min al-Qarn al-Thānī ḥatā al-Qarn al-Thāmin al-Hijrī.* [The History of Arab Literary Criticism from the Second Century until the Eighth Century Hijra] Amman, Jordan: Dār al-Sharq lil-Nashr wal-Tawzī', 1986.

Abdel Aziz, Ahmad. "Athār Lūrka fī al-Adab al-'Arabī al-Mu'āṣir." [Influences of Lorca on Contemporary Arabic Literature] *Fuṣūl* 4 (1983): 271-299.

Abdel Haq, Munsif. "Zaman al-Kitābah, Zaman al-Inṣāt." [The Time of Writing, the Time of Hearing] *Al-Karmel* 46 (1992): 52-81.

Abdel Jaouad, Hédi. "*L'amour, la fantasia* d'Assia Djebar: 'Chronique de guerre, voix des femmes.'" *Revue Celfan* 7 (November 1987-February 1988): 21-29.

Abdel Razaq. *Al-Ghurbah fī al-Shi'r al-Jāhilī.* [Exile in Pre-Islamic Poetry] Damascus: Manshūrāt Ittiḥād al-Kuttāb al-'Arab, 1982.

Abu Dib, Kamal. "Lughat al-Ghiyāb fī Qaṣīdat al-Ḥadāthah." [The language of Absence in the Modern Poem] *Al-Fikr al-Dimuqrāṭī* 3 (1988): 37-56.

Abu Salma. *Min Filasṭīn Rīshāti.* [From Palestine my Feathers] 'Akka [Acre]: Mu'assassat al-Aswār, 1980.

Abu Sana, Muhammad Ibrahim. "Maḥmūd Darwīsh Yuḥāwila Iḥrāq Asāṭīruhu." [Mahmoud Darwish Attempts to Burn his Myths] *Jarīdat al-Sharq al-Awsaṭ*, 7 October 1986.

Abu Tammam, Habib. *Dīwān Abī Tammām bi-shirāḥ al-Khaṭīb al-Ṭabrīzī.* [Collected works with Tabrizi's commentary] Cairo: Ed. Mohammad Abduh 'Azzam, 1973.

Accad, Evelyne. "Freedom and the Social Context: Arab Women's Special Contribution to Literature." *Feminist Issues* 7 (Fall 1987): 33-47.

Accad, Evelyne, and Rose Ghurayyib. *Contemporary Arab Women Writers and Poets.* Beirut: Monograph Series of the Institute for Women's Studies in the Arab World, 1985.

Adonis. *Abjadīyah Thāniyah.* [A Second Alphabet] Casablanca: Dār Tubqāl lil-Nashr, 1994.

———. "Desert: Selections from the Siege of Beirut in 1982." Pp. 134-163 in *Victims of a Map*, translated and edited by Abdullah al-Udhari. London: al-Sāqī Books, 1984.

———. "Fī al-Shi'rīyah." [On the Poetic] *Al-Karmel* 38 (1990): 136-148.

———. *Al-Kitāb: Ams al-Makān al-Ān.* [The Book] Beirut: Dār al-Sāqī, 1995.

———. *Al-Naṣṣ al-Qur'ānī wa Afāq al-Kitābah.* [The Qur'anic Text and the Horizons of Writing] Beirut: Dār al-Adāb, 1993.

———. *Muqaddamah lil-Shi'r al-'Arabī.* [An Introduction to Arabic poetry] Beirut: Dār al-'Awdah, 1983.

———. *Al-Niẓām wal-Kalām.* [System and Words] Beirut: Dār al-Adāb, 1993.

———. *Al-Shi'rīyah al-Arabīyah.* [Arabic Poetic] Second ed. Beirut: Dār al-Adāb, 1989.

———. *Al-Ṣūffīyah wal-Surriyalīyah.* [Sufism and Surrealism] Second print. Beirut: Dār al-Sāqī, 1995.

———. *Zamān al-Shi'r.* [The Time of Poetry] Beirut: Dār al-'Awdah, 1978.

Ahmed, Leila. *Women and Gender in Islam: Historical Roots of a Modern Debate.* New Haven, CT: Yale University Press, 1993.

Ahnouch, Fatima. "Assia Djebar: The Song of Writing." *World Literature Today* 7 (1996): 795-799.

Allen, Roger. *The Arabic Literary Heritage: The Development of Its Genres and Criticism.* Cambridge: Cambridge University Press, 1998.

Anis, Ibrahim. *Mūsīqat al-Shi'r al-'Arabī.* [The Music of Arabic Poetry] Cairo: n. p., 1988.

Araidi, Na'im. *Al-Binā' al-Mujassam: Dirāsah fī Ṭabī'at al-Shi'r 'ind Maḥmūd Darwīsh.* [The Embodied Structure: a Study in the Nature of Darwish's Poetry] 'Akka [Acre]: Mu'assassat al-Aswār, 1993.

Arietti, Silvano. *Abraham and the Contemporary Mind.* New York: Basic Books, Inc., 1981.

Arendt, Hannah, ed. and intro. *Illuminations: Essays and Reflections*, translated by Harry Zohn. New York: Schocken Books, 1968.

Aristotle. *Poetics*, translated by Leo Golden and commentary by O. B. Hardison. Tallahassee, FL: Florida State University Press, 1981.

Asfour, Jaber. "Ma'nā al-Ḥadāthah fī al-Shi'r al-Mu'āṣir." [The meaning of modernity in Contemporary Poetry] *Fuṣūl* 4.4 (1984): 35-56.

Assa-Rosenblum, Sonia. "M'introduire dans ton histoire: Entrée des narrateurs dans *L'amour, la fantasia* d'Assia Djebar." *Études Francophones* 12 (1996-1997): 67-77.

Auerbach, Erich. *Mimesis: The Representation of Reality in Western Literature.* Fiftieth anniversary edition. Princeton, NJ: Princeton University Press, 2003.

Averröes. *Middle Commentary on Aristotle's* Poetics, trans. Charles E. Butterworth. Princeton, NJ: Princeton University Press, 1986.

Awad, Rita. *Usṭūrat al-Mawt wal-Inbi'āth fil-Shi'r al-'Arabī al-Mu'āṣir.* [The Myth of Death and Resurrection in Contemporary Arabic Poetry] Beirut: n. p., 1978.

Ba'albaki, Ruhi. *Al-Mawrid.* [Arabic-English and English-Arabic Dictionary] third ed. Beirut: Dār al-'Ilm lil-Malāyīn, 1991.

Badr, Liana, Zakariyya Muhammad, and Munther Jaber. "Notre présent ne se résout ni à commencer ni à finir." Pp. 89-106 in *La Palestine comme métaphore: Entretiens*, translated from the Arabic by Elias Sanbar and from the Hebrew by Simone Bitton. Paris: Actes Sud, 1997.

Bammer, Angelika. "Introduction." *new formations* 17 (Summer 1992).

Belatche, Massoud. *Voix et visages de femmes dans le roman Algérien de langue française.* Washington DC: The George Washington University Press, 1982.

Benjamin, Walter. *Illuminations: Essays and Reflections*, edited by Hannah Arendt. trans. Harry Zohn. New York: Schocken, 1969.

Berger, John. *And Our Faces, My Heart, Brief as Photos.* London: Bloomsbury, 2005.

Beydoun, Abbas. "Qui impose son récit hérite la terre du récit." *La Palestine comme métaphore.*

Beydoun, Haider Tawfiq. *Maḥmūd Darwīsh: Shā'ir al-Arḍ al-Muḥtallah.* [Mahmoud Darwish: Poet of the Occupied Land] Beirut: Dār al-Kutub al-'Ilmiyah, 1991.

Bhabha, Homi K. *Nation and Narration.* New York: Routledge, 1990.

Biguenet, John, and Rainer Schulte, eds. *Theories of Translation: An Anthology of Essays from Dryden to Derrida.* Chicago: The University of Chicago Press, 1992.

Binnis, Mohammad. *Al-Shi'r al-'Arabī al-Ḥadīth.* [Modern Arabic poetry] Four vols. Casablanca: Dār Tubqāl lil-Nashr, 1991.

Blanchot, Maurice. *The Space of Literature,* translated by Ann Smock. Lincoln, NE: University of Nebraska Press, 1982.

———. *The Unavowable Community,* translated by Pierre Joris. Barrytown, NY: Station Hill, 1988.

———. *The Work of Fire,* translated by Charlotte Mandell. Stanford, CA: Stanford University Press, 1995.

———. *The Writing of the Disaster,* translated by Ann Smock. Lincoln, NE: University of Nebraska Press, 1986.

Bonn, Charles. *Le roman algérien de langue française.* Paris: Éditions L'Harmattan, 1985.

Bonner, Barbara, ed. *Sacred Ground: Writings about Home.* Minneapolis, MN: Milkweed Editions, 1996.

Borges, Jorge Luis. *Labyrinths: Selected Stories & Other Writing,* edited by Donald A. Yates & James E. Irby, pref. by André Maurois. New York: A New Directions Book, 1964.

Boullatta, Issa J., ed. *Critical Perspectives on Modern Arabic Literature.* Washington DC: Three Continents Press, 1980.

———. ed. and trans. *Modern Arab Poets 1950-1975.* London: n. p., 1976.

Bouzar, Wadi. "The French Language Algerian Novel." *Research in African Literature* 23 (1992): 51-59.

Bowman, Glenn. "A Country of Words: Conceiving the Palestinian Nation from the position of Exile." Pp. 138-170 in *The Making of Political Identities,* edited by Ernesto Laclau. New York: Verso, 1994.

Brahimi, Denise. *Maghrébines: Portraits Littéraires.* Paris: Éditions L'Harmattan, 1995.

Bsseisso, Mu'in. *Al-A'māl al-Shi'rīyah al-Kāmilah.* [Complete Works] Beirut: Dār al-'Awdah, 1981.

———. *Al-Qaṣīdah.* Beirut: Dār Ibn Rushd, 1985.

Bustani al-, Al Mu'allem Butrus. *Muḥīṭ al-Muḥīṭ.* [An Arabic-Arabic Dictionary] Beirut: Librairie du Liban Publisher, 1993.

Celan, Paul. "The Meridian." Pp. 37-55 in *Paul Celan: Collected Prose,* translated by Rosemari Waldrop. New York: The Sheep Meadow Press, Riverdale-on-Hudson, 1986.

Chalala, Elie. "The Silence of Arab Intellectuals on Algeria's Killing Fields." *Al-Jadid* 21 (1997).

Clerc, Jeanne-Marie. *Assia Djebar: Écrire, transgresser, résister.* Paris: L'Harmattan, 1997.

Cobham, Catherine. *An Introduction to Arab Poetics.* Austin, TX: University of Texas Press, 1990.

Cooke, Miriam. "Arab Women Arab Wars." *Cultural Critique* 29 (1994-1995): 5-29.

———. *Women Claim Islam. Creating Islamic Feminism through Literature.* New York: Routledge, 2001.

———. "Women Write War: The Centering of the Beirut Decentrists." Pp. 5-29 in *Papers on Lebanon.* Oxford: Centre for Lebanese Studies, 1987.

Crosta, Suzanna. "Stratégies de subversion et de la libération." Pp. 49-81 in *Littérateur et cinéma en Afrique francophone: Ousmane Sembène et Assia Djebar*, edited by Sada Niang. Paris: Editions L'Harmattan, 1996.

Dahbour, Ahmad. "Muqadamah fī Dirasāt al-Shi'r al-Filasṭīni." [A Study of Palestinian Poetry] *Al-Karmel* 23 (1987): 167-212.

———. "Muqadamah fī Dirasāt al-Shi'r al-Filasṭīni: 2" *Al-Karmel* 44 (1992): 27-63.

Darraj, Faisal. "Siyassat al-Kitābah wa Kitābat al-Siyāssah." [The Politics of Writing and the Writing of Politics] *Al-Karmel* 23 (1987): 14-34.

———. "Al-Wāqi'iyah am al-Wāqi'." [Realism or Reality] *Al-Karmel* 5 (1982): 85-123.

Darwish, Mahmoud. *'Ābirūn fī Kalāmin 'Ābir.* [We Pass through Passing Words] Second ed. Beirut: Dār al-'Awdah, 1994.

———. *The Adam of Two Edens: Selected Poems by Mahmoud Darwish*, edited by Munir Akash and Daniel Moore. Syracuse, NY: Syracuse University Press, 2000.

———. "Anta munthu al-Ān Ghayrak."[You Are No Longer Yourself] *Al Ayyām*, 16 June 2007.

———. "Al-Qatl al-Akhar wal-Abjadīyah al-Jadīdah." [The Other Killing and the New Alphabets] *Al-Karmel* 13 (1984): 4-8.

———. "Anqudhūna min hādhā al-Shi'r." [Save us from this Poetry] *Al-Karmel* 6 (1982): 4-13.

———. *Arā mā urīd.* Casablanca: Dār Tubqāl, 1990. Translated in part as *I See What I Want to See* in *Unfortunately It Was Paradise: Selected Poems*, translated and edited by Munir Akash and Carolyn Forché, with Sinan Antoon and Amira al-Zein. Berkeley, CA: University of California Press, 2003.

———.*A'rās* [Weddings]. 'Akka [Acre]: Maktabat al-Aswār lil-Ṭibā'ah wal-Nashr, 1977.

———. *'Aṣāfīr bilā ajniḥah* [Birds Without Wings]. Beirut: Dār al-'Awdah, 1960.

———. *Al-'Aṣāfīr tamūtu fī al-Jalīl* [The birds die in Galilee]. Beirut: Dār al-Adāb, 1970.

———. "Aṣbaḥtu Qādirān 'alā al-Qatl." [I have become Capable of Killing] Interview with Shirbil Dajir. *Al-Yawm al-Sābi'* 7 (1982): 48-55.

———. "Al-shā'ir lā Yaṭali'u 'alā al-Tārīkh ilā min Ba'īd." [The Poet Looks on History only from Afar] Interview. *Al-Wasaṭ* [Beirut] 192 (10-2-1995): 52-56.

———. *'Āshiq min Filasṭīn* [A lover from Palestine]. Beirut: Manshūrāt Dār al-Adāb, 1966.

———. *Awrāq al-zaytūn* [Olive leaves]. Haifa: Maṭba'at al-Ittiḥād al-Ta'wīnīyah, 1964.

———. "Bayt, Thawm, Baṣal, Mā'iz, wa Mafātīh." [House, Garlic, Onions, Goats, and Keys] *Al-Karmel* 33 (1989): 163-168.

———. "Damun lā Yaghīb." [Blood that does not disappear] *Shu'ūn Filasṭīnīyah* [Beirut] 60 (1976): 4-5.

———. *Dhākirah lil-Nisyān: al-Zamān, Bayrūt. al-Makān, Ābb.* [Memory for Forgetting: the Time, Beirut; the Place, August] Casablanca: Dār Tubqāl lil-Nashr, 1987. Translated as *Memory for Forgetfulness: August, Beirut, 1982* by Ibrahim Muhawi. Berkeley, CA: University of California Press, 1995.

———. *Dīwān.* [Collected Poems] Two vols. Beirut: Dār al-'Awdah, 1994.

———. "Fī al-lahẓah al-Marīḍah." [Within the Ailing Moment] *Al-Karmel* 9 (1983): 4-7.

———. *Fī Waṣfi Ḥālatuna: Maqālāt Mukhtārah 1975-1980.* [Assessing our Situation: Collected Essays] Beirut: Dār al-Kalimah, 1987.

———. "Ḥajar al-Wa'ī" [The Stone of Awareness] *Al-Karmel* 27 (1988): 4-12.

———. "Hal Kunnā Biḥājah ilā Kul Hādhih al-Hazā'im li-Nafham mā Huwa al-Shi'r?" [Did We Need all the Setbacks to Understand what is Poetry?] *Al-Wasaṭ* 193 (9-10-1995): 50-53.
———. *Ḥālat Ḥiṣār*. [State of Siege] Beirut: Dār Al-Rayyis, 2002. Translated in *The Butterfly's Burden* by Fady Joudah. Port Townsend, WA: Copper Canyon Press, 2007.
———. "Ḥamādah Yaksir Īṭar al-Ṣūrah . . . wa Yadhab." [Hamada Breaks the Picture Frame and Leaves] *Al-Karmel*. 43 (1992): 144-147.
———. "Ḥarīq Tishrīn wa Ḥarīq Bayrūt." [The fire of Tishrin and the fire of Beirut] *Shu'ūn Filasṭīnīyah* 50-51 (1975): 4-5.
———. *Ḥiṣār li-madā'iḥ al-baḥr* [Siege for the praises of the sea]. Beirut: Dār al-'Awdah, 1984.
———. *Hiya ughniyah, hiya ughniyah* [It's a song, it's a song]. Beirut: Dār al-Kalimah, 1986.
———. "Intifāẓah." *Shu'ūn Filasṭīnīyah* 56 (1976): 5-7.
———. "I'tirāfāt Maḥmūd Darwīsh." [The Confessions of Mahmoud Darwish] Interview. *Majallat Kul al-'Arab* [Paris], June 20 1986.
———. "Juzu' lā Jazīrah." [A part not an island] *Al-Karmel* 5 (1982): 4-7.
———. *Jidārīyah*. [Mural] Beirut: Dār Al-Rayyis, 2000.
———. Ka-Zahr al-Lawz aw Ab'ad [Like almond flowers or further]. Beirut: Dār al-Rayyis, 2005.
———. "Khalīl al-Wazīr wa Marārat al-Ḥurrīyah." [Khalīl al-Wazīr and the Bitterness of Freedom] *Al-Karmel* 28 (1988): 4-7.
———. "Kharaja Ṭāriq." [Ṭariq has left] *Al-Karmel* 13 (1984): 151-154.
———. "Al-Khurūj min al-Sāḥil al-Mutawassiṭ." [Departing from the Coast of the Mediterranean] *Shu'ūn Filasṭīnīyah* 16 (1972): 28-33.
———. "Al-Kitābah fī Darajat al-Ghalayān." [Writing at the Boiling Point] *Al-Adāb* [Beirut] 7 (1974): 2-6.
———. "Lā Bayt lil-Shi'r Khārij al-Niẓām." [No Place for Poetry outside the Systematic] *Al-Karmel* 47(1993): 133-145.
———. *La Palestine comme métaphore: Entretiens*, translated from the Arabic by Elias Sanbar and from the Hebrew by Simone Bitton. Paris: Actes Sud, 1997.
———. *Lā Ta'tadhir 'ammā Fa'alta*. [Do Not Apologize for What You Have Done] Beirut: Dār Al-Rayyis, 2004.
———. "Lā Ta'ūd ilā al-Māḍi ḥaythu Tadhaba fī al-'Awdah." [Don't Return to the Past Where you will Pass the Return] *Al-Adāb* 11 (1974).
———. "Lahum al-Layl wal-nahar lī." [The night is theirs but the day is mine] *Al-Adāb* 4 (1970): 4-7.
———. " 'Libération': Why do you Write?." *Aswār* 11 (1991): 137-139.
———. "Limādhā Kharajtu min Isrā'īl?" [Why did I leave Israel?] *Al-Hilāl* [Cairo] 3 (1971): 4-9.
———. *Limādhā Tarakta al-Ḥiṣāna Wahīdan?*. [Why have you left the horse alone?] Beirut: Riad El-Rayyis Books Ltd., 1995. Translated as *Why Did You Leave Horse Alone?* by Jeffrey Sacks. New York: Archipelago, 2006.
———. "Min Ḥaq al-Shi'r i'lān al-hazīmah." [Poetry has the Right to Proclaim Failure] Interview. *Al-Wasaṭ* 25 September 1995. 191: 52-57.
———. "Mu'īn Bssīsso lā yajliss 'alā maq'ad al-ghiyāb." [Mu'in Bsseisso does not Sit on the Seat of Absence.] *Al-Karmel* 11 (1984): 4-9.
———. The Music of Human Flesh: Poems of the Palestinian Struggle. Translated by Denys Johnson Davies. Washington, DC: Three Continents Press, 1980.

———. “Nakūn aw . . . Nakūn: Hādhā huwa al-Qarār.” [To be or . . . to be: This is the Decision] *Al-Karmel* 18 (1985): 215-217.

———. “Poetry and Palestine.” *Boundary2* 26 (1999): 81–83.

———. *Psalms*, translated by Ben Bennani. Washington, DC: Three Continent’s Press, 1994.

———. *The Raven’s Ink: A Chapbook*, translated and edited by Munir Akash, Carolyn Forché, Amira al-Zein, and Sinan Antoon. The Lannan Foundation, 2001.

———. “Ṣabāḥ al-khayr yā Mājid.” [Good Morning, Majid] *Al-Karmel* 4 (1981): 4-13.

———. *Sarīr al-Gharībah.* [The Bed of the Stranger] Beirut: Dār Al-Rayyis, 1995. Translated in part as *A Bed for the Stranger in Unfortunately It Was Paradise.* Translated as The Stranger’s Bed in *The Butterfly’s Burden.*

———. *Shay’ ‘an al-Waṭan.* [Something on the Homeland] Beirut: Dār al-‘Awdah, 1971.

———. “Saqaṭa l-Ḥabl wa-ẓalla Kamāl Nāṣir Yamshī.” [The Rope Fell and Kamāl Nāsir Continued Walking] *Filasṭīn al-Thawrah* [Beirut] 87 (1974): 26.

———. “Shu‘arā’ al-Muqāwamah Ḍid al-Muqāwamah.” [Poets of Resistance against Resistance] *Al-Adāb* 8 (1974).

———. “Thalāth Shahādāt Shafawīyah.” [Three oral testimonies] *Al-Karmel* 7 (1983): 204-233.

———. “Taraddud al-Mā’ wa-Ḥamās al-Ḥajar.” [The Hesitations of Water and the Fervor of the Stone] *Shu’ūn Filasṭīnīyah* 48 (1975): 3-7.

———. “Tarīq Dimashq.” [Damascus Road] *al-Mawqif al-Adabī* [Damascus] 1(1974): 145-156.

———. *Unfortunately, It was Paradise: Selected Poems*, translated and edited by Munir Akash and Carolyn Forché, with Sinan Antoon and Amira al-Zein. Berkeley, CA: University of California Press, 2003.

———. “‘Urs al-dam al-Filasṭīnī.” [The Wedding of Palestinian Blood] *Shu’ūn Filastīnīyah* 12 (1972): 6-7.

———. *Yawmīyāt al-Ḥuzn al-‘Ādī.* [Journal of Ordinary Sadness] Beirut: al-Mu’assassah al-‘Arabīyah lil-Nashr, 1973.

Darwish, Mahmoud, and Samih al-Qasim. *Al-Rasā’il.* [The letters] Casablanca: Dār Tubqāl lil-Nashr, 1990.

Dawood, N. J., trans. *The Koran.* New York: Penguin Classics, 1999.

Defoe, Daniel. *The History of the Devil: Ancient and Modern.* Philadelphia: D. Talcott, 1837.

Delaney, C. *Abraham on Trial: The Social Legacy of Biblical Myth.* Princeton, NJ: Princeton University Press, 1998.

De Man, Paul. “Anthropomorphism and Trope in the Lyric.” In *The Rhetoric of Romanticism.* New York: Columbia University Press, 1984.

———. *Blindness and Insight: Essays in the Rhetoric of Contemporary Criticism.* Minneapolis: University of Minnesota Press, 1988.

———. *The Resistance to Theory.* Foreword by Wlad Godzich. Minneapolis: University of Minnesota Press, 1986.

———. “Lyric and Modernity.” Pp. 166-186 in *Blindness and Insight.* Revised edition. Minneapolis: University of Minnesota Press, 1983.

———. *The Resistance to Theory.* Minneapolis: University of Minnesota Press, 1986.

Déjeux, Jean. *Assia Djebar: Romancière Algérienne cinéaste Arabe.* Québec: Éditions Naaman de Sherbrook, 1984.

———. “Francophone Literature in the Maghreb: The Problem and the Possibility.” *Research in African Literature* 2 (1992): 5-19.

———. *Littérature Algérienne contemporaine*. Paris: Presses Universitaires de France, 1975.

Derrida, Jacques. *Feu la Cendre*. Paris: Éditions des femmes, 1987.

———. "*Fors*: The Anglish Words of Nicolas Abraham and Maria Torok." Pp. xi-xlviii in *Wolfman's Magic Word*, edited by Nicholas Abraham and Maria Torok, translated by Nicholas Rand. Minneapolis: University of Minnesota Press, 1986.

———. "Freud and the Scene of Writing." Pp. 196-231 in *Writing and Difference*, translated and introduced by Alan Bass. Chicago: The University of Chicago Press, 1978.

———. "From Des Tours de Babel." Pp. 243-253 in *Theories of Translation: An Anthology of Essays from Dryden to Derrida*, edited by Rainer Schulte and John Biguenet, translated by Joseph F. Graham. Chicago: University of Chicago, 1992.

———. "Shibboleth for Paul Celan." Pp. 370-413 in *Acts of Literature*, edited by Derek Attridge. New York: Routledge, 1992.

———. *Writing and Difference*, translated and introduced by Alan Bass. Chicago: The University of Chicago Press, 1978.

Djebar, Assia. *Ces voix qui m'assiègent*. Paris: Albin Michel, 1999.

———. *Fantasia: An Algerian Cavalcade*, translated by Dorothy S. Blair. Portsmouth, NH: Heinemann, 1993.

———. *Femmes d'Alger dans leur appartement*. Paris: Éditions des FEMMES, 1980.

———. *L'Amour, la fantasia*. Paris: Éditions Albin Michel, 1995.

———. *La Disparition de la langue française*. Paris: Albin Michel, 2003.

———. *La Femme sans sépulture*. Paris: Albin Michel, 2002.

———. *La Soif*. Paris; Julliard, 1957.

———. *Le Blanc de l'Algérie*. Paris: Albin Michel, 1995.

———. "Le Discours de Francfort pour le prix de paix des librairies allemands." Oct. 2000. <www.assiadjebar.net/prizes/assia-paix.htm> (5 July 2007).

———. "Le risque d'écrire," Pp. 71-73 in *Mises en Scène d'Écrivains: Assia Djebar, Nicole Brossard, Madeleine Gagnon, France Théoret*, edited by Dominique Johnson and Sylvie Ouzilleau. Sainte-Foy, Québec: Les éditions Le Griffon d'argile, 1993.

———. *Les Alouettes naïves*. Paris: Union Générale, 1967.

———. *Les Enfants du nouveau monde*. Paris: Union Générale; 1962.

———. *Les Impatients*. Paris: Julliard, 1958.

———. *Les Nuits de Strasbourg*. Paris: Actes Sud, 1997.

———. *Loin de Médine: Filles d'Ismaël*. Paris: Éditions Albin Michel, 1991.

———. *Ombre sultane*. Paris: Édition J.C. Lattès, 1987.

———. *Oran, langue morte*. Paris: Actes Sud, 1997.

———. *Poèmes pour l'Algérie heureuse*. Alger: Société Nationale d'Édition et de Diffusion, 1969.

———. *Vaste est la prison*. Paris: Albin Michel, 1995.

Dobie, Madeleine. "The Woman as Look and the Woman as Voice: Assia Djebar and Leïla Sebbar." *Constructions* 9 (1994): 89-103.

Donadey, Ann. "Assia Djebar's Poetics of Subversion." *L'Esprit Créateur* 33 (1993): 107-117.

———. "Polyphonic and Palimpsestic Discourse in the Works of Assia Djebar." *Sub-Stance* 21 (1992).

———. *Recasting Postcolonialism: Women Writing between Worlds*. Portsmouth, NH: Heinemann, 2001.

Eagelton, Terry. *Nationalism, Colonialism, and Literature*. Derry, England: Field Day Pamphlets, 1988.

Elmessiri, Nur and Abdelwahab, eds. and trans. *A Land of Stone and Thyme: An Anthology of Palestinian Short Stories*. London: Quartet Books, 1996.

Farouq, Yasine Ahmed. *Al-Thawrah fī Shi'r Maḥmūd Darwīsh*. [Revolution in the Poetry of Mahmoud Darwish] Tunis: Dār al-Ma'rifah lil-Ṭibā'a wal-Nashr, 1989.

Farouq, Salah. "Al-Jumlah fī Shi'r *Maḥmūd Darwīsh*." [The phrase in the poetry of Darwish] *Mahmoud Darwish: An Arabic Perspective by Fourteen Critics. Al-Qāhirah* [Cairo] 151(1995): 54-60.

Faulkner, Rita. "Assia Djebar, Frantz Fanon, Women, Veils, and Land." *World Literature Today* 7 (1996): 847-855.

Felman, Shoshana and Dori Laub, M.D. *Testimony: Crises of Witnessing in Literature, Psychoanalysis, and History*. New York: Routledge, 1992.

Forché, Carolyn. "Exiled in Language." *Brick* 68 (2001): 65-66.

Fraijat, 'Adil. *Al-Shu'arā' al-Jahilīyūn al-Awā'il: Niṣūs wa-Dirūs*. [The First Pre-Islamic Poets: Texts and Studies] Beirut: Dār al-Mashriq, 1986.

Franzen, Cola, trans. *Poems of Arab Andalusia*. San Francisco: City Lights Books, 1988.

Gafaiti, Hafid. "The Blood of Writing: Assia Djebar's Unveiling of Women and History." *World Literature Today* 7 (1996): 813-822.

Garfield, Evelyn Picon. *Women's Voices from Latin America: Interviews with Six Contemporary Authors*. Detroit: Wayne State University Press, 1985.

Gaussey, Soheila. "A Stepmother Tongue: 'Feminine Writing' in Assia Djebar's *Fantasia: An Algerian Cavalcade*." *World Literature Today* 7 (1996): 457-462.

Gauvin, Lise. *L'Écrivain francophone à la croisée des langues: Entretiens*. Paris: Éditions Karthala, 1997.

———. "Writing/re-Writing the Feminine or in the Feminine: Practice Notes." *Études Françaises* 40.1 (2004): 11-28.

Geesey, Patricia A. "Collective Autobiography: Algerian Women and History in Assia Djebar's *L'Amour, la fantasia*." *Dalhousie Studies* 35 (1996): 153-167.

———. "Women's Words: Assia Djebar's *Loin de Médine*." Pp. 40-50 in *The Marabout and the Muse: New Approaches to Islam in African Literature*," edited by Kenneth W. Harrow. Portsmouth, NH: Heinemann, 1996.

———. *Writing the Decolonized Self: Autobiographical Narrative from the Maghreb*. Cincinnati, OH: The Ohio State University, 1991.

Ghali, Wa'el. "al-Ḥiṣān Yaqtaḥim al-Ashbāḥ." [The Horse Invades the Ghosts] *Al-Qāhirah* 151 (1995): 154-164.

Ghazoul, Firyal . "Lughat al-Ḍid al-Jamīl fī Shi'r al-Thamānīnāt: al-Namūthaj al-Filasṭīnī." [Aesthetic Languages in the Eighties: The Palestinian Example] *Fuṣūl* 7.1-2 (October 1986/March 1987).

Ghidani al-, Abdallah. *Al-Qaṣīdah wal-Naṣṣ al-Muḍad*. [The Qasida and the Oppositional Text] Beirut: Al-Markaz al-Thaqāfī al-'Arabī, 1994.

Gracki, Katherine. "Assia Djebar et l'écriture de l'autobiographie au pluriel." *Women in French Studies* 2 (1994): 54-64.

———. "Writing Violence and the Violence of Writing in Assia Djebar's Algerian Quartet." *World Literature Today* 7 (1996): 835-843.

Green, Mary, et al. *Postcolonial Subjects: Francophone Women Writers*. Minneapolis: University of Minnesota Press, 1996.

Green, Mary Jean. "Dismantling the Colonizing Text: Anne Hébert's *Kamouraska* and Assia Djebar's *L'Amour, la fantasia*." *French Review* 6 (1993): 959-965.

Gurr, Andrew. *Writers in Exile: The Identity of Home in Modern Literature*. Atlantic Highlands, NJ: Humanities Press, 1981.

Habibi, Imil. *Al-Mutashā'il*. [The Pessoptomist] Beirut: Dār ibn Khaldūn, 1974.

Hadidi, Subhi. "Khiyār al-Sīrah wa-Istrātajīyāt al-Ta'bīr." [The Choice of Narrative and the Modes of Expression] *Al-Qāhirah* 151 (1995): 26-36.

———. "Junūn al-Kalimāt." [The Madness of Words] *Al-Karmel* 39 (1991): 166-171.

Hadidi, Subhi, and Basheer al-Baker. "Nulle demeure pour la poésie hors un canon poétique." Pp. 63-88 in *La Palestine comme métaphore*.

Hafez, Sabry. "The Transformation of the Qasida Form in Modern Arabic Poetry." Pp. 99-120 in *Qasida Poetry in Islamic Asia and Africa: Eulogy's Bounty, Meaning's Abundance*, edited by Stefan Sperl and Christopher Schackle. Volume two. New York: E. J. Brill, 1996.

Hajjaji al-, Ahmad. *Al-Usṭūrah fil-Adab al-'Arabī.* [Myth in Arabic Literature] Cairo: Dār al-Hilāl, 1983.

Hajjam al-, Allal. "Mut'at al-Qirā'ah fī al-Rasā'il al-Filasṭīnīyah." [The Pleasure of Reading in the Palestinian *Letters*] *Al-Karmel* 48-49 (1993): 285-305.

Hallaq, Boutrous, Robin Ostle, Stefan Wild, eds. *La poétique de l'espace dans la littérature arabe moderne*. Paris : Presses Sorbonne Nouvelle, 2002.

Hamm, Jean-Jacques. "Le regard de l'objet: Sur l'oeuvre d'Assia Djebar." *Mises en scène d'écrivains: Assia Djebar, Nicole Brossard, Madeleine Gagnon, France Thoret*, edited by Dominique Johnson and Sylvie Ouzilleau. Sainte-Foy, Québec: Les éditions Le Griffon d'argile, 1993.

Hammoud, Magida. *Al-Naqd al-Adabī al-Filasṭīnī fil-Shatāt.* [Palestinian Literary Criticism in Exile] Damascus: Dār Kan'ān lil-Dirāsāt wal-Nashr, 1992.

Hamoudeh, Hussein. "'Missār al-Na'ī . . . Madār al-Ghiyāb,' 'an Shahādāt Maḥmūd Darwīsh fī Dīwānuh al-Akhīr: *Limādhā Tarakta al-Ḥiṣāna Waḥīdan*." [The testimony of Darwish in *Why have you left the horse alone?*] *Al-Qāhirah* 151 (1995): 44-53.

Hanna, Hanna Abu. "Palestinian Poetry and Diglossia." *Al-Karmel Studies in Arabic Language and Literature* [Haifa] 7 (1986): 7-70.

Harlow, Barbara. "Memory and Historical Record: The Literature and Literary Criticism of Beirut, 1982." *Left Politics and the Literary Profession*, edited by Lennard J. Davis and M. Bella Mirabella. New York: Columbia University Press, 1990.

———. "Palestine or Andalusia: the Literary Response to the Israeli Invasion of Lebanon." *Race and Class* 26 (1984): 33-43.

Hasan, Abd al-Karim. *Qaḍiyat al-Arḍ fī Shi'r Maḥmūd Darwīsh.* [Land in the poetry of Darwish] Damascus: Ittiḥād al-Kuttāb al-'Arab, 1975.

Hawi, Khalil. *Dīwān*. Beirut: Dār al-'Awdah, 1979.

Heidegger, Martin. *Poetry, Language, Thought*, trans. Albert Hofstadter. New York: Harper & Row Publishers, 1971.

Hiddleston, Jane. "The Specific Plurality of Assia Djebar." *French Studies* 58.3 (2004): 371-384.

Hosek, Chaviva, and Patricia Parker, eds. *Lyric Poetry: Beyond New Criticism*. Ithaca, NY: Cornell University Press, 1985.

Hure, Jacques. "L'écriture arabe et le mythe de Grenade." Actes du congres de la Société française de littérature générale et comparative. Aix-en-Provence, 24-26 Septembre 1986." Pp. 341-352 in *Art et Littérature*, forward by André-M. Rousseau and J. Molino, afterward by Roger Bozzetto. Aix-en-Provence, France: Université de Provence, 1988.

Husain, Rashid. *Qaṣa'id Filasṭīnīyah*. [Palestinian Poems] Ṣafā 'Amr, Palestine: Lajnat Iḥyā' Turāth Rashīd Ḥusayn, 1980.

Husain al-, Qasi. *Al-Mawt wal-Ḥayāt fī Shi'r al-Muqāwamah.* [Death and Life in the Resistance Poetry] Beirut: Dār al-Rā'id, 1985.

'Id al-, Yamna. "Aḥmad al-Za'tar li-Maḥmūd Darwīsh." [Darwish's "Ahmad al-Zatar"] *Al-Ṭarīq* [Beirut] 2-3 (1977): 133-142.

Ismael, Muhammad al-Sayyid. "Min Lahjat al-Khiṭāb ilā Lughat al-Ḥayāt: 'Ward Aqall' Namūthajan." [From the Accents of Speech to the Language of Life: the Case of "Ward Aqall"] *Al-Qāhirah* 151 (1995): 102-110.

Jaidah, Abdul Hamid. *Al-Ittijahāt al-Jadīdah fī al-Shi'r al-'Arabī al-Mu'āṣir.* [New Directions in Contemporary Arabic Poetry] Beirut: Mu'assassat Nūfil, 1980.

Jabra, Ibrahim Jabra. *Al-Riḥlah al-Thāminah: Dirāsāt Naqdīyah.* [Critical studies] Beirut: al Mu'assassah al-Arabīyah li-l-Dirāsāt wal-Nashr, 1979.

Jameson, Fredric. *The Political Unconscious: Narrative as a Socially Symbolic Act.* Ithaca, NY: Cornell University Press, 1981.

Jarrah, Nuri. "La maison est plus belle que le chemin de la maison." Pp. 169-189 in *La Palestine comme métaphore.*

Jayyusi, Salma Khadra. *Anthology of Modern Palestinian Literature.* New York: Columbia University Press, 1992.

———. ed. *The Legacy of Muslim Spain.* New York: E. J. Brill, 1992.

———. *Modern Arabic Poetry.* Anthology. New York: E. J. Brill, 1987.

———. "The Persistence of the Qasida Form." *Qasida Poetry in Islamic Asia and Africa: Classical Traditions and Modern Meanings*, edited by Stefan Sperl and Christopher Shackle. Vol. one. New York, E. J. Brill, 1996.

———. *Trends and Movements in Modern Arabic Poetry.* Leiden, Netherlands: E. J. Brill, 1977.

Jazzar al-, Muhammad al-Fikri. "Al-Wa'ī wal-Ḥasāssīyah, Shi'r Maḥmūd Darwīsh: Marḥalat mā ba'd Bayrūt." [Awareness and Feeling: Darwish's Poetry after Beirut] *Al-Qāhirah* 151 (1995): 90-101.

Johnson, W.R. *The Idea of Lyric: Lyric Modes in Ancient and Modern Poetry.* Berkeley, CA: University of California Press, 1982.

Jones, Alan, ed. and trans. *Early Arabic Poetry: Marathi and Sulūk Poems.* Vol. one. Oxford: Ithaca Press, 1992.

Kanafani; Ghassan. *Adab al-Muqāwamah fī Filasṭīn al-Muḥtallah 1948-1966.* [Resistance Literature in Occupied Palestine 1948-66] Beirut: Mu'assassat al-Abḥāth al-'Arabīyah, 1982.

———."Adab al-Muqāwamah fī Filasṭīn al-Muḥtallah: 1966-1948." *Al Athār Al Kāmilah: Al-Dirāsāt al-Adabīyah.* Beirut: Dār al-Ṭalī'a: 1980.

———. *'Ā'id ilā Ḥayfā.* [Return to Haifa] Beirut: Dār al- Ṭalī'a, 1980.

———. *Rijāl fī al-Shams.* [Men in the Sun] Beirut: Mu'assassat al-Abhāth al-'Arabīyah, 1963.

———. *Arḍ al-Burtuqāl al-Ḥazīn.* [The land of sad oranges] Beirut: Mu'assassat al-Abḥāth al-'Arabīyah, 1962.

Kelley, David. "Assia Djebar: Parallels and Paradoxes." *World Literature Today* 7 (1996): 844-846.

Khalidi, Rashid, Lisa Anderson, Muhammad Muslih, and Reeve S. Simon, eds. *The Origins of Arab Nationalism.* New York: Columbia University Press, 1991.

Khatib al-, Husam. *Ẓilal Filasṭīnīyah fī al-Tajrubah al-Adabīyah.* [Palestinian Shadows in the Literary Experience] Damascus: Dā'irat al-Thaqāfah, Munaẓamat al-Taḥrīr al-Filasṭīnīyah, 1990.

Khatibi, Abdelkabir. *Maghreb pluriel.* Paris: Denoël, 1983.

Khouri, Elias. *Dirasāt fī Naqd al-Shi'r.* [Studies in Poetics] Beirut: Mu'assassat al-Abḥāth al-'Arabīyah, 1986.

———. *Al-Dhākirah al-Mafqūdah.* [Forgotten Memory] Beirut: Mu'assassat al-Abḥāth al-'Arabīyah, 1982.

Khouri, Mounah. *Studies in Contemporary Arabic Poetry and Criticism*. Piedmont, CA: Jahan Books Co., 1987.

Kierkegaard, S. *Fear and Trembling*, translated with introduction and notes by Walter Lowrie. Princeton, NJ: Princeton University Press, 1968.

Lang, George. "Jihad, *Ijtihad*, and Other Dialogical Wars in *La Mère du printemps*, *Le Harem politique*, and *Loin de Médine*." Pp. 1-22 in *The Marabout and the Muse: New Approaches to Islam in African Literature*.

Lansari, Ahmed. *La littérature Algérienne de l'entre-deux-guerres: Genèse et fonctionnement*. Paris: Éditions Publisud, 1995.

Lauten, Kathryn M. "Discontinuous Continuities in Assia Djebar's *L'Amour La Fantasia*." *Cincinnati Romance Review* 16 (1997): 101-107.

Lee, Dennis. "Cadence, Country, Silence: Writing in Colonial Space." *Boundary 2* 3.1 (Fall 1974): 151-68.

Lee, Sonia. "Daughters of Hagar: Daughters of Mohammed." Pp. 51-61 in *The Marabout and the Muse: New Approaches to Islam in African Literature*.

Leeuwen, Richard van. "The Poet and his Mission: Text and Space in the Prose Works of Mahmoud Darwish." Pp. 255-277 in *Conscious Voices: Concepts of Writing in the Middle East*, edited by Priska Furrer and Johann Christoph Burgel Stephan Guth. Beirut: Orient Institut der DMG, 1999.

Levenson, Jon D. "Abusing Abraham: Traditions, Religious Histories, and Modern Misinterpretations." *Judaism* 47 (Summer 1998): 259-277.

"Libération: 'Why Do You Write?'" 1991. In *Aswār* 11: 139.

Lu'abi al-, Abdellatif. "Al-Kitābah li-Filasṭīn fī al-Wa'ī wa-Allāwa'ī." [Writing for Palestine in the Conscious and the Unconscious] *Al-Karmel* 12 (1984): 309-315.

Luji al-, Abdel Rahman. *Al-Īqā' fī al-Shi'r al-'Arabī*. [Rhythm in Arabic Poetry] Damascus: Dār al-Ḥaṣad lil-Nashr wal-Tawzī', 1989.

Lukács, Georg. *The Historical Novel*, trans. By Hannah Mitchell and Stanley Mitchell. Boston: Beacon Press, 1962.

Ma'arri al-, Abu al-'Ala. *Saqṭ al-Zand*. [The Fall of Fire] Beirut: Dār Ṣadir, 1963.

Mahmoud, Husni. *Shi'r al-Muqāwamah al-Filasṭīnīyah: Dawruhu wa Waqā'i'uhu*. [Palestinian Resistance poetry: Its Role and Reality] Three vols. Amman, Jordan: Al-Wakālah al-'Arabīyah lil-Tawzī' wa al-Nashr, 1984.

Mahwi, Ibrahim. "Al-Lughah Mithl Filasṭīn Tuwaḥḥid mā lā Yattaḥid," [Language like Palestine Unites that which Resists Unity] *Al-Qāhirah* 151 (1995): 122-125.

Malti-Douglas, Fedwa. *Woman's Body, Woman's Word: Gender and Discourse in Arabo-Islamic Writing*. Princeton, NJ: Princeton University Press, 1991.

Martínez-Montávez, Pedro. *Al-Andalus, España, en la Literatura Árabe Contemporánea: La Casa del Pasado*. Madrid: Editoriale MAPFRE S.A., 1992.

Marx, Karl. *The Eighteenth Brumaire of Louis Bonaparte*. New York: International Publishers, 1963.

Marx-Scouras, Danielle. "Muffled Screams/Stifled Voices." *Yale French Studies* 1 (1993): 172-182.

Massad, Joseph. "Conceiving the Masculine: Gender and Palestinian Nationalism." *Middle East Journal* 49 (Summer 1995): 467-483.

Memmi, Albert, ed. *Écrivains francophone du Maghreb: Anthologie*. Paris: Éditions Seghers, 1985.

Mernissi, Fatima. *Beyond the Veil: Male-Female Dynamic in Modern Muslim Society*. Bloomington, IN: Indiana University Press, 1987.

———. *The Veil and the Male Elite: A Feminist Interpretation of Women's Rights in Islam*. Trans. Mary Jo Lakeland. Reading, MA: Addison-Wesley Pub. Co, 1991.

Monroe, James T., ed. and trans. *Hispano-Arabic Poetry*. Berkeley, CA: University of California Press, 1974.

Mortimer, Mildred. *Journeys through the French African Novel*. Portsmouth, NH: Heinemann, 1990.

Muhammad, Ibrahim Abdel Rahman. "Min Uṣūl al-Shi'r al-'Arabī al-Qadīm: al-Aghrāḍ wal-Mūsīqā." [Poetic Conventions of Early Arabic Poetry] *Fuṣūl* 4.2 (1984): 24-41.

Muhammad, Ramadan Bassttawissi. "Al-Ḥadāthah fī Shi'r Maḥmūd Darwīsh." [The Modern in Darwish's Poetry] *Al-Qāhirah* 151 (1995): 38-43.

Murdoch, Adlai H. "Rewriting Writing: Identity, Exile, and Renewal in Assia Djebar's *L'Amour, la fantasia*." *Yale French Studies* 2 (1993): 71-93.

Mutanabbi al-, Abu Tayyib. *Dīwān Abī al-Ṭayyib al-Mutanabbi*. Cairo: Ed. Abd al-Wahāb 'Azzām, 1994.

Muwafi, Abd al-Aziz. "Thunā'īyāt al-Arḍ/al-Mar'āh wa-intihāk al-Muqadas: Qirā'ah fī Dīwān *A'rās*." [The Coupling of Land/Woman: A Reading of Darwish's *Weddings*] *Al-Qāhirah* 151 (1995): 62-69.

Nabulsi al-, Shakir. *Majnūn al-Turāb: Dirāsah fī Shi'r wa Fikr Maḥmūd Darwīsh*. [A Study of the Poetry and Thought of Darwish] Beirut: al-Mu'assassah al-'Arabīyah lil-Dirāsāt wal-Nashr, 1987.

Naficy, Hamid. *Home, Exile, Homeland: Film, Media, and the Politics of Place*. New York: Routledge, 1998.

Nancy, Jean-Luc. *The Inoperable Community*, edited and translated by Peter Connor, Lisa Garbus, Michael Holland, and Simona Sawhney. Minneapolis: University of Minnesota Press, 1991.

Naqash al-, Raja. *Maḥmūd Darwīsh, Sha'ir al-Arḍ al-Muḥtallah*. [Darwish, Poet of the Occupied land] Beirut: al-Mu'assassah al-'Arabīyah lil-Nashr, 1972.

Narain, D. "Writing 'Home': Mediating between 'the Local' and 'the Literary' in a Selection of Postcolonial Women's Texts." *Third World Quarterly* 26.3 (2005): 497-508.

Nawwab al-, Muthaffar. *Watarīyāt Laylīyah*. [Night Strings] n.p.i.

Ngate, Jonathan. *Francophone African Fiction: Reading a Literary Tradition*. Trenton, NJ: Africa World Press, 1988.

Niang, Sada. *Littérature et cinéma en Afrique francophone: Ousmane Sembène et Assia Djebar*. Paris: Édition L'Harmattan, 1996.

Nietzsche, Friedrich. *The Birth of Tragedy*, translated by Walter Kaufmann. New York: Vintage, 1967.

Niranjana, Tejaswini. *Siting Translation: History, Post-Structuralism, and the Colonial Context*. Berkeley, CA: University of California Press, 1992.

Nufferi al-, Muhammad Ibn 'Abd al-Jabbar. *Kitāb al-Mawāqif wa Kitāb al-Mukhāṭabāt*, edited and commented by Arthur John Arberry. Cairo: Maktabat al-Mutannabi, 1935.

O'Riley, MF. "Place, Position, and Postcolonial Haunting in Assia Djebar's *La Femme sans sepulture*." *Research in African Literatures* 35.1 (2004): 66-68.

Page, Andrea. "Rape or Obscene Copulation?: Ambivalence and Complicity in Djebar's *L'Amour, la fantasia*." *Women in French Studies* 2 (1994): 42-52.

Parmenter, Barbara McKean. *Giving Voice to Stones: Place and Identity in Palestinian Literature*. Austin, TX: University of Texas Press, 1994.

Paz, Octavio. "Translation: Literature and Letters." Pp. 152-162 in *Theories of Translation: An Anthology of Essays from Dryden to Derrida*, edited by Rainer Schulte and John Biguenet. Chicago: The University of Chicago Press, 1992.

Qabani, Nizar. *Qaṣā'id Maghḍūb 'Alayha*. [Ill-Fated Poems] Beirut: Manshūrāt Nizār Qabānī, 1986.

Qadi al-, Mohamad. *Al-Arḍ fī Shi'r al-Muqāwamah al-Filasṭīnīyah.* [Land in the Palestinian Resistance Poetry] Tunis: al-Dār al-'Arabīyah lil-Kitāb, 1982.

Qamhieh, Mufid Mohamad. *Al-Ittijāh al-Insānī fī al-Shi'r al-'Arabī al-Mu'āṣir.* [The Humanist Bent in Contemporary Arabic Poetry] Beirut: Dār al-Afāq, 1981.

Qasim al-, Afnan. *Mass'alat al-Shi'r wal-Malḥamah al-Darwīshīyah: Maḥmūd Darwīsh fī Madiḥ al-Ẓill al-'Ālī.* [The Question of Poetry and the Darwishian Epic: Darwish's *Madiḥ al-Ẓill al-'Ālī*] Beirut: al-Mu'assassah al-'Arabīah lil-Nashr, 1987.

Qasim, Samih. *Al-A'māl al-Nājiẓah.* [The Complete Works] Vol. six. Cairo: Dār Su'ād al-Ṣabāh, 1993.

Qays, Imru'. *Dīwān.* ed. Abu Suwaylim. Amman, Jordan: Dār 'Ammār, 1991.

Qur'an. [*Al-Qur'ān al-Karīm*] Medina, Saudi Arabia: Majma' al-Mallak Fahid li-Tibā'at al-Muṣḥaf al-Sharīf, 1413 Higra.

Rahman, Najat. Interview with Mahmoud Darwish. Ramallah, Palestine. 9 and 10 April 1996.

Rahman, Najat, and Hala Kh. Nassar. *Exile's Poet, Mahmoud Darwish: Critical Essays.* Northampton, MA: Interlink Publishing, 2007.

Razouq al-, Salih. "Defeat in Modern Arabic Poetry." *Al-Ma'rifah* 273-74 (1984).

Rayyis al-, Riad Najib. *Al-Fatrah al-Ḥarijah: Naqd fī Adab al-Sitīnāt.* [The Critical Period: Criticism in the Literature of the Sixties] Second revised edition. London: Rayyis Books ltd., 1992.

Robbins, Bruce. "Homelessness and Worldliness." *Diacritics: A Review of Contemporary Criticism* 13 (1983): 69-77.

Rothe, Arnold. "L'Espace du harem dans *Ombre sultane.*" Pp. 49-60 in *Mises en Scène: Assia Djebar, Nicole Brossard, Madeleine Gagnon, France Théoret,* edited by Dominique Johnson and Sylvie Ouzilleau. Sainte-Foy, Québec: Les éditions Le Griffon d'argile, 1993.

Roy, Jean-Louis, and Jean-Louis Joubert, ed. *Littératures francophones du monde arabe: Anthologie.* Paris: Nathan, 1994.

Rubiera Mata, María Jesús. *Literatura Hispanoárabe.* Madrid: Editoriale MAPFRE S.A., 1992.

Rushdie, Salman. *East, West: Stories.* New York: Pantheon Press, 1994.

Sabbah, Fatna A. *Woman in the Muslim Unconscious,* translated by Mary Jo Lakeland. New York: Pergamon Press, 1984.

Safadi al-, Muta', and Elie Hawi, eds. *Mawsū'āt al-Shi'r al-'Arabī.* [Selections of Pre-Islamic Poetry] Beirut: Dār al-Sha'b, 1970.

Said, Edward W. *Culture and Imperialism.* New York: Vintage, 1993.

———. "Intellectual Exile: Expatriates and Marginals." *Grand Street* 12 (1994): 113-124.

———. *Reflections on Exile and Other Essays.* Cambridge: Harvard University Press, 2002.

———. "Talāḥum 'Assīr lil-Shi'r wa lil-Dhākira al-Jāmā'īyah." [A difficult Meshing of poetry and Collective Memory] *Al-Qāhirah* 151 (1995): 22-24.

Said, Edward W., and David Barsamian. *Culture and Resistance: Conversations with Edward W. Said.* Cambridge, MA: South End Press, 2003.

Said, Edward W., and Hamid Dabashi. *Dreams of a Nation: On Palestinian Cinema.* New York: Verso Press, 2006.

Saleh, Fakhri. "Isti'ārāt al-Arḍ al-Kubrā: 'an al-Shi'r al-Filasṭīnī al-Mu'āṣir." [On Contemporary Palestinian poetry] *Al-Karmel* 38 (1990): 166-179.

Saleh, Muhammad Ibrahim. "Aḥmad al-Za'tar." *Al-Qāhirah* 151 (1995): 126-153.

Samti al-, Abdallah. "Maḥmūd Darwīsh wa-Mawāqīt al-Qaṣīdah: Jamālīyāt al-Zaman al-Naṣṣī: Muqāranah Waṣfīyah Simyā'īyah." [Mahmoud Darwish and the Times of the Qaṣīdah: A Semiotic Comparison] *Al-Qāhirah* 151 (1995): 70-89.

Sanbar, Elias. "Bilād Tantaqil." [Travelling Countries] *Al-Karmel* 48-49 (1993): 276-284.

Saunders, Rebecca, ed. *The Concept of the Foreign: An Interdisciplinary Dialogue*. Lanham, MD: Lexington Books, 2003.

Sayyab, Badr Shaker. *Inshūdat al-Maṭar*. [The Song of Rain] Third ed. Beirut: Dār al-'Awdah, 1983.

Schwartz, Regina M. *The Curse of Cain: The Violent Legacy of Monotheism*. Chicago: University of Chicago Press, 1997.

Schwarz-Bart, André. *Le Dernier des Justes*. Paris: Éditions du Seuil, 1959.

Selao, Ching. "Impossible Autobiography: Towards a Derridian Reading of *L'Amour, la fantasia* by Assia Djebar." *Études Françaises* 40.3 (2004): 129+.

Sells, Michael, ed. and pref. *Desert Tracings: Six Classic Arabian Odes by Alqama, Shanfara, Labid, Antara, al-Asha, and Dhu al-Rumma*. Middletown, CT: Wesleyan University Press, 1989.

Shammas, Anton. *Arabesques*, translated by Vivian Eden. New York: Harper and Row, 1988.

Shanati al-, Mahmoud Salih. "Khuṣūṣīyāt al-Ru'iyah wal-Tashkīl fī shi'r Maḥmūd Darwīsh." [The Particular Vision and Form of Darwish's Poetry] *Fuṣūl* 4-7 (October 1986-March 1987).

Shawk, Ali. "Ihtimamāt Mithūlūjīyah wa-Istiṭrādāt Lughawīyah: Al-Qism al-Thālith." [Mythological and Linguistic Interests: Part 3] *Al-Karmel* 26 (1987): 4-38.

———. "Naḥnū wa Hūmīrūs." [Homer and Us] *Al-Karmel* 36-37 (1990): 4-35.

Shawsheh, Farouq. "Maḥmūd Darwīsh 'Āshiq al-Trūbādūr.'" [Darwish, Lover of the Troubadours] *Al-Adāb* 2 (1974).

Shepherd, Danielle. "*Loin de Médine* d'Assia Djebar: Quand les porteuses d'eau se font porteuses de feu." *Littérateur et Cinéma en Afrique Francophone: Ousmane Sembène et Assia Djebar*, edited by Sada Niang. Paris: Éditions L'Harmattan, 1996.

Shimon, Samuel. Interview with Mohamed Choukri. *Banipal* 5 (Summer 1999).

Shukri, Ghali. "'Asfūr al-Jannah am Ṭā'ir al-Nār?" [The Bird of Paradise or Fire?] *Al-Qāhirah* 151 (1995): 9-21.

Shuri al-, Mustafa Abdel Shafi. *Shi'r al-Rathā' fīl-'Aṣr al-Jāhilī*. [Mourning Poetry in the Pre-Islamic Era] Beirut: al-Dār al-Jam'īyah, 1983.

Sobh, Mahmoud. "La Poeisía Árabe, la Música y el Canto." *Anaquel de Estudios 'Arabes* 6 (1995): 149-184.

Sperl, Stefan, and Christopher Shackle, eds. "Introduction." Pp. 1-62 in *Qasida Poetry in Islamic Asia and Africa: Classical Traditions and Modern Meanings*, edited by Stefan Sperl and Christopher Shackle. Vol. one. New York: E. J. Brill, 1996.

Steiner, George. *After Babel: Aspects of Language and Translation*. New York: Oxford University Press, 1975.

———. *Real Presences*. Chicago: University of Chicago Press, 1991.

Suleiman, Khalid A. *Palestine and Modern Arab Poetry*. London: Zed Books, 1984.

Talahite, Anissa. "North African Writing." Pp. 13-30 in *Writing and Africa*, edited by Msiska and Hyland. London: Longman, 1997.

Tawfiq, Majdi Ahmad. "Al-Munūlūj wal-Diyalūj: Qirā'ah fī Dīwān Maḥmūd Darwīsh." [Monologue and Dialogue: A Reading of Darwish's work] *Al-Qāhirah* 151 (1995): 112-121.

The Holy Bible: Revised Standard Edition. New York: New American Library, 1962.

Trabulsi, Amjad. *Naqd al-Shi'r 'ind al-'Arab ḥata al-Qarn al-Khāmis lil-Hijrah*, [Arabic Poetics until the Fifth Century Hijra or the Eleventh Century A.D.] translated by Idris Belmalīh. Casablanca: Dār Tubqāl lil-nashr, 1993.

Tuqan, Fadwa. *Dīwān Fadwā Ṭūqān*. Beirut: Dār al-'Awdah, 1984.

Tuqan, Ibrahim. *Dīwān Ibrahim Ṭūqan*. Beirut: Dār al-'Awdah, 1988.

Udhari al-, Abdullah, ed. *Modern Poetry of the Arab World*. London: n. p., 1986.

Uthman, I'tidal. "As'ilat al-Thaqāfah: As'ilat al-Qaṣīdah fī Zaman al-Ma'sāt al-Mulhāt." [Questions of Culture, Questions of the Qaṣīdah in the Time of the Tragicomic] *Ibdā'* 7-8 (1990): 23.

———. "Naḥwa Qirā'ah Naqdiyah li-Arḍ Maḥmūd Darwīsh." [Toward a Critical Reading of Land in Mahmoud Darwish's Work] *Fuṣūl* 5.1 (1984): 196.

Verthuy, Maïr. "Histoire, Mémoire et Créations dans l'Oeuvre d'Assia Djebar." Pp. 25-36 in *Mises en Scène: Assia Djebar, Nicole Brossard, Madeleine Gagnon, France Théoret*, edited by Dominique Johnson and Sylvie Ouzilleau. Sainte-Foy, Québec: Les éditions Le Griffon d'argile, 1993.

Wazen, Abduh. "Maḥmūd Darwīsh li *al-Ḥayāt*: Lā anẓuru ilā maḍīy bi-riḍā." [I do not look to my past with satisfaction] *Al Ḥayāt*, 10-11 December 2005.

White, Hayden. *The Content of the Form: Narrative Discourse and Historical Representation*. Baltimore, MD: The Johns Hopkins University Press, 1987.

Wiessbort, Daniel. ed. *Translating Poetry: The Double Labyrinth*. Iowa City, IA: University of Iowa Press, 1989.

Woodhul, Winifred. "Exile." *Yale French Studies* 1 (1993): 7-15.

———. "Feminism and Islamic Tradition." *Studies in Twentieth Century Literature* 17 (1993): 27-43.

———. *Transfigurations of the Maghreb: Feminism, Decolonization, and Literatures*. Minneapolis: University of Minnesota Press, 1993.

Worton, Michael, and Judith Still, eds. *Intertextuality: Theories and Practices*. Manchester: Manchester University Press, 1990.

Wylie, Hal, Eileen Julien, and Russel J. Linnemann. *Contemporary African Literature*. Washington DC: Three Continents Press, 1983.

Xavier, François. *Mahmoud Darwich dans l'exil de sa langue*. Paris: Autres Temps, 2004.

———. *Mahmoud Darwich ou la nouvelle Andalousie*. Paris: Esquilles, 2002.

Yeshurun, Helit. 1997. "Je ne reviens pas, je viens." Pp. 107-167 in *La Palestine comme métaphore*.

Yousef al-, Yousef Sami. *Al-Shi'r al-'Arabī al-Mu'āṣir*. [Contemporary Arabic Poetry] Damascus: Ittiḥād al-Kuttāb al-'Arab, 1980.

Yousefi al-, Mohammad Lutfi. *Fī Bunyat al-Shi'r al-'Arabī al-Mu'āṣir*. [The Structure of Contemporary Arabic Poetry] Tunis: Sirass lil-Nashr, 1985.

Zaki, Ahmad. *Al-Asāṭir: Dirāsāt Ḥaḍarīyah Muqaranah*. [Myths: Comparative Studies] Cairo: n. p., 1975.

Zayyad, Tawfiq. *Dīwān Tawfiq Zayyād*. Beirut: Dār al-'Awdah, 1971.

Zeidan, Joseph T. *Arab Women Novelists: The Formative Years and Beyond*. New York: State University of New York Press, 1995.

Zimra, Clarisse. "Hearing Voices, or, Who are You Calling Postcolonial? The Evolution of Djebar's Poetics." *Research in African Literatures* 35.4 (2004): 149-159.

———. "Not so Far from Medina: Assia Djebar Charts Islam's 'Insupportable Feminist Revolution'," *World Literature Today* 7 (1996): 823-833.

———. "'When the Past Answers Our Present': Assia Djebar Talks about *Loin de Médine*." *Calaloo* 16 (1993): 116-131.

———. "Writing Woman: The Novels of Assia Djebar." *SubStance* 21 (1992).

Appendix

Translations of Selected Poems by Mahmoud Darwish

Crypts, Andalusia, Desert

So you continue your lyric in my name.
Did I choose my mother your voice?
Desert and desert.
Let the earth extend its oval. And these strange doves
strange doves. And believe my short journey to Cordoba.
And my separation from the sand and the ancient poets,
and from trees that were no woman.
The beginning is not our beginning, and the last smoke is ours
and if the kings they entered a village corrupted it,
so do not cry, my friend, a wall dissembles
and believe my short journey to Cordoba.
And continue your lyric in my name.
Did I choose my mother your voice? Desert and desert.

It's effortless and difficult this egress of the doves
from the wall of language,
so how do we pass to the small orange grove?
It's effortless and difficult this ingress of the doves
to the wall of language,
so how do we bide before the lyric in the crypt? Desert and desert.
I remember that I will dream again of the return.
—To where my friend?
—To where the doves have flown clapping the wheat
and opening the sky
to tie this space with one chaff in Galilee
—Did you survive, then, my friend?
—I was dropped from the presence of god like a strand

in my mother's long dress
kindled, I lit . . . and I didn't go out[1]
—And why do you want to journey to Cordoba?
—Because I don't know the path. Desert and desert.

Sing of the similarity between a question and another question
that follows it
so that one collapse may protect my collapse from a final collapse
I am one thousand years from the Arabic moment,
I build on sand what the wind carries
from battles and desires and perfume from India.
I remember the path of silk
to Cham.
I remember a Samarkand school,
and a woman picks dates from my words and falls into the river
—Do they kill the horses?
—And the smoke which seeps from our blood toward the echo
—Do you die a lot?
—And I live a lot, and I hold my shadow like a ripe apple
and the long road wraps itself around me
like a noose of dew
and realize, my friend, that we chase Caesar. Desert and desert.

Sing of my spreading on earth's corpse like manna. Yes the gypsies
hate farming
but they farm the horses on two guitar strings
and they do not fill the vaults with wheat like ancient Egypt,
nor do they ride to Andalusia
singularly;
and sing of the fields in which sun and heart run and never tire . . . and Desert

and desert! From one thousand years to the light I came.
They opened the lonely door of confinement so I fell upon light.
My pace is narrow, and the distances are white, white,
and the door is a river,
They opened the lonely door of confinement so I came out.
I found a path so I walked.
Where do I go? To the issue I said: I'll teach my freedom how to walk, she leaned on me, I straightened up, and straightened her up, and we toppled the old orange seller, and I got up,
and I carried her
over my back like they carry countries on camels and lorries, and I walked. And in the grove of oranges I tired, so I called: military police! I cannot go to Cordoba!
And I bent my back over a step
and I lifted down my freedom like a sack of coal and escaped to the crypt;
does the crypt resemble my mother your mother? Desert and desert.

What time is it now?

---

1 Please note that all ellipses are in the original poems.

No time for the crypt
What time is it?
No time
In the orange groves we believed the women selling ancient swords,
and those who go about their day listening to lyric and don't lie on the bread,
a desert in the heart,
tear the veins of my ancient heart in a Gypsy song that rides to Andalusia
and sing of my separation from the sand and the ancient poets,
and from trees that were no woman
and don't die now, please! Don't break like mirrors, don't hide like a homeland
and don't drop like rooftops and cliffs
because they will steal you like me a martyr
because they will know the relation between the doves and the crypt
and they will feel that the birds are the spread of the morning on earth and the river is a hairpin for a woman who suicides.
And wait for me little by little so I can hear the sound of my blood
cross the street that explodes
(I almost survived)
—You will not win!
—I will walk
—To where my friend?
—To where the doves have flown clapping the wheat
to uphold this space by a chaff that waits.
So you continue your lyric in my name
and don't cry, my friend, for a string lost in the crypts.

It's a song
It's a song!

Special thanks to Jeffrey Michels for his editing of this poem.

How many times does our issue end?

He contemplates his days in cigarette smoke,
he glances at his pocket watch:
If I could I would slow down the minutes
so I can delay the ripening of wheat!
and he leaves himself irritable and weary:
It is time for the harvest
the spikes are heavy, and the scythes are neglected, and the country
is distant now from its prophetic gate way.
Lebanon's summer speaks to me of my vines in the south
Lebanon's summer speaks to me of what lies behind nature
but my path to god begins
from a star in the south

—Are you speaking to me my father?
—They signed an agreement in Rhodos, my son!
—And how does it concern us, how does it concern us, my father?
—And the issue has ended
—How many times does our issue end, my father?
—The issue has ended. They did their duty:
They fought enemy fighter planes with broken guns.
And we did our duty, we distanced ourselves from the chinaberry
so we wouldn't disturb the helmet of the military leader.
And we sold the rings of our wives so they can hunt birds
my son!

—Will we stay here, then, my father?
beneath the willow of wind
between skies and sea?

—My son! Everything here
will resemble something there
we will resemble ourselves in the nights
it will burn us the eternal star of resemblance
my son!

—My father, ease the words for me!
—I left the windows open
for the coo of doves
I left my face on the edges of the well
I left the words
strung over the closet's string
speaking, I left darkness
to its night wrapping the wool of my awaiting
I left a cloud
on fig trees hanging its wear
and I left a dream

renewing itself in itself
and I left peace
alone, there on the land

—Were you dreaming while I was awake my father?
—Come. We will return my son!

To my end and to its end

—Are you tired from walking
my son, are you tired?
—yes, my father
the night has been long on this path
and the heart has flowed onto the land of your night
—You still have the lightness of a cat
climb unto my shoulder,
we will cross in a little while
the last forest of terebinth and oak trees
this is the north of Galilee
and Lebanon is behind us,
and the sky is ours
all of it from Damascus
to the wall of beautiful Acre
—Then what?
—We return to the house
do you know the path my son
—Yes my father:
east of the carob of the main street
a small path narrows to a cactus
in the beginning, then it leads to the well
wider and wider, then it looks
upon the orchard of my uncle "Jamil"
the seller of tobacco and sweets,
then loses its way on a threshing floor before
it straightens and sits in the house,
in the form of a parrot,
—Do you know the house, my son
—I know it like I know the path:
Jasmine surrounds an entrance from iron
and light steps on the stone stairs
and sunflower watches what is behind the place
and familiar bees prepare breakfast for my grandfather
on a dish of bamboo,
and in the courtyard a horse, a well, and a willow tree
and behind the fence tomorrow pages our leaves

—Are you tired my father,
I see sweat in your eyes?
—I'm tired my son . . . will you carry me?
—Like you used to carry my, my father
and I will carry this longing
to my beginning and its beginning
and I will walk this path
to my end . . . and its end!

A Rhyme for *Mu'allaqāt*[2]

No one guided me to myself. I am the guide,[3]
I am the guide to myself between the sea and the desert.
From my language I was born
on the path of India between two small tribes upon which abides
the moon of ancient religions and the impossible peace
and it is incumbent upon them to learn the celestial sphere of the neighboring Persians
and the grand apprehensions of the Romans, so that the heavy time may descend
from the Arab's tent. Who am I?
This is the question of the others that has no answer. I am my language I,
and I am *mu'allaqatun*[4] . . . *mu'allaqatān*[5] . . . ten, this is my language,
I am my language. I am what the words said:
Be
my body, so I was for its tone a body. I am who
said to the words: be the crossing of my body with
the eternal desert. Be so I can be as I say!
No land over earth bears me, so my words bear me
ascending, parting from me, and they build the dwelling of their passage before me
in my debris, in the debris of the enchanting world around me,
Upon a wind I stood still. And my long night became longer for me
this language of mine is pendants[6] from stars encircling the embraces
of the beloved: migrated
they took the place and migrated
they took time and migrated
they took their scents from the clay
and the sparse pasture and migrated
they took the words and the fallen heart migrated
with them. Will the echo expand, this echo
this white, resonant mirage for a name
which the unknown fills with hoarseness, and which the wind fills with divinity?
The sky sets a window upon me so I look: I don't
see anyone besides me
I found myself upon its surface
like it was with me, and my gaze
does not depart from the desert,
from wind and sand are my steps
and my world is my body and all that my hands possess
I am the traveler and the path

---

1. *Mu'allaqāt* are the oldest collection of ancient Arabic *qaṣīdahs* or poems. Believed to be seven and later ten, chosen as the best poems, and written in gold, they were hung at the wall of Ka'bah shrine in Mecca. Hence their names *mu'allaqāt* which means to be hung or suspended.

2. The Arabic word "*dalīl*" which I translated as guide is rich in meaning and can signify sign, mark, evidence, proof, testimony, witness, clue, key, reference, index, etc.

3. *Mu'allaqatun* is the singular, indefinite form for *Mu'allaqāt*.

4. *Mu'allaqatān* refers to two.

5. The Arabic word for necklaces "*qalā'id*" can also mean exquisite poems.

gods look upon me and pass, and we don't prolong
our talks of what is to come. No tomorrow in
this desert except what we saw yesterday,
so I will raise my *mu'allaqah* so that circular time will break
and beautiful time will be born!
From the excess of the past emerges tomorrow
I left her myself filled with its present
and travel emptied me
from the shrines. For the sky its people and its wars
But I, I have a doe for a wife, and I have the palm trees
mu'allaqāt in the book of sand. Past is what I see
for one a kingdom of dust and his crown. So let my language
triumph over time and the enemy, over my descendents,
over me, over my father, and over disappearance that does not disappear
this is my language and my miracle. A magical wand.
The gardens of Babel, my obelisk, my first identity,
and my polished metal
and the sacred of the Arab in the desert,
who worships what flows
from rhymes like stars on his cloak,
and he worships what he says

it is necessary for prose then,
it is necessary for divine prose for the prophet to triumph . . .

A traveler told another:
We won't return the way . . .

I don't know the desert,
but I grew on its limits words
The words said their words, and left
like a separated woman, I left as her broken spouse,
I did not keep except the rhythm
I hear it,
and I follow it,
and I raise it a dove
in the passage to the sky,
the sky of my song,
I am the son of the Syrian coast,
I live it a journey or shrine
between the people of the sea,
but the mirage draws me east
to the ancient nomads,
I bring the beautiful horses their water,
I take the pulse of the alphabets in their echoes,
and I return a window facing two ways
I forget who I will be so I can be
a people in one, and contemporary
to the praises of the unfamiliar mariners beneath my windows,
and the letter of the warring to their own:
we won't return like we left
we won't even return . . . now and then!

I don't know the desert,
no matters how I visit its foreboding,
And in the desert the invisible said to me:
Write!
I said: On the mirage there is other writing
He said: Write so that the mirage becomes greener
So I said: I'm short of absence
And I said: I have yet to learn the words
He said to me: Write so you will know them,
and to know where you were, and where you are
and how you came to be, and who you'll be tomorrow,
put your name in my hand and write
to know who I am, and pass a cloud
in the expanse
So I wrote: whoever writes his story inherits
the land of words, and possesses significance thoroughly!

I don't know the desert,
but I take leave of her: peace
to the tribe east of my song: peace
to the multiply descended on a sword: peace

to the son of my mother beneath a palm tree: peace
to the *mu'allaqah* that guards our stars: peace
to the people passing memory to mine: peace
to the peace upon me between two *qaṣīdahs*:
a *qaṣīdah* written
and another whose poet died desiring!
Am I myself?
Am I here . . . or there?
In every "you" I,
I am you the interlocutor, it is not exile
to be you. It is not exile
to be the I in you. And it is not exile
for the sea and desert
to be the song of the traveler for the traveler:
I won't return, like I left,
I won't even return . . . now and then!

Poetic planning

There was for the stars no role
except they
taught me how to read:
I have a language in the sky
and on earth I have a language
Who am I? Who am I?

I don't want an answer here
Perhaps a star will fall upon its image
Perhaps the forest of chestnuts will rise
and raise me toward the galaxy, at nighttime,
and say: you will stay here!

The *qaṣīdah* above has the power
to teach me whatever it wishes
such as opening a window
and arranging my domestic affairs
between myths. It has the power
to marry herself to me . . . time

And my father below carries an olive
tree of a thousand years,
that is neither eastern
nor western.
Perhaps he will rest from the conquerors,
and will incline toward me a little,
and will gather for me Lilly of the Valley

The *qaṣīdah* distances itself from me,
and enters the port of sailors who adore wine,
and who do not return to the same woman twice,
and who do not carry longing to anything
nor sadness!

I did not die after a passion
But a mother sees the reflections of her son
in a carnation and fears the amphora from wounding it,
then weeps to distance the event
before its advent,
then weeps to return me from the lures of the path
alive, so I can live here

The *qaṣīdah* is in between, and it has the power
to light the nights with the breasts of a young woman,
and it has the power to light with the apple of two bodies,
and it has the power to return,
with a cry of a gardenia, a homeland!

The *qaṣīdah* is between my hands, and it has the power
to command the affairs of myths,
through the work of my hands, but I
since I found the *qaṣīdah*, displaced myself
and asked her:
Who am I?
Who am I?

I see my apparition coming from afar

I look upon what I want, like a dwelling's lanai
I look upon my friends as they carry their evening
post: bread and wine,
and some novels and records

I look upon sea gulls, and lorries of soldiers
changing the trees of this place.

I look upon the dog of my neighbor
from Canada, immigrant from a year and a half

I look upon the name "Abi Tayyib al-Mutannabi,"
traveling to Egypt from Tiberia
over the horse of *nashīd*

I look upon the Persian rose rising
over the iron fence

I look upon what I want, like a dwelling's lanai

I look upon trees guarding the night from itself
and guarding the sleep of those who wish me dead

I look upon the wind searching for the home of wind in itself . . .

I look upon a woman sunbathing in herself

I look upon a procession of ancient prophets
as they climb barefoot toward Orshalim
And I ask: Is there a new prophet
for this new age?

I look upon what I want, like a dwelling's lanai

I look upon my image running from itself
to the stone ladder, carrying my mother's scarf
fluttering in the wind: what will happen if I returned
a child? And I returned to you . . . and I returned to me

I look upon an olive branch hiding Zachariah
I look upon words no longer in "Lisān al-'Arab"

I look upon Persians, Romans, Sumerians,
and the new refugees

I look upon the necklace of one of the poor of Tagore
pounded by the carriages of the handsome prince

I look upon a hoopoe weary from the blame of a king

I look upon what nature hides:

What will pass . . . what will pass after the ash?

I look upon my body fearful from far

I look upon what I want, like a dwelling's lanai

I look upon my language after two days. A little absence is enough
for Aeschylus to open the door for peace,
A short speech is enough
for Anthony to declare war,
A woman's hand in mine is enough
for me to embrace my freedom
and for my body to begin anew its ebb and flow

I look upon what I want, like a dwelling's lanai

I look upon my apparition
coming
from
afar . . .

Index